TRAUMA Redeemed

A Biblical Response to Medicalized Suffering

Julie Ganschow, Ph.D.

ISBN: 979-8-9889591-0-6

The fictional case study of "Sally" in this book is created to illustrate biblical counseling principles. Any resemblance to actual persons, living or dead, or real events is purely coincidental.

Edited by Jenna Bogard

Cover design by Sydney Lucero, incorporating AI-generated art from Grok.

Published by Pure Water Press

Dedication

This book is dedicated with gratitude and prayer
to those who bear the weight of catastrophic suffering
and the counselors who guide them to Christ's redeeming hope.

Table of Contents

Endorsements

"Biblical counselors urgently need reliable guidance in understanding trauma, and Dr. Julie Ganschow has provided just that. With a clear awareness of secular modalities, she presents a thoroughly biblical framework, offering practical applications and insightful questions to engage the hearts of the hurting. Every biblical counselor would benefit from owning and applying this book. Her chapter on the church's vital role in the care process is especially heartwarming."

Pastor Matthew Statler, Teaching Elder
Sierra Vista Baptist Church
Sierra Vista, AZ

In "Trauma Redeemed," Dr. Julie Ganschow provides a detailed understanding and a practical approach to trauma, one of the most discussed topics in current culture. Not only does she leave no stone unturned, she also makes it abundantly clear that in order to have proper understanding and a truly effective counseling approach—that God can heal and strengthen the soul of the wounded, one must have a biblical anthropology, a right phenomenology, and a sound theology that informs the Christian presupposition and approach. Dr. Ganschow does not simply make the claim that Christ is superior and sufficient, but she clearly shows how this claim is true. Likewise, she does not steer away from empirical evidence or claims of scientific and clinical knowledge about trauma. Instead, she rightly shows how the true science available points believers to the creator of all natural knowledge—God Himself—and His Word, and she destroys arguments that are raised against God yet are promoted as scientific fact. Sadly, far too many people have accepted and believed a great deal of scientism surrounding the concept of trauma. Ultimately, this book will point the reader to Jesus, who Himself suffered and endured profound trauma in order that those who put their faith in Him can escape the worst and eternal trauma known to mankind. Any Christian who seriously considers helping those who have been through some of life's most difficult trials and suffering should utilize this book as an essential counseling reference.

Dr. Daniel Berger II, Lead Pastor
Faith Fellowship Church
Clarence, NY
Director of Alethia International Ministries and
Faith Counseling Center

One of the fundamental presuppositions of a biblical counselor is that we live in a fallen world with fallen people. Sometimes, the world falls hard on a person, and they experience severe trauma. The Bible would call trauma suffering, and sometimes the suffering is severe. Dr. Ganschow has shown in "Trauma Redeemed" that suffering has been medicalized at the expense of what the Scriptures say about life in a fallen world and what the Scriptures say about suffering and genuine hope in the Lord Jesus Christ. The book painstakingly takes a biblical counselor like me through various and often contradictory theories by providing a case study of what treatment looks like. The case study then progresses to the unchangeable Word of God for treatment. The book is written with compassion, empathy and care for those experiencing severe trauma.

Pastor/Elder Bruce Roeder
ACBC Counselor
The Vine Community Church

Acknowledgments

This book is the fruit of many hands and hearts who have supported me in this journey. I am deeply grateful to my biblical counseling colleagues whose works have shaped my approach. To the Reigning Grace Counseling Center staff for their wisdom and encouragement, and my mentors in the biblical counseling community who deserve special thanks for their faithfulness to Scripture.

To my family, especially my beloved husband, Larry, your steadfast love, endless encouragement, and patience made this work possible. I am also thankful for the countless survivors of catastrophic suffering whose courage inspired me to write *Trauma Redeemed.* Finally, I give all glory to God, whose Word is the foundation of this book and the hope for every wounded soul.

Introduction

The Crisis of Trauma in Our Time

In 1988, David Powlison wrote, "Counseling continues to be compromised significantly by the secular assumptions and practices of our culture's reigning psychologies and psychiatries."[1] He might write the same thing today. One expert said we are living in Traumaville.[2] "Trauma" is suddenly everywhere, and more people are seeking help than ever to overcome something traumatic in their past or present. As a result, counselors are being inundated with calls to integrate "trauma-informed" practices and to embrace "clinically-informed biblical counseling," which falls under the umbrella of what is called trauma-informed care (TIC). However, this integration often leads to confusion and a departure from the sufficiency of Scripture.

Defining Trauma: A Biblical Perspective

What *is* trauma? While secular definitions abound, biblically, trauma is a form of undergoing or suffering distress of the soul, trouble, severe pain, or affliction (Mal. 1:13; 2:13, 16; 2 Tim. 2:8–10; 4:5; James 5:10). It is sorrowful suffering, anguish, or catastrophic suffering that can be both physical and emotional and comes from living in a fallen world. To experience trauma is to suffer sadly and be in a dire situation (Luke 22:15; 24:46; Acts 1:3; 3:18; 17:3; 1 Cor. 12:26; Heb. 2:18; 9:26; 13:12; 1 Pet. 2:19, 23; 3:17; 4:15, 19). As biblical counselors, our work is to help someone who has experienced or witnessed something horrible, violent, shocking, disturbing, or painful with the spiritual and emotional effects of such events.

The Medicalization of Suffering

Because of the significant shift toward the medicalization of suffering, there has been a move away from biblical terminology for these experiences and gravitation toward terms like post-traumatic stress disorder (PTSD) and complex post-traumatic stress disorder (C-PTSD). Unfortunately, some who consider themselves biblical counselors promote a clinically-informed or trauma-informed approach that integrates physiological and psychological interventions into their counseling. These are secular methodologies, which are rooted in evolutionary, bio-deterministic theories. Adopting a blend of psychology and biblical counseling (integration) creates confusion for the counselee. It fails to address the issues of the heart that are at the core of human suffering.

A Call to Biblical Sufficiency

This book is a call to return to the sufficiency of Scripture in helping those victimized or harmed by evil, violence, and suffering, which we understand to be "trauma." It is written out of deep concern for my colleagues and the next generation of biblical counselors who may be swayed by the allure of such worldly wisdom (Col. 2:8). Many biblical counselors are reading blogs and articles and listening to the podcasts of people who believe they are promoting biblical truth, unaware they are espousing therapies contrary to the sufficiency of Scripture. To be clear, I have no personal ill will toward those promoting these methodologies, nor is this a personal attack on them. Having read their books and articles and listened to their podcasts, I am confident that we all desire to help people deal with and overcome the effects of the horrific events they have suffered. My concern is how we go about it.

Ultimately, this book is a call to return to biblical sufficiency. The Bible provides a comprehensive framework for understanding and addressing catastrophic suffering.

The Journey Ahead

In the following chapters, we will examine the secular view of catastrophic suffering, its flaws, and its limitations. More importantly, we will explore a biblical model of care for those impacted by deep human suffering. We will examine the effects of the fall on mankind, the need for a new identity in Christ, and the importance of redefining terms from a biblical perspective. My goal is to provide a comprehensive biblical framework for understanding and addressing the anguish of the soul. At the end of each chapter are questions that will encourage you to *Consider and Apply* the contents of the chapter for yourself and your biblical counseling ministry.

Remember, by standing on the sufficiency of Scripture and relying on the transforming power of the Holy Spirit, we offer hope and help that surpasses the limitations of secular and integrated approaches and provides a pathway to healing that addresses the whole person. God's Word is sufficient, sufficient for even this.

Consider and Apply

1. What motivated you to explore a biblical approach to "trauma" counseling?
2. How do you see the current trends in trauma counseling aligning or conflicting with biblical principles?
3. What are your initial thoughts on the sufficiency of Scripture in addressing catastrophic suffering?

CHAPTER 1

The Fall of Mankind and the Roots of Suffering

As we embark on this journey to understand trauma from a biblical perspective, starting at the very beginning is essential. The roots of all suffering, including trauma, can be traced back to the fall of mankind. By examining the theological foundations of suffering, we can gain a deeper understanding of human brokenness and the pervasive impact of sin on our lives and relationships.

Theological Foundations of Suffering

As I counsel women, I am frequently asked, "Why did this happen to me?" "Why did I have to suffer this way?" The short answer is that it is a consequence of the fall. In Genesis 3:1–6, we find the scriptural account of the fall of humanity into sin. Eve was deceived by the lies of the serpent, her desire for the fruit of the forbidden tree, the pleasure of having what she wanted, and the desire to be wise (1 John 2:16). She disobeyed God, ate the fruit, and then gave some to her husband, Adam. This one action created both theological and relational changes for us all.

Theologically speaking, MacArthur says, "The willful decision of Adam and Eve created a state of rebellion between the creation and their Creator."[3] When Adam sinned (Gen. 3), creation fell from its pristine condition and became sinful. Whereas God initially blessed creation (Gen. 1:22, 28; 2:3), Adam's deliberate disobedience to God's command to eat nothing from the tree in the center of the Garden brought curses upon creation (Gen. 3:14–16). God cursed the serpent (Gen. 3:14–15) and the earth (Gen. 3:17–19). Humanity was also placed under a curse and now would experience physical and spiritual death (Gen. 2:17; Eph. 2:1–5).[4]

While those after Adam did not choose to be born in the kingdom of Satan, Adam's sin brought death, and his sin is passed on to every person in every generation with only one exception, Jesus Christ (Rom. 5:12–15a, 16b, 17; 2 Cor. 5:21; Heb. 7:26). We are now born under God's wrath, in bondage to the kingdom of sin and Satan (Rom. 1:18; 3:23; 6:16–23; Eph. 2:1–2).

> The Bible makes it clear that the fall brought sin into every subsequent person's life: "Therefore, just as through one man sin entered the world, and death through sin, and thus death spread to all men, because all sinned" (Rom. 5:12). One's capacity for sin is inborn. A person is a sinner before he has the opportunity to sin. All have inherited the effects of Adam's fall.[5]

Sin and Its Consequences: Understanding Human Brokenness

In the fall, we became inherently corrupt and totally incapable of choosing or doing what is acceptable to God apart from divine grace (Rom. 5:12, 19; 8:8). This is known as total depravity. Total depravity does not mean we are as bad as we might be, for we have already seen that God's common grace (unmerited favor) restrains unredeemed sinners from fully realizing their sinful potential. Every one of us has the potential to commit the worst of sins since the fall affects every aspect of us (all aspects of the heart, including the will, emotions, desires, conscience, and thoughts). We are hopelessly lost and have no power within ourselves to recover holiness. Historically, this radical corruption of the soul has been called *total inability*.[6]

The theological effects of the fall have also affected us relationally. The moment Adam and Eve disobeyed God, all relationships worsened. The relationship between God and people changed. Because of their sin, they were immediately separated from God, and their fellowship was broken (Rom. 5:12). Was that traumatic for them? We can never know what that was like because we were born separated from God. The closest we can come to an understanding would be the total destruction of a significant relationship due to something horrible we did.

The Bible reveals how Adam and Eve responded to their sin; they experienced guilt and fear and sought cover for their bodies and souls to hide their sin and shame from God (Gen. 3:7–10). At that moment, *for the first time,* they knew fear and anxiety, guilt, shame, and a desire to hide from each other and God. We cannot imagine what this was like for them, to one moment be sinless and the next moment to experience feeling and knowing sin, but I think that experience would be traumatic!

The Impact of the Fall on Creation and Relationships

As a result of the fall, the relationship between man and woman changed. Adam and Eve looked at each other differently with their newly opened eyes. They were exposed to each other in the condition of sin, and an immediate disruption of their relationship took place. Whereas before they sinned, they were completely comfortable with their bodies, and with the exposure being unclothed brought. After the fall, they wanted to hide their nakedness from each other. MacArthur states, "Sin instantly destroyed their innocence. Even the holy gift of their physical relationship was polluted with a sense of shame. Gone was its purity. Now present were wicked and impure thoughts they had never known before."[7] "Instead of knowing good and evil, the couple now know [sic] that they are naked. This is hardly the knowledge for which they bargained. What was formerly understood to be a sign of a healthy relationship between the man and the woman (2:25) has become unpleasant and shameful."[8]

The first couple also experienced an immediate corruption of the conscience, which brought them into conflict, and for the first time, they experienced division. As evidence of the changed relationships between Adam and Eve, God, and the first couple, we see the first incidence of blame-shifting when God confronts Adam for his sin. First, Adam is devious and defensive, and he minimizes his participation in eating the forbidden fruit by blaming Eve for his disobedience. Then, he blames God for giving the woman to him (Gen. 3:12). When God confronts Eve, she blames the serpent for their disobedience (Gen. 3:13). All this sin was new to them.

While Scripture doesn't explicitly tell us that it was "traumatic," as human beings, it must have been disturbing and shocking to suddenly know the feelings of sinfulness. To instantly know fear, guilt, shame, and the desire to hide spiritually and physically. It is hard to imagine anything worse than being separated from God and suddenly knowing sin, but that was not the end of their upsetting revelations.

Everything about their known world changed when Adam and Eve were removed from the Garden and unable to return. Men and women would now have to work for food to stay alive. All they had known before was "tending" in the Garden; there was no "work" as we understand it. Their food grew in abundance, and they tended to what grew. No weeds or pests were eating the food they were growing. There was no drought, no scorching sun to wither the plants, and no need to water for things to grow. Now, not only are they removed from the Garden and barred from it, but they must also labor for their food. Under the curse, the Earth opposes Adam, and he must physically till the ground and clear the rocks, trees, and weeds to grow his food. He now battles the elements, pests that will compete for his food, and varying amounts of sun and water. Weeds try to choke out his garden. Not only this, but the animals that previously lived among them peacefully now wanted to kill and eat them! All of creation fell in every way possible. Do you think this was distressful for them?

In addition, Adam and Eve faced other hardships and trials. Part of God's curse on women was that they would now bear children in pain. Any woman who has ever given birth knows the pain and sometimes the physical trauma of labor and delivery. However, God, in His mercy, has so wired our bodies that the memory of the pain of childbirth fades over time. Another relational aspect of the curse was that all women would struggle with the battle of self-will, bringing with it the desire to rebel against God's authoritative order, and men would desire to misuse the authority they were given to dominate their wives sinfully. Another tragedy that befell our biblical ancestors was when Cain killed Abel. Adam and Eve experienced the evil of one child murdering the other, lying about it, and trying to cover it up. As a result, they lost one son to homicide and the other son to banishment (Gen. 4:1–16).

The effects of the fall on mankind echo throughout biblical history. Job's story could be considered a case of significant catastrophic suffering. The loss of his wealth and entire family, save one, the medical calamities that befell him, and then the miserable counsel of his friends all combined to create a situation of significant suffering. And who can ignore Joseph's story; it is full of horror and adversity. In Genesis 37:18, we read that his brothers plotted to kill him. His life from that moment on was one ordeal after the next. First, his brothers throw him in a hole, leaving him for dead (Gen. 37:21–24). Reconsidering that plan, they decide to sell him to a caravan of Ishmaelites for twenty shekels of silver (Gen. 37:26–28). Finally, Joseph is sold again, this time to Potiphar in Egypt, where he is a slave for thirteen years. Within that period, Joseph spent at least two years in prison for a crime he didn't commit.

Throughout the Old Testament, we see the history of the Israelites come to life, and in those pages, we find an astonishing number of events that would be considered traumatic. The Hebrews were frequently at war with other nations beginning in Genesis 14. Joshua, King Saul, and David experienced war, which was plentiful and bloody. 1 Samuel 18:7 says, "Saul has slain his thousands and David his ten thousands." The combat was up close, often hand-to-hand with swords and clubs. Warriors saw the faces of the men they were slaying. And yet, while the Bible acknowledges physical and emotional responses to suffering, we do not find any specific references in the Bible referencing signs or symptoms of what is today called post-traumatic stress disorder (PTSD.) Some wrongly claim Psalm

38 is David's experience of PTSD.[i] While David is indeed suffering, his angst in Psalm 38 is partly due to his own sin (v 3, 18) and being abandoned and tormented (vs. 11–12). There is no reference to experiencing the consequences of war in this intense lament. One article in the *Journal of Pastoral Care and Counseling* claims that David played the harp when the evil spirit (sent by God) came upon Saul (1 Samuel 16:14–23) because "Saul had begun to experience a type of panic and stress attack that continued to reoccur and deeply affected his life. Because of the exposure to heavy combat and killing, Saul had begun to develop PTSD wherein he re-experienced unwanted memories and emotional distress plagued him."[9] There is no evidence that Saul's plight had anything to do with his military experiences. In fact, the Scriptures make it clear that he was suffering because the Lord sent an evil spirit to terrorize Saul (1 Samuel 16:14).

The Hebrews were in bondage as enslaved people for 400 years, and the Scriptures say they were compelled to labor rigorously. As a result, their lives were bitter with hard labor in mortar and bricks and all kinds of labor in the fields (Ex. 12:40–41).

Another traumatic result of the fall was what we would consider sex trafficking. Few stories are more horrific in the Bible than those found in Genesis 19 and Judges 19. Both narratives describe men giving women to other men for sex. For example, Lot offered his daughter and said she was a prize because she was an innocent virgin. The Levite offered his concubine to the crowd for their use, and they abused her so severely that she died.

In Judges 21, we see the Israelites destroying the inhabitants of Jabesh-Gilead. They killed this city's men, women, and children. This whole period in Israel's history is bleak in which every man did what was right in his own eyes (Judg. 17:6–21:25).

We read about the rape of Dinah by Shechem in Genesis 34 and the rape of Tamar by her half-brother Amnon in 2 Samuel 13. Amnon's treatment of Tamar in this entire narrative is despicable. First, he lures her in under the guise of being ill and needing her to make him food- in his bedroom. Next, he wants her to feed him at his bedside, and when she complies, Amnon's lust is so great that he brutally rapes her despite her pleadings. When he finishes violating her, he dismisses Tamar, telling his servant to throw her out of his room, treating her like a common prostitute.

After two centuries of existence as a nation, the northern tribes of Israel were ruled by a succession of nineteen wicked, idolatrous kings. Some reigned briefly,

---

[i] This article claims Ps. 30: 1-3 could be David's PTSD response https://thewarriorsjourney.org/challenges/king-david-ptsd/, this article cites several Psalms as "evidence" of David's PTSD: https://crumilitary.org/ptsd-prayers-king-david/, and this post provides journaling based on David's Psalms for PTSD. https://www.bible.com/reading-plans/32169-surviving-trauma/day/1

but violence, assassinations, and cruelty characterized the entire period. First, the ten northern tribes of Israel were conquered by the Assyrians and taken captive. Next, Israel was conquered by the Babylonians (586 BC), the Persians (538 BC), the Greeks (332 BC), the Maccabees (164 BC), and the Romans (63 BC). Every time they were conquered, it was brutal. The soldiers would march in and sack the city. They would demolish it and massacre the inhabitants; those left were taken as booty. They became slaves or worse. In 2 Kings, chapters 6–7, we read the narrative of when the Arameans laid siege to the city of Samaria. So severe was the famine caused by the siege that the Bible says the women were eating their children.

The metanarrative of salvation history is laced with loss. Many of God's people suffered from poverty and persecution (Ps. 107:4–9). For example, the prophet Zechariah (son of Jehoiada) was stoned (2 Chron. 24:20–22; Matt. 23:35). According to tradition, Manasseh, king of Judah, had the prophet Isaiah executed by having him sawn in two (Heb. 11:37). Uriah the prophet was killed with the sword (Jer. 26:23; cf. 1 Kings 19:10), and the Bible reveals that many, many more people experienced abuses, trauma, and horrific manners of death.

In Romans 8:22, Paul, who details his sufferings and the trials he experienced after coming to saving faith in Christ (2 Cor. 11:23b–28), reminds us that creation itself is groaning under the weight of sin and suffering, or trauma (Rom. 8:20-22). All human beings in every culture worldwide experience the trauma of sickness, pain, plagues, wars, violence, and death. So, you can see that the Bible reveals that God's people have always suffered trauma; Christians are not exempt from suffering.

Understanding the theological reasons for suffering provides a solid foundation for addressing all suffering and cataclysmic events. However, to fully grasp the complexities of catastrophic suffering in counseling, we must examine how modern culture has responded. This leads us to our next discussion on the medicalization of suffering.

Consider and Apply

1. How does understanding the fall of mankind help you make sense of affliction and suffering?
2. Name specific ways the biblical narrative of sin and redemption provides comfort to those who have experienced deep suffering and pain.
3. How can you compassionately and understandingly communicate the theological reasons for suffering to your counselees?

CHAPTER 2

Trauma and the Medicalization of Suffering

Defining Trauma: Cultural and Psychological Perspectives

In the previous chapter, we explored the theological foundations of cataclysmic suffering. Now, we turn our attention to the medicalization of suffering, examining the secular approaches that have shaped modern trauma counseling. Let's begin by identifying the cultural and psychological perspectives of trauma. The word trauma means "wound" and comes from Greek antiquity. The meanings attested at the time include being severely hurt, physical wounds, wounding, (military) defeat, and psychic wounds.[10] Webster's Dictionary defines trauma as "an injury (such as a wound) to living tissue caused by an extrinsic agent, a disordered psychic or behavioral state resulting from severe mental or emotional stress or physical injury, an emotional upset."[11] Another source says trauma "results from exposure to an incident or series of events that are emotionally disturbing or life-threatening with lasting adverse effects on the individual's functioning and mental, physical, social, emotional, and/or spiritual well-being."[12] In the Introduction, I said that trauma can be both physical and emotional. The above collection of definitions supports the idea that a person who has suffered or witnessed something horrible, violent, shocking, disturbing, or painful can be emotionally and physically affected by what they have endured. Simply stated, trauma is the secular term used to describe those effects.

There is one more important source we need to look at for a definition of trauma: the Diagnostic and Statistical Manual of Mental Disorders (DSM). This book, compiled and published by the American Psychiatric Association, contains all the formal classifications of mental health disorders. The DSM is currently in its

Fifth Edition with Text Revisions (DSM-5-TR). It is the secular counselor's source of authority and is often called the "bible" of psychiatry.

Secular mental health professionals have collected and categorized the thoughts, feelings, and behaviors that occur in many, but not all, who have experienced something traumatic and placed them into diagnostic categories in the DSM. It is of utmost importance to understand that the diagnoses in the DSM are constructs. A construct is an abstract concept; it's a social theory created and agreed upon by consensus to help us make sense of the objective world. The DSM itself is a social construct. Sociologist Susan P. Robbins writes,

> Given the dual processes of consensus and authority that are used to create the categories and specific diagnoses that are included and excluded, it is crucial to recognize that the ***DSM is, first and foremost, a socially constructed document. Rather than being based on demonstrable advances toward a scientific understanding of mental distress, it reflects not only the views and interests of the members appointed to the DSM task force, but also the interests of those that provide funding for and benefit from its creation and widespread use.*** Inherently ideological in nature, it also reveals the prevailing social, cultural, historical, and political climate in which psychiatry was able to invent itself as a medical specialty with the authority to define a broad array of life's problems and human suffering as being located within the psychopathology of the individual, rather than in the larger social, cultural, and political context. [13](Emphasis added)

It is essential to recognize that the DSM is not a book based on scientific discovery but instead on the evolution of cultural norms and may be heavily influenced by the pharmaceutical industry.[14] Dr. Jenn Chen quotes from a paper written by The Council for Evidence-Based Psychiatry of the United Kingdom, which says,

> Psychiatric diagnostic manuals such as the DSM and ICD are not works of objective science, but rather works of culture since they have largely been developed through clinical consensus and voting. Their validity and clinical utility are therefore highly questionable, yet their influence has contributed to an expansive medicalization of human experience.[15]

I am also troubled that human problems have been redefined into medical problems. I am specifically concerned that human suffering has been removed from horrific experiences and medicalized into what we call trauma disorders. *Trauma, as we understand it today,* is a psychological construct that is commonly used to describe the feelings and emotions associated with enduring one or more distressing or catastrophic events. The DSM-5-TR defines traumatic events as involving actual or threatened death, serious injury, or sexual violence...[16]

Having established a foundational understanding of trauma from various cultural and psychological perspectives, we now turn to the lived experiences of trauma. This shift will enable us to explore how individuals perceive and process traumatic events in different ways.

Trauma Experienced: The Phenomenology of Trauma

"The especially sinister side of trauma is that, even when the event has ended, it is[sic] only begun to shatter one's key assumptions about oneself and one's relation to others in the world... The disintegration of one's perception of self and the world disrupts one's normal pattern of functioning."[17]

Phenomenology is the philosophy of experience. It studies conscious experience as experienced from the subjective or first-person perspective. It establishes a new way for people to think about themselves and the world around them. In phenomenology, it is posited that human beings' lived experience is the ultimate source of all meaning and value.[18] In a moment, you will read about common ways people experience trauma.

While initially, trauma was associated with the effects of war or natural disasters, the understanding of trauma has become elastic, encompassing a wide variety of experiences. Today, "'Trauma' is understood as a state of being negatively overwhelmed. It is the experience of terror, loss of control, and helplessness during a stressful event that threatens one's physical and/or psychological integrity."[19]

Jon G. Allen, in his book *Coping with Trauma: A Guide to Self-Understanding,* helps us by saying that trauma is the "subjective experience of the objective events that constitute the trauma...The more you believe you are endangered, the more traumatized you will be."[20]

Many who experience something horrific have "after-shocks" related to what they have endured. It is unclear why a distressing event in and of itself should lead to a "trauma response" in one individual and not another. However, some phenomenological researchers think the context in which a horrific event occurs, or what the individual's experience or expectation of "normal," may be related to whether an event is processed as trauma.[21] As individuals, we bring our unique perspectives, belief systems, and experiences into every situation. In addition, what is normal or abnormal is subjective and can be contextual.

For example, a young woman who grew up in a home where marital fidelity was the norm will marry with the assumption and expectation of fidelity. If her husband commits adultery, he will disrupt her assumptions and violate her expectations, distressing and potentially traumatizing her. Even if her husband repents and returns to fidelity, she may no longer assume he will remain faithful. Her "normal" has been altered, and she will no longer take faithfulness for granted as she did before his infidelity. She has lost trust in him and has no interest in repeating the emotional distress (trauma) she experienced upon learning of his adultery. Her "normal" is now distrust, fear, sorrow, and perhaps anxiety.

In contrast, a young woman grew up with infidelity as the ordinary course of life. One or both parents were unfaithful, and while each adultery revelation perhaps caused a temporary uproar, cheating was expected. When she married, while she perhaps hoped her husband or her marriage would be different, when her husband commits adultery, it is an ordinary and expected course of life. While she will probably be angry and upset, this young woman will likely not experience the same emotional distress as the woman who grew up where fidelity was the expectation and the norm.

A more extreme example is a child who grew up in a typical American suburb compared to a child who grew up in a war-torn region of the Middle East. For the American child, one day of having missiles destroy your neighborhood is unimaginable and abnormal, which is partly why it is so traumatic. The American child will likely experience distressing effects such as terror, nightmares, flashbacks of the event, heightened startle reflexes, and other reactions that will dissipate with time. For the Middle Eastern child, incoming missiles may be a daily occurrence and are now processed as usual. This child, who initially responded with distress, has grown accustomed to the sights and sounds of war and is less affected by those initial terrified responses. Instead, he or she will more likely experience feelings of hopelessness and depression.

Domestic violence, including physical, verbal, emotional, spiritual, sexual, or mental abuse, can also result in distressing after-effects. An isolated incident or ongoing physical abuse can cause long-term harm to the body. Still, abusive behaviors don't have to be physical to provoke a response. Verbal abuse is biblically understood as reviling (1 Cor. 5:11) or sword words (Prov. 12:18). Receiving these words can, over time, drastically change a person. Biblically, it is understood as oppression and can be as distressing (Eph. 4:29;[ii] Prov. 12:13[iii]). Emotional or mental abuse is a cruel form of mistreatment in which one person exercises harsh control over another person or misuses authority or power against someone. and harmful as physical abuse to some people (James 2:6; Gen 16:6[iv]).[v,vi]

Bullying can also lead to significant affliction and distress. The Bible doesn't speak directly to bullying, but we can find the essence of bullying in various places (Gen. 37; 1 Sam. 17; Matt. 27:11–56; Luke 10:35–37). Proverbs 6:16–19 helps us understand the prideful, wicked heart of the bully. Ultimately, the bully wants to demonstrate power over a weaker or vulnerable person. They enjoy inflicting pain on others and dominating them. Being bullied at home, school, or work can be so tormenting that the recipient takes their own life. It is essential to realize that bullying isn't only experienced by kids on the playground or school bus; adults are also mistreated by those who use harassment, manipulation, and intimidation to make themselves feel powerful or to get what they want. Bullies are of all ages and come from all walks of life. The constant tension and fear of encountering the bully, along with the experience of being bullied, can lead to significant suffering and emotional upset.

Children are typically put in foster care due to abuse or neglect in their homes. Some kids have been beaten or sexually abused or have gone without basic needs of food, clothing, shelter, and cleanliness. Unfortunately, a child's suffering and hardship often persists after they enter the foster care system. First, everything familiar to them, except what the social worker put in the plastic trash bag, is gone. Second, when a child is placed in foster care, they instantly lose connection to their birth family. Siblings are often separated and placed in different

---

ii Strong's G4550 of poor quality, bad, unfit for use, worthless (A. V. corrupt) G4550, sapros: of poor quality, bad, unfit for use, worthless (James Strong, Strong's Exhaustive Concordance, Blue Letter Bible, accessed March 26, 2024, https://www.blueletterbible.org/lexicon/g4550/kjv/tr/0-1/).

iii Strong's H6588, pesha': transgression against individuals (James Strong, Strong's Exhaustive Concordance, Blue Letter Bible, accessed March 26, 2024, https://www.blueletterbible.org/lexicon/h6588/kjv/tr/0-1/).

iv Strong's H6031, 'ānâ: humble, mishandle, afflict: individual (James Strong, Strong's Exhaustive Concordance, Blue Letter Bible, accessed March 26, 2024, https://www.blueletterbible.org/lexicon/h6031/kjv/tr/0-1/).

v Strong's H3905, s.v. lachats: oppress: (James Strong, Strong's Exhaustive Concordance, Blue Letter Bible, accessed March 26, 2024, https://www.blueletterbible.org/lexicon/h3905/kjv.

vi William Joseph McGlothlin, International Standard Bible Encyclopaedia, ©2022 Blue Letter Bible "Oppression" "In Jas 2:6, "oppress" is the rendering of katadunasteuo, "to exercise harsh control over one," "to use one's power against one." https://www.blueletterbible.org/search/Dictionary/viewTopic.cfm?topic=IT0006579

foster homes. Third, they enter an existing family system, have new "brothers and sisters" in their foster home, go to a new school in a new neighborhood, and have new teachers and classmates. Fourth, the sad reality is that far too many children are sexually and physically abused in their foster homes by foster parents and other foster children.

Adding to their distress, they may be moved from temporary home to temporary home, repeating this cycle numerous times before reuniting with their parent, being adopted, or aging out of the foster care system at 18. Those who age out of foster care are turned out to the world, leaving 20% homeless. Often unprepared for life, relatively few get a college education, and more than 70% of females become pregnant before turning 21 years old.

Living in poverty causes significant suffering. An economic downturn can increase poverty as the rising cost of living makes it difficult for income to cover basic expenses. Many people with jobs do not have enough money to pay their bills, buy gasoline to get to work, and put food on the table. In addition, social programs are often stressed beyond their ability to help everyone with their needs. Statistically, Americans now live paycheck to paycheck and live beyond their means. One adverse financial event can cause a cascade of problems, such as economic collapse, leading to defaulting on rent or a mortgage and homelessness.

Both the process of descending into homelessness and the experience of living on the streets can severely distress a person. Stories abound about the difficulties of being homeless—freezing in the winter, no relief from the heat in the summer, little protection from the elements, and insufficient clothing and footwear all take their toll on a person. The lack of appropriate food and medical care is also problematic. None of these issues consider the danger of living on the streets. Homeless people can struggle with erratic and violent behaviors toward those around them due to untreated ailments or drug abuse. Sexual and physical assault, sex trafficking, prostitution, robbery, and murder are common among the homeless (2 Kings 6:24–29; Job 30:3; Prov. 22:7).

Children and teens experience the afflictions that accompany homelessness with and without a parent. Suppose the parent becomes homeless due to financial collapse or drug and alcohol addiction. The children often are homeless with their parent(s) for a time and experience the difficulties of living on the streets. Having a parent with the life-dominating problem of physical addiction to drugs or alcohol can add other hardships to the life of a family. The addicted person is unreliable and often unemployed. Abuse and neglect are common, introducing emotional and sometimes physical affliction into the family system. In extreme situations, children are sold for sex by their parents to get money for drugs or alcohol. If the parent is jailed, the kids go into the foster care system, which can be another significant source of extreme suffering.

Human trafficking for labor or other purposes can be horrific for the migrants. Beginning in the year 2000, the southern border of the United States was open, and millions of people crossed into our country illegally. They made harrowing journeys from Mexico, India, Turkey, Russia, China, Cuba, Haiti, Brazil, Colombia, and Nicaragua, among other South American countries, by paying the drug cartels, human traffickers, and smugglers to get them to the US border and into the country. Sadly, for many illegal migrants, the cost was much more than monetary. Far too many of them paid with their lives. Some who made it across the border reported having been raped, starved, and left for dead, among other horrors. Small children and youth have reported that their parents abandoned them, leaving them to make the harrowing trip alone and at the mercy of the cartels. We've seen the stories and videos of toddlers being dropped over the border wall or floated across the Rio Grande on a raft by traffickers. Some families started together, but the parents died or were killed along the way. As a result, migrants likely experienced significant forms of catastrophic suffering on their journey and after they arrived at their destination in America.[22]

Even legal immigration can be emotionally distressing. Leaving behind all that is familiar and beginning again in a new country with different traditions and customs is very unsettling. If the migrant does not speak the language, this also can lead to fear and distress. In addition, if the immigrant encounters difficulty with housing and getting a job and is victimized by unscrupulous people, that may cause tremendous fear and persecution.

The consequences of war often bring unbelievable suffering. Thanks to technology, the Iraq and Afghanistan wars were viewed on our televisions. Many of our sons and daughters served and fought in those hot and sandy places, and they have experienced emotional harm from their tours of duty. While watching from the safety of our homes, we could not imagine what they were experiencing. They saw their friends and buddies blown up, sometimes being covered with their blood while comforting them as they took their last breaths or carrying them to safety with bullets flying overhead. Most of us can't fathom shooting people, dropping bombs on villages and compounds, or taking human life in combat.

Once home, these brave men and women often experience post-war distress. They live in a constant state of hyper-alertness. They are the people who always sit with their backs to the wall, their eyes constantly scanning the room, looking for threats. They hate crowds and loud booms and are tortured by the fireworks in which the rest of us delight. They struggle not to react out of the terror those pops and booms provoke. At home at night, they lie on the floor, against the wall and facing the door, trying to shove away the memories and fears that haunt them as they attempt to sleep. They suffer from what one physician called "over-remembrance," in which they recall, with vivid clarity, through flashbacks and nightmares, what they experienced in war.[23]

Veterans often numb themselves with alcohol and legal or illegal drugs just to function. The parents, spouses, and children who are so grateful to have them home are often confused by the person their loved one has become. The formerly docile and happy person may now be aggressive and angry. The son or daughter who previously had an optimistic outlook might now be sullen and depressed. The family is upset, and the veteran cannot talk about why they are the way they are. They have no concept of processing or expressing what they have experienced.

There are also the extreme hardships resulting from physical injuries sustained in combat. Our warriors come home missing limbs, experiencing blindness, hearing impaired, or utterly deaf from the sounds of war. They have traumatic brain injuries (TBI) from bullet penetration, concussion, violent impact, or shock waves from the explosive blast from improvised explosive devices. They arrive wheelchair-bound or with prosthetic limbs to homes they can no longer navigate because they are not built for disabled people. They experience their losses many times daily while simply trying to function, all while grappling with the other aspects of post-war distress.

Medical trauma is a genuine, experienced phenomenon. A person who experiences severe illness requiring invasive or life-altering treatment can experience physical reactions, emotional distress, feelings of depression, anxiety, and grief. During the COVID-19 pandemic, patients in the ICU (Intensive Care Unit) and restrained while on ventilators have described their experiences to healthcare professionals. Most were semi-conscious and delirious from medication or the illness itself and experienced vivid hallucinations and terrifying dreams. Due to the frequent changes in ICU staff and lack of familiar faces, there was a sense of extreme confusion. Many say they have ongoing emotional issues from their prolonged hospital stay.

The aftermath of a church or school shooting, bombing, or the 9/11 terrorist attacks can vary from sleeplessness and anxiety to debilitating terror. Likewise, those who have lived through natural disasters such as severe earthquakes, floods, volcanic eruptions, or tsunamis are also afflicted to varying degrees. However, we observe that many people who experience catastrophic devastation, whether on a short-term or long-term basis, display similar groups of behaviors as a result of the incident.

An unfortunate and increasingly common cause of extreme distress is sexual assault or sexual abuse. Sexual assault is forced sex of any kind. It includes rape and any sexual encounter that is not consensual. It may or may not be violent, but it will be coercive and include an adult or other child insisting on or demanding sexual acts. Sexual abuse and assault can occur outside of or within the context of marriage. Sadly, within the church, New Testament Scriptural imperatives such as Ephesians 5:22 and 1 Corinthians 7 are increasingly being used to justify emotional, verbal, and sexual abuse in Christian marriages, causing incredible suffering in the spouse who endures such treatment. The curse of sin caused humans to become perverse, selfish, self-centered, and ungodly in every respect, and this is at the root of sexual abuse in our culture, even among Christians. Notably, there are dozens of warnings in Scripture regarding sexual sin and its consequences.

Sex trafficking is a horrific and often violent aspect of sexual abuse and assault. It occurs when one human being is bought or sold to another to engage in commercial sex acts against their will. Sex trafficking is another tragic source of horrific suffering. Tragically, 60% of women who age out of foster care enter the sex industry. The consistently cited risk factor for vulnerability to being trafficked is a child who has been in foster care, the child welfare system, and the juvenile justice system. Many have already been sexually abused, physically abused, and neglected in their birth home or foster home.

Some trafficked kids are runaways, and others are turned out of their homes by their parents or guardians because they are considered too troublesome or disobedient. Other trafficked youth are abandoned by those who are charged to care for them. The reasons vary and can include the mother getting a new boyfriend or husband who does not want her child around or the parents' drug use renders them unwilling or unable to care for the child. Dr. Gerassi and Dr. Nichols cite a sad statistic: "A third of runaway or throwaway youth are recruited into prostitution within 48 hours of leaving home."[24] All of these people would be at high risk of being diagnosed with Post-Traumatic Stress Disorder (PTSD).

While the previous examples highlight various forms of trauma, a detailed case study can offer a more comprehensive understanding of the long-term effects of catastrophic experiences. Let's delve into Sally's story to see how complex suffering unfolds over time. Sally's journey will be a recurring theme throughout this book, enabling us to explore various aspects of devastation and recovery in greater depth.

Sally: A Case Study in Catastrophic Suffering

Sally lived with her mom, dad, and older brother Billy. Her mom worked from home, and her dad was an elder in their local church. Sally had a wonderful life. Even though her brother was three years older than her, they played together all the time. They would climb trees, play tag, and pretend to be pirates. They would swim in the pond on their property all summer long. Theirs was a life of innocence and fun.

When Sally was 9, Billy and his best friend lured her into their clubhouse to play a game. Sally liked games and, as you can imagine, she adored her big brother. She was excited to be allowed into Billy's clubhouse, as it was ordinarily off-limits to her. What started as excitement quickly turned to confusion as her brother grabbed her and forced her to the floor of the clubhouse. Sally was very confused. Billy was her trusted best friend; what was going on?

Confusion became fear and then terror as Billy held her down, and his friend ripped off her favorite yellow summer shorts with the daisies on them. Once her shorts were off, her brother's best friend and then Billy raped her repeatedly. The look on Billy's face as he held her down so his friend could rape her was frightening. When it was his turn, she didn't recognize her brother. She'd never seen him like this!

Sally tried so hard to get away from them. She squirmed and tried to move, but she was held fast. Sally started to scream, and they stuffed her favorite shorts in her mouth so she couldn't make a sound. Sally was afraid she would suffocate, so she stopped trying to scream. She was terrified and in pain from how they were holding her to the floor of the clubhouse. She could smell the woodsy smell of the playhouse. The clubhouse floor was rough wood, and it hurt her back. Her private parts hurt, too, from what they were doing to her.

Eventually, Sally stopped fighting and let them do what they wanted. She went away to a place in her mind where this wasn't happening. She started thinking about playing pirates, of being big and strong. When it was over, Sally was numb. Her body hurt, her soul was aching, and her heart was broken. Before they let her go, they threatened her to be silent about the assaults, or they would kill her. After what they did to her in the clubhouse, Sally believed them. She was terrified of being hurt again.

This was only the beginning. Every opportunity that they could get Sally alone, the boys would have sex with her. After a while, they began taking Sally into the woods, and they forced Sally to allow their other friends to have sex with her and do unspeakable things. At first, Sally was very afraid. Some boys were rough with her, but others were not so bad. Sally even started liking it some of the time. When she didn't, she found it easier each time to go to that special place in her mind where the bad things didn't happen.

Sally wanted to please Billy, yet she hated him. She longed to tell her parents what was happening to her, but she felt guilty because she had long since stopped struggling and fighting back. Sally didn't always want to do the things they wanted her to do, but she wanted to be liked. She wanted the boys to be nice to her.

As you can imagine, Sally was deeply impacted by these assaults. After the very first incident in the clubhouse, Sally began to change. The formerly bright and sunny little girl became quiet and anxious. She started to wet the bed at night and didn't want to be alone. She demanded the light be left on in her bedroom at night, and sometimes, she would get out of bed and sleep on the floor with her back against the door so her brother would not sneak in and hurt her again.

Her parents were at first confused but became angry and annoyed with Sally over the changes in her behavior and demeanor over time, especially since when they asked what was going on, Sally stood silently, terrified of telling her parents what her brother had been doing to her. She began lying and hiding things, and when disciplined for her actions, she really started acting out. As time passed, she was failing school, was caught stealing, getting into fights and other kinds of trouble, and rebelling against her parents at home.

The sexual assaults and being prostituted by her brother continued until, at age 13, Sally became pregnant. Billy was furious with her. He took her for an abortion and then again threatened her into silence. In the car on the way back home, he held a knife to her neck and told her he would slit her throat if she ever disclosed anything to anyone.

Sally had complications after the abortion, and this is how her parents learned she had been pregnant and aborted the baby. Her parents were shocked and horrified. They demanded to know the baby's father, but remembering what Billy said kept her quiet. Besides, Sally had no idea who the father was. After the abortion, Sally's behavior became so disruptive she essentially lived in lockdown in her room, her only visitor, Billy, after everyone else had gone to sleep.

At age 15, Sally opened her bedroom window one night and slipped into the darkness. Very quickly, Sally was swept into a life of commercial sex work and forced into a brutal life of sex trafficking, pornography, and drug abuse. This is a fate that awaits a third of runaway or throwaway kids.

Sally made her way across the country, sometimes alone and other times as the captive of a boyfriend who was more often than not a man who sexually exploited her. There were a few peaceful times in her life when kind people would take her in, and she would receive medical care and briefly enroll in school. However, it never lasted. Something or someone would drive her back to the streets and commercial sex work. This was Sally's life until she arrived at a rescue mission at age 23, physically and emotionally beaten, ill, desperate, addicted, and without hope. She also needed medical services for numerous injuries and a sexually transmitted disease. She arrived physically addicted to drugs and alcohol and has been through physical withdrawal under medical supervision.

Sally received good care from the staff at the Mission. It was the first time she had not stolen or begged for food in many years. The Mission staff noticed Sally was hyper-vigilant, always alert and waiting for something to happen. Loud noises or unexpected sounds or movements startled her—she would overreact and sometimes physically jump up or try to run out of the room in a panic. The other residents were often awakened by Sally's screams or yelling in her sleep from nightmares when she was able to sleep, that is. It was not unusual for Sally to be awake for a day or two until she physically passed out from exhaustion.

The staff noticed there were times when Sally appeared to be somewhere else in her mind, especially during a challenging therapy session. The staff psychologist determined Sally was having what secular psychology calls dissociative episodes—a form of disconnection from reality. Sally will say she "goes away" in her mind or "floats above" what is happening. The psychologist told Sally that dissociation allows her to block out and detach in her mind to avoid experiencing the emotional responses of the event. She would also have terrifying flashbacks, appearing to be watching something like a horror movie behind glassy eyes. Sally would sweat, tremble, and make scary noises, unaware that it was happening. She can't or won't talk about what's happened, even when the gentlest person tries to get her to open up. These things and other distressing events occur repeatedly.

Sally is a difficult resident in the Mission. She lives by her emotions and has fleshly responses to her internal pain, like sinful anger, rage, and anxiety. And you can see this in her life as she interacts with the other residents and staff. She often has significant outbursts of anger and times when she is physically and verbally out of control. She appears to have a lot of guilt but won't talk about it. The therapist said Sally displays low self-esteem. She doesn't seem to think much of herself, says negative things about herself, and calls herself names. Along with these things, Sally frequently appears quite anxious and fearful. Her countenance is downcast, and she rarely makes eye contact with anyone, leading the staff to conclude that she is ashamed. Overall, it is very clear that Sally is suffering.

The mission had a program that, among other services, provided trauma-informed counseling. Sally was matched with a female counselor who provided therapy. Based on her history and behaviors, Sally was labeled as having PTSD or complex PTSD.

The Rise of Medicalization: How Catastrophic Suffering Became a Medical Issue

The label of post-traumatic stress disorder (PTSD) was first added as a diagnosis in DSM-III in 1980. The DSM-III task force initially opposed its inclusion due to its connection to the Vietnam War. Proponents of its inclusion in the DSM, the Vietnam Veterans Working Group (VVWG), argued that the stress symptoms in the proposed disorder had been around since the late 1800s when they were called "railway spine."[25] They indicated that veterans had been observed to be suffering from the effects of war since WWI when soldiers were diagnosed with "shell shock." They further argued that returning veterans often faced severe adjustment problems. They enlisted the support of psychiatrists and social workers known for their work with vets and bolstered their efforts by providing scientific support for the claims.[26] The DSM working group was eventually persuaded when parallels were drawn between the veterans' responses and others who had experienced different traumas, such as rape or natural disasters. "The DSM-III defined PTSD as a syndrome erupting in response to a 'stressor that would evoke significant symptoms of distress in almost everyone.'"[27]

Post-Traumatic Stress Disorder (PTSD)

Briefly, psychologists and integrated counselors often diagnose suffering people who have been grievously harmed with PTSD. Symptoms include but are not limited to the intrusion of memories of the event, such as flashbacks and nightmares; avoidance of stimuli associated with the event; negative alterations to cognition and mood; partial amnesia concerning the event, negative beliefs, loss of trust, and changes in reactivity, such as heightened startle response lasting more than four weeks after the traumatizing event.[28]

Like other mental illness diagnoses, post-traumatic stress disorder (PTSD) is a construct, an abstract concept or shared idea of something that is not physically real but supported by general agreement.[29] Unfortunately, the diagnosis includes the term "disorder," which communicates the idea that the traumatized person is suffering from an incurable medical disease.[30] PTSD has no organic cause, although those diagnosed with it often have significant physical problems. Physical symptoms can be very pronounced, including fatigue, weakness, headache, hyperventilation, indigestion, nausea, and vomiting. Additionally, there may be an increase or decrease in heart rate, muscle spasms, and cold sweats. More severe physical symptoms may include chest pain, recurrent dizziness, and seizures. Sleep disturbances are among the most enduring symptoms of traumatic stress. They are particularly common with severe and prolonged trauma while also increasing one's risk of developing traumatic stress and contributing to worse general health and quality of life.[31] The symptoms of PTSD can pop up months or even years after a traumatic incident. PTSD can be challenging to identify because it's happening in the person's mind. It can look and feel like depression or rage and can affect everything from how the person sleeps to their relationships at home and work.[32] Sleep disturbances, in particular, stand out as some of the most persistent effects of traumatic stress, especially in cases of severe or prolonged suffering. Such disruptions not only linger but can heighten vulnerability to further distress, often correlating with poorer overall health and a diminished quality of life.

Diagnosing PTSD

In general, a formal PTSD diagnosis is given by a mental health specialist. Sometimes, they will do a basic interview, while others administer an initial screening questionnaire asking about the individual's emotional state, sleeping habits, and issues, as well as any problems with anger or rage. One such tool, the PCL-5, is a 20-item self-report measure assessing DSM-5-TR PTSD symptoms (e.g., intrusions, avoidance, negative cognitions, and mood, alterations in arousal and reactivity) on a 0-4 scale (0 = 'Not at all,' 4 = 'Extremely'), with a total score range of 0-80.[33] This tool is used on those suspected of having PTSD by the Los Angeles County Department of Mental Health[34] as well as the Veterans' Administration.[35] Scores of 31-33 or higher suggest probable PTSD, though a clinician must interpret it alongside a full interview.[36] The patient may also require laboratory testing to rule out any underlying medical conditions that could be causing their symptoms. When Sally was at the rescue mission, she was sent for therapy because of the behaviors she was displaying. The therapist administered the PCL-5 to evaluate her struggles after she learned of the years of sexual abuse by her brother Billy and his friends.

Depending on the results of the initial questionnaire, the patient may be referred for a more comprehensive interview or screening with the Clinician-Administered PTSD Scale for DSM-5 (CAPS-5), Treatment-Outcome Post Traumatic Stress Disorder Scale (TOP-8), or the PTSD Symptom Scale Interview (PSS-I and PSS-I-5). Regardless of the assessments used, the evaluations will gather information regarding the traumatic event and the client's symptoms since it happened. For example, surveys that seek the client's thoughts and feelings may be included, along with information from a spouse or partner. Although it's uncommon, it is not out of the question that testing could be done that observes the client's bodily reactions to mild reminders of their trauma. For Sally, the PCL-5 screening with the therapist revealed a score well above 33, prompting a referral for a CAPS-5 interview to confirm the impact of her trauma.

Per the DSM-5-TR, a person experiencing a post-traumatic stress response will have experienced a trauma (A) and then experience symptoms from four different clusters.[37] These clusters include intrusion (B), where the trauma reemerges through memories, nightmares, or flashbacks; avoidance (C), marked by efforts to evade trauma-related thoughts or reminders; negative alterations in cognitions and mood

(D), involving distorted beliefs, persistent negative emotions, or detachment; and alterations in arousal and reactivity (E), such as hypervigilance, anger, or sleep disturbances.[38] The individual over age six will have been exposed to actual or threatened death, serious injury, or sexual violence (A) whether directly to the self, witnessing it as it occurred to others, learned of actual or threatened violent or accidental death of family member or friend, or repeated or extreme exposure to aversive details of the traumatic event.[39] Sally's repeated assaults by Billy and his friends, alongside his death threat with a knife at age 13, meet this trauma threshold, driving the symptoms assessed in her PCL-5 screening years later.

The first symptom cluster (B) is intrusion symptoms. The traumatic event is persistently re-experienced through unwanted or upsetting memories accompanied by emotional and physical distress of the re-experience.[40] This might include nightmares with themes related to the event(s), or flashbacks of events that occur (and feel like they are happening in real-time) when they least expect them.[41] Dissociation and detachment may also occur when horrific memories or bodily sensations become too much to bear. Naturally, the sufferer wants to avoid these experiences. During her PCL-5 screening with the therapist at the Mission, Sally reported nightmares of her brother Billy raping her in the clubhouse, which were rated '4—Extremely' for the relentless distress they caused, and flashbacks where she sweats and trembles as if pinned to the rough wooden floor again, reflecting the assaults that still haunt her.

The second cluster of symptoms (C) is avoidance. It is a desperate attempt to escape the grip of painful thoughts or feelings tied to the trauma, shutting out memories that threaten to flood back with torment. They steer clear of places, people, or things that remind them of the past—perhaps a street where it happened, a face that saw it, or a sound that reminds them of the pain. In their effort to protect themselves, they might refuse to speak of it, avoiding conversations that come too close or turn from anything that stirs the emotional and physical distress they dread. So fierce is this need to hide that they build walls around their heart, determined to keep the terror at bay.[42] Sally's desire to avoid all thoughts about Billy's assaults and her life on the streets was evident as she met with the therapist for the PCL-5 screening. No matter how gently the therapist approached the subject, Sally refused to reveal any more about her life than she already had. She also avoided anything that reminded her of her years on the streets, reflecting her isolation and fear of triggers tied to those years of abuse.

The third cluster (D) is related to negative alterations in cognition and mood. Some post-traumatic stress sufferers experience difficulty with memory, especially recalling key aspects of the trauma, particularly if they tend toward mentally checking out as a coping attempt. They will be unable to remember specific events, dates, and times of traumatic events, struggle with feelings of depression, anxiety, wanting to isolate, and a lack of pleasure in things they formerly enjoyed. In addition, their behaviors make it difficult for them to maintain relationships with others. Some refer to being emotionally numb and feeling detached from others. Many individuals experience negative feelings about themselves and others, often describing an inability to experience positive emotions.[43] Sally reported persistent shame and guilt about her assaults from age 9 to 15 during her PCL-5 screening, rating them '4—Extremely' for believing she was to blame. Her detachment from others and anxiety scored high, too, as she isolated herself and felt numb, reflecting the trauma's deep mark on her mind and mood.

The fourth cluster of symptoms (E) involves alterations in arousal and reactivity. Individuals with PTSD often experience heightened states of alertness and reactivity following their trauma. This can manifest as irritability or aggression, where they may have angry outbursts or engage in physical aggression. They might also exhibit risky or destructive behavior, participating in dangerous activities without regard for their safety. Hypervigilance is common, where they are excessively watchful and alert for potential threats, often feeling on edge. Additionally, they may have a heightened startle reaction, being easily startled by sudden noises or movements. Difficulty concentrating is another symptom, where they struggle to focus on tasks or maintain attention. Finally, difficulty sleeping is prevalent, with problems falling or staying asleep or experiencing restless sleep. These symptoms must persist for more than one month and cause significant distress or impairment in social, occupational, or other important areas of functioning.[44] During her PCL-5 screening, Sally reported frequent angry outbursts and reckless behavior, scoring high on hypervigilance and difficulty sleeping, which prompted further evaluation to confirm the impact of her trauma.

Whereas the initial PTSD diagnostic criteria were limited to direct personal exposure to a horrific event (connected to something like combat or violent rape), the diagnosis has experienced a conceptual bracket creep over the years. Beginning with DSM-IV, a PTSD diagnosis extended to those who witnessed or were exposed to others' trauma.[45] In DSM-5-TR, the diagnosis was further extended to merely learning that a traumatic, violent event occurred to a close family member or friend.[46] The current landscape connects PTSD to things like "repeatedly overhearing jokes in the workplace,"[47] "little things occur that can make you a little upset or annoyed," or walking down the street and seeing a shirt with a familiar pattern on it that spoils your good mood and brings on a feeling of anxiety.[48]

The difference between a normal response to traumatic events and a response given the PTSD label depends on the *length* of *time* a person experiences the stress response and the *degree* to which they experience it. A person is described as having PTSD when standard techniques that attempt to lessen the impact of the trauma do not work, such as the military veteran who cannot escape the distress of war.

Bracket creep regarding PTSD is of concern to researchers. They posit that "if anything can now qualify as a traumatic event, then trauma becomes an all-purpose idiom of distress -- a trope for misfortune in contemporary life... [and] blurs the distinction between traumatic stressors and ordinary stressors. It medicalizes more of human experience while trivializing genuinely traumatic events."[49] A recent article in *The Chicago Tribune* points out this is not a mere terminological fad. The article states, "It reflects a steady expansion of the word's meaning by psychiatrists and the culture at large. And its promiscuous use has worrying implications. When we describe misfortune, sadness, or even pain as trauma, we redefine our experience. Using the word "trauma" turns every event into a catastrophe, leaving us helpless, broken, and unable to move on."[50]

Complex Post Traumatic Stress Disorder (C-PTSD)

The secular diagnosis of Complex Post-Traumatic Stress Disorder (C-PTSD) was first formulated in 1997 by Judith Herman, Harvard professor of clinical psychology. The American Psychological Association (APA) has twice rejected formal requests to recognize C-PTSD for inclusion in the DSM due to a lack of evidence.[vii] The committee determined that C-PTSD shares enough of the same criteria with PTSD, or is PTSD co-occurring with borderline personality disorder, and thus, C-PTSD is not a discrete diagnosis in DSM-IV or DSM-5. This decision is controversial among trauma treatment providers because many believe that while the experiences of both disorders are closely related and all the diagnostic core symptoms of PTSD are found in C-PTSD, they claim that in C-PTSD, there are additional symptoms related to trauma not captured by the original diagnosis. While "simple PTSD" is said to occur when a person experiences a single incident of acute trauma such as a sexual assault, witnessing or experiencing a shooting, an auto accident, or other horrific act, Herman says C-PTSD applies to those who endure or experience prolonged and multiple traumas. These include ongoing childhood sexual assault, sex trafficking, multiple deployments into war zones, or witnessing

[vii] For a detailed explanation of the controversy of the diagnosis of C-PTSD and the lack of scientific evidence, see Scheeringa, *The Trouble with Trauma*, chapter 3 (pp. 83–141).

constant domestic abuse.[51,52] Based on her extensive history of being sexually abused as a child into adulthood and the signs and symptoms she displayed, Sally was given the diagnosis of C-PTSD.

Christian Counselor Rachel Rosser specializes in working with women suffering from complex trauma. She defines C-PTSD as "...a condition that results from chronic or long-term exposure to emotional trauma over which a victim has little or no control and from which there is little or no hope of escape."[53] It is repetitive trauma in which the victim is directly harmed, such as child sexual abuse or sex trafficking.

Bessel van der Kolk, the author of *The Body Keeps the Score*, is considered the premier secular expert on treating complex trauma. He says,

> The traumatic stress field has adopted the term "Complex Trauma" to describe the experience of multiple and/or chronic and prolonged, developmentally adverse traumatic events, most often of an interpersonal nature (e.g., sexual or physical abuse, war, community violence) and early-life onset. These exposures often occur within the child's caregiving system and include physical, emotional, and educational neglect and child maltreatment beginning in early childhood.[54]

In his book, *The Body Does Not Keep the Score,* Dr. Michael Scheeringa, an expert in PTSD research, painstakingly addresses 42 claims about neuroscience, 51 claims about treatment, and 29 claims about related issues made by van der Kolk. He found that much of the analysis of the evidence used to support the claims in van der Kolk's book was faulty or completely lacking![55] Astonishingly, numerous claims contained citations for studies that had nothing to do with trauma or PTSD.[56]

The problem, again, is that there is zero objective scientific data or a single published case report to support the creation of this disorder. No one has documented a patient's pre-event symptoms and personality as compared to their post-event symptoms and personality in such a way that it fits with C-PTSD. Instead, it is a diagnosis "based primarily on a certain class of people defined by specific types of experiences as opposed to the types of symptoms patients showed." [57] Scheeringa states, "[Herman] created the myth that these types of patients show a 'prodigious array of psychiatric symptoms' that are all due 100 percent to their trauma experiences and nothing else."[58]

According to supporters of the C-PTSD construct, those victims who suffer from the effects of complex trauma can experience and demonstrate numerous additional problems to those affected by PTSD. Despite the lack of the most fundamental scientific evidence and the exclusion of C-PTSD as an official diagnosis in the DSM-5-TR, the C-PTSD concepts are used extensively by trauma counselors and those researching the effects of trauma on the mind and body.

The United States Department of Health and Human Services says,

> Victims suffering from complex trauma often experience depression, anxiety, self-hatred, dissociation, substance abuse, despair, and somatic ailments. Individuals exposed to this type of trauma are also at heightened risk for self-destructive and risk-taking behaviors as well as re-victimization and tend to experience difficulty with interpersonal and intimate relationships.[59]

Dr. Frank Ocher, another secular expert in C-PTSD, says:

> Complex PTSD is characterized by 1) severe and pervasive problems in affect regulation; 2) persistent beliefs about oneself as diminished, defeated, or worthless, accompanied by deep and pervasive feelings of shame, guilt, or failure related to the stressor; and 3) persistent difficulties in sustaining relationships and in feeling close to others. The disturbance causes significant impairment in personal, family, social, educational, occupational, or other important areas of functioning.[60]

Rosser thinks that there is a difference in the thoughts and behaviors of those suffering from PTSD and C-PTSD. She says complex trauma sufferers "…exhibit a fragmented identity with an abiding sense of shame, unstable interpersonal relationships, distorted perceptions and a false narrative of their life, disassociation and compartmentalizing, emotional volatility, self-destructive behaviors, somatic disorders, and a distrust of God."[61] She also identifies self-sabotage as common with sufferers of complex trauma in that these women may repeatedly seek out abusive relationships in which they are the victim or the rescuer.

While the experiences and phenomenology may be very real to the sufferer, no objective scientific evidence supports the notion that their etiology is biological.

Diagnosing Trauma Through Brain Imaging

Those who embrace a clinically-informed counseling (CIC) model believe we should avail ourselves of current "evidence-based research" done by treatment providers and researchers currently attempting to qualify and quantify PTSD and other effects of trauma through brain science. However, brain science, specifically neuroscience and neurology, are relatively new fields of study in medicine. Despite the advances of modern medicine, we still know very little about the brain. One area of study is brain imaging, a relatively new technique that subjects the brain to various forms of energy to create maps that reveal the structure and function of the brain.

These scans, like MRI and fMRI, measure changes in brain structure, activity, or blood flow, hoping to reveal differences between a "normal" brain and one affected by trauma. Some researchers claim "abundant evidence" of altered brain areas tied to fear and anxiety. However, others question the results, citing small sample sizes, bias, and even flawed scans, like one of a dead salmon showing activity.[62] For more details, see the appendix, "Understanding the Medical Frameworks of Trauma: An Optional Deep Dive."

There is no universal agreement among scientists that brain scans prove that PTSD and complex trauma cause structural changes or any pathological diseases of the brain. Any claims of this kind cannot be scientifically validated at this time. In fact, Scheeringa notes that any differences in the brain of trauma-exposed people versus those who have not been exposed to trauma are "unreplicable."[63]

Remember, the DSM identifies PTSD as a mental health condition and lists it as an anxiety disorder primarily consisting of memories, emotions, intense and disturbing thoughts, and feelings. It is not a problem of the brain; it is a problem of the mind. Dr. Daniel Berger notes that neuroimaging has its limitations because no scientific tool can directly observe the mind. As a result, he says, "It (neuroimaging) cannot reveal causes and effects – those must be inferred- or evaluate experiences and thoughts."[64] This is vitally important to consider as we think about how to help those who live with the effects of one or more traumatic incidents.

The Brain and the Mind

Since Aristotle's time, people have debated the difference between the brain and the mind. The materialist view posits that the mind is comprised of the brain's physical processes. Neuroscientist Dr. Caroline Leaf believes the mind is separate and inseparable from the brain. She says the mind works through the brain, but it is not the brain.[65] Some people say the mind is the brain in action. It has also been said that the mind is the decision-making power of the brain or the brain at work. Still, others argue that the mind is merely an illusion of the brain, suggesting that the mind itself doesn't exist. In the materialist view, which is the prevailing position of the medical sciences and secular psychology, most argue that the mind and the brain are essentially the same thing. These scientists do not consider humans to be both material and immaterial. They operate from a materialist perspective and do not believe there is anything about us beyond what can be seen, touched, scanned, or examined manually or under a microscope.

Culturally, the mind is often mistakenly associated with the brain as an organ, but biblically, it is understood differently. The organ of the brain is a physical, outer-person reality. It is not the mind and stands in contrast to the mind. To be most biblical, which makes us most accurate, we should speak of the brain as the outer person and the mind as the inner person. Dr. Greg Gifford rightly states that if you conclude the mind is an organ, you will confuse the treatment of people. [66]

We can draw from both the Old and New Testaments to conclude that the biblical concept of the mind refers to the inner person, being the seat of emotions and affections. It is an aspect of the heart. For example, in the Old Testament, the word *lêb* is often translated as "heart." It encompasses the thoughts, intentions, mind, will, and emotions.[viii] The New Testament Greek word *nous* refers to intellect or understanding. The word *dianoia* is used for thoughts and reasoning.[ix] A. Craig Troxel says, "The heart includes and encompasses the mind with all its cognitive abilities, like reasoning, meditating, remembering, and believing. This is why the words "heart" and "mind" often appear together in Scripture (Phil 4:7). In such instances, they are not being contrasted but coordinated."[67] As you will see, this is critical when considering counseling methodologies for those who have suffered catastrophic suffering.

[viii] lēḇ, Strong's H3820 - inner man, mind, will, heart, understanding, 1. inner part, midst 2. heart (of man), 3. soul, heart (of man), 4. mind, knowledge, thinking, reflection, memory, 5. inclination, resolution, determination (of will), 6. Conscience, 7. heart (of moral character), 8. as seat of appetites, 9. as seat of emotions and passions. https://www.blueletterbible.org/lexicon/h3820/kjv/wlc/0-1/, accessed 11/11/24.

[ix] *Dianoia,* Strong's G1271 – I. The mind as a faculty of understanding, feeling, desiring, II. Understanding, III. mind, i.e. spirit, way of thinking and feeling, IV. thoughts, either good or bad.

Predicting Trauma by The Adverse Childhood Experiences (ACEs) Questionnaire

The ACEs is a commonly used diagnostic screening tool used by clinicians to measure trauma and compound trauma resulting from adverse childhood experiences (ACEs) such as abuse, neglect, and household dysfunction. The CDC believes ACEs "can have a tremendous impact on future violence victimization and perpetration, and lifelong health and opportunity."[68] In the report titled "What Is the ACE?" the Minnesota Department of Mental Health describes how they use this tool in a telephone survey and how the results are calculated:

> Exposure to any single ACE condition (sexual abuse, physical abuse, emotional abuse, mental illness of a household member, problematic drinking of a household member, illegal street drugs used by a household member, divorce or separation of parents, domestic violence, incarceration of a household member) is counted as one point. If a person experienced none of the conditions in childhood, the ACE score is zero. Points are then totaled for a final ACE score. It is important to note that the ACE score focuses on the number of ACE conditions experienced. Also, the ACE conditions used in the ACE survey reflect only a select list of experiences.[69]

If the participant scores four or higher, researchers "predict" if they will experience various lifelong problems and adverse life events, ranging from smoking and unintended pregnancy to diabetes to depression and anxiety.

Sally: A Case Study in Catastrophic Suffering- The ACEs

Sally was given the ACEs *questionnaire upon entering a previous secular treatment and recovery facility after one of her arrests for prostitution. Sally scored six on her ACEs questionnaire. According to the theory, when a child like Sally experiences one or more ACEs or "toxic stresses," how their genes work can be changed. This affects learning and behavior in ways that lead to difficulty in successfully negotiating everyday social interactions (which, according to this theory, explains why Sally was so troubled in school and at home) as well as toxic stress causing the release of a hormone that shrinks the limbic system —the amygdala, and hippocampus—which are part of the brain where memories and emotions are stored. According to the theory, this explains why Sally has such a flat affect and wildly fluctuating emotions.*

The ACEs framework assumes Sally's struggles (anger, dissociation) are inevitable brain-based outcomes, ignoring her heart's response to sin—both hers and others' against her (Rom. 5:12; Ezek. 36:26). While ACEs label Sally's pain as a brain problem, Scripture sees her as a whole person, body and soul, broken by sin yet redeemable by grace. The staff at the facility told Sally her high ACEs score meant she'd always struggle socially, offering pills, not peace, while overlooking her heart's cry for forgiveness.

How can this simple assessment, which typically contains 9–12 questions, accurately predict the future of a child who has experienced adversity, hardship, or affliction? The theory is grounded in the evolutionary perspective on human development. Medical science has a widely accepted view of how the body and brain have evolved. Bessel van der Kolk states, "The brain is built from the bottom up. It develops level by level within every child in the womb, just as it did in the course of evolution."[70] Dr. Bruce Perry explains, "When a baby is born, his or her brain is not fully formed" but continues to develop. Research has shown that a child's brain is extremely malleable.[71] He further states, "Like a series of building blocks, each portion of the brain that develops provides a foundation for further development, so the brain's higher functioning abilities depend entirely on those early, basic 'building blocks' of development."[72]

Perry, van der Kolk, and other evolutionary scientists, biologists, and neuroscientists support the 1960s theory of Dr. Paul MacLean, who described the brain as having three parts: the reptilian brain (the most primitive part that controls basic body functions), the mammalian brain (the limbic system that controls emotional responses), and the rational brain (the prefrontal cortex that controls language and reason). (You will read more about this in the section on the Polyvagal Theory.) The tri-part brain theory, while now discredited, continues to be used in therapeutic approaches and is widely used to explain the effects of trauma on the developing brain.[73]

Developmental traumatology is a newer field of study that systematically investigates the psychiatric and psychobiological effects of abuse on children. Currently, there is little research on the neurobiological effects of trauma and PTSD on developing children. The only comparative models are provided by studies done on the neurobiological effects of overwhelming stress in animal models and studies done on adults diagnosed with PTSD.

Developmental traumatology theory states that when a child experiences sexual abuse or other ACEs, the trauma changes how the brain develops and grows. Dr. Perry believes, "Everything that develops in the mind after that point will be influenced by the brain's reaction to that traumatic experience. As a result, the brain will grow in an unbalanced and unstable manner."[74] The result is a lasting consequence on the victim's ability to function as an adult.[75] Mary Francis Bowley, who works extensively with adult victims of sex trafficking, says when a child is sexually abused, "The damage from just one incident of trauma, such as sexual abuse, is life-altering. She may experience a stunting to her emotional development."[76] Bowley believes that a woman who has experienced ongoing child sexual abuse can experience damage to all parts of her brain. The damage's severity depends on the frequency and severity of the trauma she experienced. In her experience as both a victim and survivor of abuse and sex trafficking, she says the victim does not process danger like someone who did not experience childhood trauma. Therefore, as an adult, a child abuse victim struggles to assess risks to her safety adequately.[77] These theories are accepted and promoted as factual, spreading widely online despite conclusive scientific evidence. One trauma-focused domestic violence blogger wrote,

> For those who go through this [trauma] as children, because the brain is still developing and they're just beginning to learn who they are as an individual, understand the world around them, and build their first relationships - severe trauma interrupts the entire course of their psychologic and neurologic development.[78,79]

However, a significant concern with the data collected through the ACEs tool is that "one hundred percent of the dozens of ACEs studies have been cross-sectional."[80] Cross-sectional studies are done on adults, meaning the study subjects were examined *after* their traumatic experiences. Because there was no data on the subjects from before the trauma (surveys, brain scans), there is no clinical or objective comparison to be made. Therefore, if any neurological abnormalities are present, it is impossible to determine how, when, or to what extent to attribute those changes. Traumatic stress may adversely affect the development of their biological stress systems. However, causation cannot be proven as the completed studies were entirely based on the cross-sectional analysis of limited data with zero power to determine causality.[81] Additionally, many of the subjects studied had received or were receiving treatment for some form of mental illness, including psychoactive medications.[82,83,84,85] Scheeringa states,

> The key question surrounding this set of facts about the neurobiology of trauma and PTSD is not about whether the neurobiological differences exist. The key question is how those neurobiological

> differences originated. *Did those neurobiological factors exist before trauma exposure and serve as vulnerability factors? Or did those neurobiological factors develop as a consequence of trauma exposure?*[86]

In his follow-up book, *The Body Does Not Keep the Score,* Scheeringa states that while trauma does occur more frequently in children with biological, psychological, social, or environmental vulnerabilities or who are born into families with difficulties, the interpretation of collected data is frequently invalid due to violation of the principle of exchangeability.[x] He reiterates, "One hundred percent of the ACE studies that have been cited by activists in every single legislative resolution and government program are cross-sectional studies."[xi]

Clinicians attribute research in epigenetics to the findings that support their theory, which suggests that ACEs alter how the brain develops and grows. Research in epigenetics, the study of how environment and experiences affect the expression of a person's genes, is one of the most active areas of scientific research today. Despite what we hear in the media, very little is known about the human genome at the molecular and functional levels. What we do know for a fact is that our genetic code is inherited from our parents. The color of our eyes, our height, and other physical traits are encoded in our genes. Unfortunately, epigenetics has been used to promote the extraordinary claim that trauma permanently changes and damages the brain.

According to the theory, how their genes work can change when a child lives under continual stress (ACEs) without help or support from a caregiver. This is called the toxic stress response. Scientists say that their research shows that although the DNA itself is not altered, experiences can lead to changes in the genome as

---

[x] The principle of exchangeability is a fundamental concept in statistics and causal inference, especially within observational studies and randomized controlled trials. It posits that two groups being compared (such as treatment and control groups) should be similar in all relevant aspects except for the treatment or exposure being studied. This principle is crucial in ACEs research to ensure that comparisons between groups (e.g., those with high ACEs versus those with low or no ACEs) are valid and meaningful. Addressing these challenges necessitates careful study design, robust statistical methods, and a nuanced understanding of the complex interplay between ACEs and various outcomes. By maintaining exchangeability, ACEs research can more accurately identify causal relationships between early adverse experiences and later life outcomes. Researchers must be diligent in controlling contradictory and invalid variables and employing appropriate methods to ensure their findings are valid and reliable.

[xi] Michael Scheeringa, "The Body Does Not Keep the Score: How Popular Beliefs About Trauma Are Wrong," Self-Published, 2024, p. 75. Scheeringa provides detailed data on a qualitative review he conducted of 22,175 studies. His summary conclusion after review of the data was that "cross-sectional studies not only possess zero power to determine causal effects (as the ACEs state), but they are inevitably flawed because they violate the principle of exchangeability."p.75

minute chemical tags that turn the genes on and off are added and removed from the genes in response to the environment in which the child is living. So, how the child's body reads the DNA sequence and whether and how genes release the information they carry leads to the toxic stress response.[87] Some researchers suggest toxic stress disrupts aspects of brain growth, causing physiological changes that impact the child's development. For example, learning and behavior are said to be affected in ways that lead to difficulty in successfully negotiating everyday social interactions. Toxic stress also triggers the release of a hormone that shrinks the part of the brain where memories and emotions are stored. [88,89,90,91]

Until recently, epigenetic shifts were thought to be permanent, a concept known as biodeterminism. However, research reveals that, unlike genetic mutations, which are permanent, epigenetic changes are temporary and reversible. Dr. Scheeringa has evaluated both the claims and the evidence and has determined that the evidence does not support the claims that toxic stress has lifelong effects, as claimed by some researchers.[92] He emphatically states that "there is absolutely zero evidence that trauma can alter hard-wired developmental capacities."[93] He confidently states this because no objective scientific evidence supports these claims. Instead, reliable research indicates that the tags in the genome that turn genes on or off provide a way of adapting to changing conditions without causing permanent changes in our genomes.[94,95] This is good news in that while experiencing childhood trauma may temporarily affect the body, there are no lasting, permanent effects or biological changes.

> The central premise of the toxic stress and ACE theories that psychological stress damages the brain, alters anatomical brain structures, and permanently disrupts hardwired neurocircuitry that has evolved through centuries of human development is an extraordinary claim. Extraordinary evidence in humans to support the toxic stress theory is lacking in pre-trauma prospective studies in humans.[96]

Researchers who promote the theory of biological embedding also claim that biomarkers associate a high ACEs score with elevated risk and stress-related chronic health problems, including heart disease, cancer, stroke, chronic bronchitis, emphysema, diabetes later in life, and premature death. They have labeled this the "social brain" concept. The "social brain" has become a popular term to describe the involvement of several brain regions in mediating social behaviors, accounting for the difficulty these children experience with inappropriate conduct in school and, ultimately, the workplace. The theory suggests that these problems affect individuals emotionally, cognitively, and socially well into adulthood.[97] However, this is not universally agreed upon among secular professionals. For example, Steve W. C. Chang, Ph.D., an associate professor of Psychology and Neuroscience at Yale University, says the social brain concept can be misleading. Moreover, considering the brain's complex functions, he believes this concept is imprecise and does not entirely support the current research claims.[98] Dr. Scheeringa, who has devoted well over twenty-eight years to researching PTSD and may have more direct experience working with young children exposed to trauma and PTSD, considers the toxic stress claims to be "an extraordinary notion that is not true."[99]

It is also theorized that toxic stressors elevate the likelihood of suicide, drug or alcohol abuse, and other self-harm risks, including increased vulnerability to being sex trafficked. [100] However, association is not causation. Moreover, researchers admit they don't understand the mechanisms that would cause those physical responses. Scheeringa says,

> If ACE theory is true, tell us, please, what's the biological mechanism of how ACEs cause a horde of physical and mental conditions? A more plausible theory to explain why individuals who develop diseases as adults experienced stressful events in childhood is that many bad things do not happen at random in nature, but they are not causal of each other.[101]

As we have already seen, research conclusions are often flawed and unreliable despite being touted as factual and conclusive in various books on trauma and, of course, on the internet. Even though the theories are unproven, published research papers are filled with statements such as "it is thought," "research suggests," "these data suggest," "outcomes may suggest," or "it is hypothesized that." Dr. Scheeringa, upon examining the claims and analyzing the evidence, states, "There is absolutely zero evidence that humans are so fragile that psychological stress and trauma, which are extremely common, can derail hard-wired, genetically driven human development that has created humans for millions of years."[102]

The Polyvagal Theory

Another theory closely connected to trauma-informed care is the polyvagel theory. The polyvagal theory (PVT) is an evolutionary construct that builds upon Darwin's 140-year-old observations. Dr. Stephen Porges, a

Professor of Psychiatry at the University of North Carolina, developed PVT. Porges, whose research intersects psychology, neuroscience, and evolutionary biology, introduced PVT in 1994. This evolutionary theory plays a featured role in *The Body Keeps the Score* and is the premise under which virtually every current secular therapy and treatment for PTSD and C-PTSD is based. "PVT is an attempt to explain the relationship between parasympathetic activity and behavior from an evolutionary perspective. It aims to provide an understanding of the connections between brain and body processes."[103] Because PVT is based on theories about the evolution of the species, we must declare at the outset that, as Christians who hold to biblical anthropology, the basis of PVT claims and associated research are oppositional to our belief system.

PVT has been a personal interest and area of study since I discovered its connection to trauma-informed counseling, and I have conducted extensive research on it over the past several years. An internet search for PVT will yield a minimum of 120,000 references, including articles, blogs, and self-help materials that instruct the reader how to "activate" or stimulate the "ventral vagus complex," a term unique to this theory. Numerous podcasts by therapists and Christian counselors promote this scientifically unfounded and, most certainly, unbiblical theory.

Polyvagal theory (PVT) posits that trauma impacts the nervous system through the vagus nerve, which connects the brain to the body, driving responses like fight, flight, freeze, or even dissociation. It links brain regions such as the amygdala, hippocampus, and medulla to a "social engagement system," suggesting that physiological states, rather than the mind alone, shape behavior, fear, and memory, potentially rewiring these areas in response to threats. However, critics such as Scheeringa and Grossman argue that PVT oversimplifies the brain's complexity, lacking robust evidence to support its evolutionary claims or role in social engagement. For a deeper exploration, see the appendix, "Understanding the Medical Frameworks of Trauma: An Optional Deep Dive."

Complementary to PVT, the Adverse Childhood Experiences (ACEs) questionnaire predicts the long-term effects of trauma based on early hardships, while trauma-informed care (TIC), which we will examine next, incorporates these insights into treatment. Together, these approaches emphasize brain changes and physiological interventions, framing suffering as a medical issue. Yet, this focus may overlook the heart's deeper spiritual needs, reducing a complex human experience to biological fixes.

Let's return to Sally's story to see how she would respond to the PVT.

Sally: A Case Study in Catastrophic Suffering — The Polyvagal Response

Sally arrived at the rescue mission at 23, physically broken, addicted to drugs and alcohol, STD-infected, and scarred from years of trafficking and abuse since childhood. After failed secular treatments and arrests, labeled with Complex PTSD and other DSM terms, she's now detoxed, clean, and sober, yet still wrestling with deep emotional wounds. Sally has made enough progress in her current treatment program that she is allowed day passes to leave the mission for the church and to take brief trips to the store or on a social outing. Although she has had difficulty going out on her day passes, she forces herself to attend her 12-step groups and some social gatherings.

Typically, while in public, Sally continually scans the room, looking for someone who might be a threat. She stays on the edges of any crowd, refusing even to use the restroom while in public. She keeps her back to the wall whenever possible.

According to PVT, Sally's nervous system subconsciously engages in neuroception (which, according to Porges, is the ventral vagus system's ability to detect safety and danger) and scans her environment for safety cues or potential threats. When Sally determines she is secure and safe, she can engage in social behaviors because she feels calm and relaxed. Her heart rate variability (HRV) is higher, indicating an adaptive autonomic nervous system. She is comfortable interacting with and relating to others. Her face is uplifted and expressive, and her voice intonations are lighthearted. She is emotionally happy and feels at peace.

On this occasion, while Sally is happily chatting with a friend, she thinks she recognizes the face of a man who bought her for sex entering the crowded room. She remembers him because he was very rough and cruel to her. But there are so many people, and she is so far away from the door that she can't be sure it's him.

According to Porges's theory, neuroception has determined that a threat may be at hand, and Sally's social engagement system is called upon to invalidate the danger. When her social engagement system can't invalidate the threat, her sympathetic nervous system goes into overdrive, resulting in adrenaline, epinephrine, norepinephrine, and cortisol being dumped into Sally's system. These increase her heart rate and respiration, decreasing her heart rate variability (HRV).

Sally begins to experience anxiety, fear, and perhaps anger. She excuses herself from the conversation and carefully moves around the room's perimeter, back against the wall. Her facial expressions change from calm and relaxed to tense and fearful as she searches the crowd to see if it is actually a former assailant in the crowd. She is hyper-aware and mentally prepared to fight or take flight. Suddenly, he is standing next to her, and she is face-to-face with one of the men who was particularly cruel to her. She feels trapped and desperately wants to get away from him.

Porges theorizes that Sally's dorsal vagal complex is now activated. She will mentally withdraw and feel frozen, numb, hopeless, dizzy, and trapped or "not here" (dissociation). She may become immobilized or "freeze." Anyone observing Sally will notice that she stops engaging, and her facial expressions decrease. You might perhaps describe her as having a "blank" or faraway look on her face. Her eyes may appear fixed and "spaced out." Serotonin, dopamine, and endorphins have been released, and her heart rate variability is very low in this state.

Sally has experienced what Porges calls the "freeze" response. He and van der Kolk describe this as the old vagus nerve generating immobilization in the reptilian brain that Sally (and we) share with mankind's ancient ancestors. They say the "freeze" response is only enacted when our more evolved systems fail. The freeze response is said to characterize many traumatized people.

Porges suggests that once a person is traumatized the way Sally has been, the body can remember that experience and become "stuck" in the "fight, flight, or freeze" response. This creates further social and relational problems for someone traumatized as they realize they live on a plane of hypervigilance, constantly scanning for danger signs, or are so emotionally numbed out that they cannot enjoy the ordinary pleasures of life. Once the threat is eliminated, her body will return to a state of safety, and the ventral vagal system will be reactivated over the next 20 minutes. Her heart rate and respiration will gradually slow down, leaving Sally completely exhausted.

Trauma-Informed Care (TIC)

The polyvagal theory has had a significant influence on trauma-informed care, and current treatments for trauma in secular and Christian counseling are based on the trauma-informed care (TIC) model. TIC is an organizational structure and treatment framework. This systems-level approach recognizes and responds appropriately to the neurological, biological, and psychological symptoms that result from experiencing trauma. TIC understands, recognizes, and responds to the effects of all types of traumas, including the person's need for safety and security. TIC does not treat specific symptoms or syndromes.[104] Like PVT, TIC has its etiology in evolutionary theory. So it makes sense that the Office for Mental Health and Addiction Services says, "The treatment of specific mental health symptoms and syndromes requires evidence-based therapeutic and sometimes pharmacological approaches"[105] rather than spiritual/biblical approaches.

Sally's suffering-related responses are classified as mental illnesses. Therefore, the only option for how to view people like Sally, with so-called problems of the mind (brain), and the only option for how to fix or treat her maladies is through medical and psychiatric intervention. Sally was prescribed treatments that included talk and behavioral therapy along with psychoactive medications to try and manage the symptoms of her "diseased" and "disordered" mind and the resulting problems. The result of accepting these theories as factual medicalized her experience of suffering. Throughout the years, Sally received several different therapies and medications under the banner of CBT.

On a practical level, the TIC approach involves therapy, medical treatment, medications, and social support. It focuses on the survivor's strengths and empowers them by building trust in the counseling process.[106] TIC also emphasizes physical, psychological, and emotional safety for both consumers and providers, helping survivors build a sense of comfort and control. A key part of the goal is avoiding re-traumatizing the person during counseling. It is considered to be a crucial part of a victim's recovery.[107] This doesn't sound bad, does it? No biblical counselor would be against building a sense of safety and security in their counselee, and no one would intentionally retraumatize a hurting person. However, where this breaks down for those providing biblical care, is under the TIC model, the human experience (phenomenology) is medicalized, and science or scientism[xii] is elevated as the ultimate authority, which is a significant concern for biblical counselors.

Trauma-informed care (TIC) offers evidence-based treatments like cognitive-behavioral therapy (CBT), cognitive processing therapy (CPT), and prolonged exposure therapy (PET), aiming to reduce PTSD symptoms through talk, exposure, or restructuring thoughts. Other options, like Eye Movement Desensitization and Reprocessing (EMDR) or Narrative Exposure Therapy (NET), target trauma's emotional impact, while drugs like ketamine or MDMA are researched despite risks and controversy. These secular approaches, rooted in behavioral or cognitive theories, focus on symptom relief, potentially for someone like Sally, but lack data for sex trafficking survivors and often ignore spiritual needs. For details, see the

---

[xii] *Merriam-Webster Dictionary* (2024), s.v. "scientism." "Scientism is qualified by the recognition that many of the events that require explanation are not simple physical or physiological processes, but complex phenomena that can be explained only by taking into account the cultural significance they undoubtedly possess, such as "the meaning of words," "the morals of the story," "the significance of gestures and facial expressions," "the challenges and obligations and social opportunities," and "all the intricacies that make up a functioning culture." See John Kekes, *The Nature of Philosophical Problems: Their Causes And Implications*, (Oxford, United Kingdom: Oxford University Press, 2014), 137, https://doi.org/10.1093/acprof:oso/9780198712756.001.0001. accessed 11/13/24.

appendix, "Understanding the Medical Frameworks of Trauma: An Optional Deep Dive." Some counselors integrate these, yet Scripture offers a fuller hope (Col. 2:8).

I am concerned that this medicalization—redefining human problems into disorders—creates confusion for counselees. It fails to address the issues of the heart at the core of human suffering, as Scripture does (Prov. 4:23). Sally's story shows this: she was given secular labels to explain her hyper-vigilance and dissociation; her previous therapists considered them to be brain-driven, yet her wounds and problems remained. Sally's problems are spiritual—guilt, shame and a broken soul needing Christ's redemption, not clinical fixes. Adopting secular methodologies, even in "clinically-informed biblical counseling," departs from the sufficiency of Scripture, which offers a comprehensive framework for understanding and addressing catastrophic suffering.

The biblical counseling approach is distinctly different from the TIC approach. Biblical counseling is not based on human wisdom, psychology, opinions, experience, or behavioral concepts (Isa. 55:8–11) but on the belief that Scripture is sufficient to address all aspects of life, including the emotional and psychological issues commonly associated with catastrophic suffering. It seeks to bring the full range of biblical truth to focus on the counselee's need (Heb. 4:12). Biblical counseling methodology focuses on spiritual growth and change. It includes prayer, Bible study, and the use of Scripture-saturated, extra-biblical resources related to the spiritual needs of the counselee, which will enable them to grow in maturity as part of the healing process. Counselees are taught how to apply biblical principles to daily life and are given practical advice based on biblical teachings.[108]

In his book *Saving Abnormal,* Dr. Daniel Berger states, "Psychiatric phenomenology is the humanistic attempt to explain the fallen/broken condition of the human soul- a person's self-perception of life/awareness/consciousness /personhood- within an allegedly scientific framework. This perspective is less of a suggested worldview and more of a forced belief system shrouded in medical authority and statistical data."[109]

With this in mind, let's take another look at when Sally came face-to-face with the man from her past, this time through the lens of biblical counseling.

Sally: A Case Study in Catastrophic Suffering — The Biblical Response

Sally begins to experience anxiety, fear, and perhaps anger as she thinks she recognizes the face of a man who bought her for sex entering the crowded room—a man she remembers for his cruelty. From a biblical perspective, Sally's response reflects the deep wounds of her soul, a heart burdened by the sins committed against her since childhood, and the lingering effects of living in a fallen world (Rom. 8:22–23). Scripture tells us that "a heart at peace gives life to the body, but envy rots the bones" (Prov. 14:30), and Sally's lack of peace—rooted in memories of violence and betrayal—manifests in her body as fear and anxiety. She excuses herself from the conversation and carefully moves around the perimeter of the room, keeping her back to the wall. Her facial expressions shift from calm and relaxed to tense and fearful as she searches the crowd, trying to discern if this is indeed a former assailant. She is hyper-aware, her senses sharpened not by a subconscious neural circuit but by a heart conditioned by years of danger and mistrust.

Suddenly, he is standing next to her, face-to-face—one of the men who was particularly cruel to her. Sally feels trapped and desperately wants to escape. Her response isn't a physiological "freeze" response but a profound human reaction to evil—a soul crying out under the weight of suffering and the consequences of sin (Ps. 55:4–5). Her body and spirit are intertwined, as God created humans as embodied souls (Gen. 2:7), and the extreme suffering and abuse she endured have left a lasting mark on both. She withdraws inwardly, feeling numb, hopeless, and distant—not because of a dorsal vagal shutdown but because her heart, overwhelmed by fear and pain, struggles to find refuge. To those observing, Sally's face grows blank, her eyes distant and fixed, as if she's no longer fully present. This isn't a reptilian instinct but a reflection of a soul wrestling with despair, echoing the psalmist's cry: "I am feeble and utterly crushed; I groan in anguish of heart" (Ps. 38:8).

Biblically, Sally's experience isn't a failure of evolved systems but a vivid illustration of living in a broken world where sin has corrupted human relationships (Rom. 3:23). Her hypervigilance and withdrawal aren't just bodily reactions; they reveal a heart conditioned to expect danger rather than trust, a mind shaped by memories of abuse rather than the renewing hope of God's promises (Rom. 12:2). Scripture doesn't attribute this to a stuck nervous system, but to the spiritual battle within and around her (Eph. 6:12). The catastrophic suffering of her past has taught her to scan for threats, distancing her from the joy and rest God desires for His people (Matt. 11:28–30). Yet, unlike secular theories that might leave her trapped in a cycle of physiological responses, there is hope. When the threat passes, Sally's exhaustion isn't just a return to homeostasis but an opportunity for God's grace to restore her soul. Over time, as she clings to Christ, her heart can find peace (Phil. 4:6–7), her body can rest, and her spirit can heal—not through neural resets, but through the transformative power of God's Word and Spirit (2 Cor. 12:9–10).

CHAPTER 3

Biblical Anthropology and Human Nature

Anthropology: Understanding Human Nature

Anthropology is the study of humans and human life or the belief about mankind and human nature. A person's anthropological view has everything to do with how they approach helping suffering people. Therefore, it is vital to the discussion when considering a counseling methodology to help people with wounded bodies and souls.

There are two very different and mutually exclusive approaches to understanding and defining human nature, and the counselor's anthropological views will determine what they believe about the problem. For example, are post-trauma issues a spiritual problem, or are they a mental illness? Without an agreed-upon authority and source of what is accurate about the human soul and the human condition, counseling (whether biblical or secular) cannot progress.

The counselor's anthropological views will also directly affect how they see the people they counsel. Are they patients, clients, or counselees (fellow Christians on the road of progressive sanctification)? Furthermore, the counselor's anthropological views will determine if they approach suffering therapeutically or biblically. So, for counseling to be successful, there has to be agreement on anthropology.

One viewpoint is humanistic and evolutionary. It assumes the anthropological position that humans evolved from something, whether primordial ooze or apes, over billions of years. This presuppositional belief undergirds the psychiatric system and its truth and knowledge claims. The psychiatric system redefines human nature and confines it to a therapeutic view of man. This dangerous anthropology ignores the immaterial aspect of each human being and supports only a materialist view of mankind. In the materialist view, the mind and brain are considered one, and the operations of the mind are aspects of brain function. In this philosophy, man has no soul, so his "mental life" is part of his physical substance. Therefore, they believe the only options to help those with complex trauma and PTSD are the medical and psychological approaches.

The biblical anthropological view is the study of the human story as it is lived out with, before, and by God. It views humans as beings with material and immaterial aspects meant to have a relationship with God. It is primarily focused on the nature of humanity - how man's immaterial and material aspects relate to each other.

Genesis 1 and 2 both document the origin of human life. Genesis 1:26–28 provides the account of the creation of humankind upon the Earth. The Bible teaches that on the sixth day of creation, man was created from the dust of the ground (Gen. 2:7), and woman was created from the rib God took from man (2:21–22). We are the crown of God's creation. Christian anthropology states that God created mankind in His image (Imago-Dei), sin-free and with a rational nature, intelligence, and will.[110]

To be made in the image and likeness of God means "man is like God and represents God."[111] This makes us unique and distinct from anything else God created. It is significant that while all creation may be beautiful, and much of it is intelligent, only humans can reflect God's moral and spiritual qualities. Barnhouse states, "This is a moral likeness – 'righteousness and true holiness' (Ephesians 4:24), and an intellectual likeness – 'renewed in the knowledge after the image' (Colossians 3:10)."[112] The *Holman Old Testament Commentary on Genesis* says humankind is "a combination of dust and divinity."[113]

The Imago-Dei creates a moral responsibility within us to be righteous (Gen. 1:26–28; Eph. 4:24). We are morally like God in that we possess an innate knowledge of right and wrong; we are spiritually like God in that we have an immaterial nature and are mentally like God in our capacity to think and reason.[114] Additionally, we are relationally like God in our ability to relate to Him and to one another, experiencing interpersonal harmony to a higher degree than what animals experience with each other.[115] Finally, even a casual reading of Psalm 139 informs us that we are fearfully and wonderfully made. However, God did not stop there; He declares that we are His workmanship (Eph. 2:10)!

Sally: A Case Study in Catastrophic Suffering- Identity

Sally was raised in a Christian home and heard these truths faithfully preached from the pulpit each week. She sat in church each Sunday morning and Wednesday night alongside her brother, even during the years Billy was assaulting and prostituting her. Her inner conflict was enormous as what she heard and sometimes read in the Bible told her she was created in God's image, yet other image-bearers treated her with such contempt and brutality when they met in the woods.

Body and Soul: An Inseparable Unity

We have looked at one facet of what it means to be created in the Imago-Dei, our physical nature (Gen. 2:7), and some of the responsibilities that result from being made in God's image and likeness. However, we must also examine another aspect of our nature, which significantly affects our anthropology and how we counsel. To have biblical anthropology means we accept that we are dual beings; we are both material and immaterial, consisting of both a spiritual and physical reality. The body and soul are inseparably intertwined; we are embodied souls. When God created Adam (Gen. 2:7), He "breathed into his nostrils the breath of life; and man became a living soul (KJV)."

The Bible makes a distinction between the outer aspects of a person, which is the material or physical part of them that is subject to decay (2 Cor. 4:16), and the inner aspects of a person, which refers to the immaterial aspect of a person, understood biblically as the heart, and includes their thoughts, beliefs, desires, will, soul, mind, and emotions, as well as their spirit. Jay Adams, the father of the modern biblical counseling movement, held a duplex view of a person that emphasizes the unity of the elements (meaning they are folded together rather than their separability).[116] Adams writes,

> Let us first consider Hebrews 4:12. There, we are told, "God's Word, the Bible, is likened to a sharp, flashing two-edged sword that is able to penetrate deeply enough to divide between soul and spirit, just as it can divide between joints and marrow." "See" say those who advocate triplexity, "if the Scriptures affirm the possibility of dividing soul from spirit, so should we." But the fact is that the Greek doesn't do any such thing. The KJV (and some subsequent translations) mislead the English reader. The point is not that the soul is divided from the spirit, or joint from marrow. Rather, what is said is that God's word splits the spirit and also the soul, the joints and also the marrow.... The true idea is that God's Word penetrates deeply enough into man's innermost being to cut open and lay bare his desires and thoughts.[117]

More importantly, the Scriptures argue for a dual or dichotomous view of a person. The two words *soul* and *spirit* are used interchangeably throughout the Bible, and nowhere does Jesus or Paul argue for a three-part composition of a person. The Hebrew word for soul is *nephesh* (neh'-fesh), used 276 times in the New American Standard Bible.[xiii] In the New Testament, the Greek word for soul is *psyche*. Strong defines the psyche or soul as "the seat of the feelings, desires, affections, aversions (our heart, soul, etc.); the soul as an essence that differs from the body and is not dissolved by death (distinguished from other parts of the body)."[xiv] Strong's definition supports the two-part distinction of material/organic and immaterial/inorganic and identifies the heart as the same thing as the soul. The word "heart" captures all the aspects of the inner person. This is why it is critical to have a biblical theology of the soul and not a theology of the soul as seen through the lens of psychology.

Sally: A Case Study in Catastrophic Suffering- Identity (continued)

Sally knew in her soul that she was made in the image of God; she grew up hearing it in church. However, over time, the conflict within her was won by her flesh. She could not continue to believe there was a loving God who made her in His image. She believed she was every dirty and filthy thing the boys told her she was. In one of her therapy sessions, Sally was told her problems were related to her self-esteem and her mental illness. She didn't have a spiritual problem; there was something wrong with her mind that made her feel and act the way she did.

The Interplay Between Body and Spirit

Very often, when a trauma occurs, there is damage to the physical body. Depending on the type of trauma, there may be a need for emergency treatment or surgery to repair broken bones, stop severe bleeding, remove internal organs, or attend to gunshot or stab wounds. When the body experiences such a shock, the inner, immaterial aspect of the person is also affected. Our material bodies and immaterial spiritual nature constantly interplay. Organic problems in the outer man (physical body) can contribute to people's difficulties on an emotional level (inner man). This interplay is the realm of the biblical counselor, who is charged

---

xiii Strong's Lexicon "H5315 – nephesh," Blue Letter Bible, accessed 5/9/2019. https://www.blueletterbible.org/search/search.cfm?Criteria=Soul&t=NASB#s=s_primary_0_1

xiv Strong's Lexicon, "G5590 – psyche," Blue Letter Bible, accessed 5/9/2019. https://www.blueletterbible.org/lang/lexicon/lexicon.cfm?t=kjv&strongs=g5590

with addressing how all aspects of a person, including their medical issues, affect the immaterial part of them.

For the biblical counselor, faith in the authority, inerrancy, and sufficiency of the Bible for all things pertaining to the soul must be paramount. God's Word reveals why it is not wisdom but pure foolishness to look to man for solutions to our problems. As Isaiah 55:8–9 (NIV) declares, "For my thoughts are not your thoughts, neither are your ways my ways," declares the Lord. "As the heavens are higher than the earth, so are my ways higher than your ways and my thoughts than your thoughts." Colossians 2:8 also warns, "See to it that no one takes you captive through philosophy and empty deception, according to the tradition of men, according to the elementary principles of the world, rather than according to Christ." This biblical anthropology informs how we approach people and their problems, recognizing that humans are created in God's image as embodied souls (Gen. 2:7, 1 Thess. 5:23).

Christians who profess a belief in the Bible cannot righteously accept secular answers about people and problems or apply secular solutions for issues that affect the inner man. It is helpful to recognize that even the issues associated with severe affliction are, as Paul says in 1 Corinthians 10:13, "common to man." Therefore, if they are common to man, then we know that the Bible must have the answers to issues related to human suffering and the after-effects. Just as secular scientists' or researchers' anthropology directly affects how they perform research, biblical counselors' anthropology informs our methods. When we see a struggling person as someone created in God's image, we can go to the One who made him or her for wisdom and knowledge on how to help. No one knows creation better than its Maker.

One of the outcomes of our counseling is to help ease the pain of violence done to the soul through progressive sanctification — addressing the thoughts, beliefs, and desires of the heart that lead to biblical change (Rom. 12:2; Eph. 4:22–24). While biblical counselors do not reject valid medical and scientific facts or ignore legitimate scientific discoveries, we must choose to establish God as the highest authority regarding who and what people are and how to help them. The consequences of accepting a differing anthropological view of humankind are devastating. Outside of the dual-nature view, with the plethora of mental illnesses and emotional problems facing the trauma survivor, the psychologist becomes the soul physician, replacing the minister and biblical counselor and diminishing the sufficiency of the Scriptures. Winston Smith writes, "Divorced from a truly biblical understanding of the heart as the seat of human motivations and behavior, the gospel and the commands of God are superficial and ineffective, only vaguely relevant to 'psychological problems,' and irrelevant to 'physiological problems.'"[118]

Biblical counselors are accused by clinically-informed counselors and other secular counselors of being reductionistic in their approach to trauma counseling, primarily because we emphasize the sufficiency of Scripture and are wary of systems of counseling that integrate secular psychological theories and self-regulation techniques such as grounding, holding ice cubes, and breathing techniques. We are erroneously accused of minimizing the impact trauma has on the body-spirit-soul connection. To be clear, ignoring the visible external evidence of internal trauma (chronic pain, headaches, gastrointestinal issues, unexplained physical ailments, weight loss or gain, anxiety, fear, increased irritability, changes in sleep patterns, etc.) would be irresponsible. The biblical counselor has an ethical obligation to refer to a medical professional to rule out organic illness as the cause of physical suffering. In addition to moral concerns, to ignore it would be cruel and not in keeping with the compassion we see in Christ when He encountered suffering people (e.g., Matt. 9:36).

Very often, the counselee is given a clean bill of health; there is no medical explanation for their suffering. Because of the dual natures of man—body and soul—it is important to note that even when there is no medical explanation for their chronic pain, anxiety, or sleep disturbances, their spiritual and emotional struggle is worthy of attention. We must conclude that the counselee is experiencing manifestations of spiritual struggles affecting the body. We acknowledge their pain as real because it is real to them. We can show them how to rest in the knowledge that God knows both the origin and solution for their pain and that He means to use it for their good and His glory (2 Cor. 12:7–10).

Therefore, the question must be asked: is the answer to physical suffering that originates in the spiritual nature to redirect the energy of the counselee's suffering to tapping, EMDR, micro-current neurofeedback, holding ice cubes, or snapping rubber bands on their wrist? Or can we help them ease the pain of violence done to their soul by addressing the thoughts, beliefs, and desires of their heart? Sean Perron says,

> There is nothing wrong with telling an anxious person who is worked up to "take a breath." The Bible is filled with moments that instruct us to stop dwelling on disordered thoughts and look to God. Be still and know that I am God. Stop panicking. Calm down. And look to Jesus.

> Selah.
>
> So why then do I think teaching breathing exercises (or muscle relaxation) as a counseling method is unhelpful?
>
> When we use a method, we are always using it in service to a methodology. Methods are not neutral and come laden with philosophical and theological purposes. Taking a breath to be still when worked up is one thing. Breathing routines to reduce anxiety is another.
>
> Counseling is intensive discipleship and there is a reason the Bible NEVER instructs us on how to breathe to produce peace. This means we can obtain perfect peace without it. Jesus breathed upon his disciples the Holy Spirit. He never taught them to breathe properly.
>
> When breathing exercises become a regular part of discipleship, it teaches bad theology. It is teaching the body needs to be prepared by these techniques before sanctification happens. This is not how the Bible teaches change when it comes to fear and anxiety. God gave food and sleep to help Elijah when he was exhausted, terrified of Jezebel, and despairing of life itself. God didn't send him an angel to teach him Diaphragmatic Breathing.
>
> God keeps in perfect peace those whose mind is set on Him. Peace is the fruit of the Spirit, not fruit of the body.
>
> When breathing exercises become a regular part of discipleship, it is subtly teaching people to place their faith in that method rather than in Christ. They learn exercises are the first thing that calms them down. Breathing or muscle relaxation becomes the entryway to peace. This ought not to be.[119]

While clinically-informed counselors advocate for "deep breathing" as a cure to eliminate anxiety, biblical counselors don't focus on regulating the counselee's diaphragm or peddling self-help techniques. Instead, we point them to the God who holds their breath in His hand (Job 12:10). We don't endorse a system like "inhale for 4, out for 6." Rather, we suggest they take a couple of slow breaths, then pray, hear, or recite His Word (Phil. 4:6–7). Breathing serves as a means to refocus on dependence upon God, not as a mechanism for self-sufficiency.

This approach does not imply that we merely instruct counselees to read Scripture and pray as a simplistic remedy for genuine emotional, physical, and mental distress. On the contrary, recognizing humans as embodied souls, we assist counselees in discerning how spiritual struggles manifest in physical symptoms, such as tension or rapid breathing. Grounded in Scripture, we engage suffering individuals with truth and compassion, not as detached clinicians but as fellow bearers of human frailty (Matt. 22:37–38). Through biblical wisdom and the ministry of the Holy Spirit, we confidently, empathetically, and humbly engage both body and spirit through biblical wisdom and the Holy Spirit's ministry.

Sally: A Case Study in Catastrophic Suffering-Biblical Counseling Begins

Sally's biblical counselor, Abigail, met with her for the first time and listened to her tragic story of immense suffering. Abigail acknowledged that Sally had suffered horrific wounds to both her body and her soul and assured her that while she may not be able to relate to everything Sally would disclose to her, God would understand. Together, they would seek biblical solutions to Sally's problems and suffering.

After prayer, Abigail asked Sally to discuss her understanding of God and salvation. Sally talked about her early years in the church, enjoying Sunday School, Vacation Bible School in summer, and her recollection of her dad leading family devotions. She could clearly articulate the Gospel, and as the discussion went on, Abigail was confident Sally understood what the Bible teaches about Creation, the Fall, and Redemption in Christ, but refrained from affirming Sally's salvation because, at this point, she was not sure she was regenerated.

Abigail also asked about Sally's previous counseling and the various clinical diagnoses she received. Sally recalled being diagnosed with PTSD, C-PTSD, major depressive disorder (MDD), dissociative disorder (DID), substance use disorder (SUD), generalized anxiety disorder (GAD), and borderline personality disorder (BPD). Abigail asked Sally if she understood what each of those diagnoses was intended to convey about her. Sally admitted she really didn't know other than she was "a mess." She was told she couldn't "stay stable" without her medicine, and that she used drugs because she had things wrong with her brain. Abigail responded with compassion and asked Sally if she was interested in hearing what God says about her, to which Sally agreed.

Abigail focused on biblical anthropology, emphasizing Sally's creation in God's image and her worth as His workmanship. She showed Sally from the Scriptures that God breathed life into her soul and that she is a purposeful creation of God to begin to address her feelings of worthlessness (Gen. 2:7; 1:26-27; Eph. 2:10). Abigail asked Sally to read Psalm 139:13-16 to help her to see her unique value in Christ, and start to shift her focus from "trauma victim" to someone created according to God's intentional design. This deeply affected Sally as it countered the materialist view Sally was presented with in therapy, that she's a random product of evolution and that "something is wrong with her mind."

She further explained to Sally that she was made in the Imago Dei, which means Sally is "like God and represents God," possessing moral, spiritual, and relational qualities unique among creation (Eph. 4:24; Col. 3:10). This challenged the secular narrative Sally received in therapy—that her worth is tied to her "self-esteem" or mental state. Abigail explained to Sally that she is a dual being, material and immaterial (Gen. 2:7; 2 Cor. 4:16), with her heart as the seat of her thoughts, beliefs, and desires (Prov. 4:23). Abigail understood that Sally's feelings of worthlessness exist in part because the sins committed against her body (abuse, trafficking) have scarred her soul, distorting her beliefs about her identity. Abigail explained that if Sally is willing, they will look at her life and situation as a spiritual struggle rather than through secular diagnoses in a fallen world (Rom. 8:22-23) and seek biblical solutions to heal.

General Revelation: Insights from Creation

While a complete theological discussion on general revelation and common grace is beyond the scope of this section of the book, it is wise to summarize these vital doctrines as they pertain to biblical counseling and the subject at hand.[xv] General revelation and common grace are frequently cited in the debates between biblical and integrated counselors. In fact, the current division within the biblical counseling movement stems from differing views on these concepts, especially as debates over secular trauma research and counseling influence them.

In an article written for *Christianity Today*, Christian counselor Nate Brooks says the Bible doesn't tell us everything we need to know about trauma care and that God desires that we consult other resources to *really* understand how to heal trauma

[xv] I refer you to MacArthur and Mahue and their book, Biblical Doctrine: A Systematic Summary of Bible Truth, or John Frame's Systematic Theology: An Introduction to Christian Belief for a full and robust treatment of common grace, and to a summary article by Dr. Samuel Stephens, "General Revelation: A Decisive Doctrine for the Biblical Counseling Movement" found at https://biblicalcounseling.com/resource-library/articles/general-revelation/.

and other hurts.[120] He goes on to say that we need knowledge from things found in the natural world (general revelation) to address the phenomenology of catastrophic suffering. Another influential Christian counselor says, "Wise counseling requires that evangelical faith be carefully integrated with the theories, therapeutic methods, and professional roles of the modern psychologies."[121] Brooks and other Christian counselors promote incorporating experience, research, investigation, observation, and other scientific and pseudo-scientific "truths" into counseling. They consider it general revelation.

However, it is rightly understood that general revelation is not about the revelation of general truths such as what is discovered or uncovered through the sciences; it is the revelation *of God by* God through His works to a general audience (Ps. 19:1). It is God who does the revealing, not man, not science. General revelation is authoritative enough to reveal and condemn man's sins but not enough to save man *from* sin (Rom. 1:18-20). Millard Erickson defines general revelation as "God's communication of himself to all persons at all times and in all places, specifically through nature, history, and the inner being."[122]

While Christian counselors advocate for the integration of general revelation with biblical counseling, suggesting that insights from the natural world can enhance our understanding of trauma and healing, this perspective is not without controversy. Critics argue that such an approach misinterprets the true nature of general revelation. Samuel Stephens nicely summarized this in his workshop on general revelation delivered at the 2021 ACBC Annual Conference. He said,

> In the context of counseling, general revelation has been used in ways that often distract from its true nature. Commonly it has been misused to allow for the integration of extra-biblical resources under the banner of "all truth is God's truth." However, a correct understanding of general revelation does not promote a "discovery" of truth outside of the Bible but speaks to an unveiling of the truth by God about His character, nature, and sovereignty.[123]

Why not incorporate extra-biblical resources? Shouldn't we want all the available data on a given problem? Yes, when the source is proven, reliable, tested, and unchanging. While this is true of the Bible, it is not true of modern science and psychology's consistently evolving theories and methodologies. The biopsychosocial position elevates worldly knowledge to be as true as what is found in Scripture (i.e., "All truth is God's truth.") This is a common position for integrated counselors and undermines the authority and superiority of the Bible. Heath Lambert states,

"Biblical and Christian counselors debate the necessity of secular counseling resources and the sufficiency of biblical resources because of different theological commitments about the contents of Scripture."[124] "Scientific theories are not the same thing as general revelation. General revelation (like special revelation) refers to an infallible action of God (or to the content revealed through that action). Scientific theories are the fallible interpretations of what Christians know to be God's created works."[125]

While insights from the natural world can offer valuable observations, historic biblical counseling emphasizes that genuine and reliable counsel comes from Scripture alone. Maintaining this distinction ensures that biblical counseling remains firmly grounded in the authority of God's Word, providing a solid foundation for addressing all aspects of human life and problems.

Common Grace: God's Goodness in a Fallen World[xvi]

While the doctrines of general revelation and common grace are closely related, they are not the same. In his Systematic Theology, Louis Berkhof says that general revelation is the means by which common grace operates.[126] Common grace is non-salvific and is given to everyone without exception. We see God's common grace in the world around us: He sends sun and rain to bless the Earth and its inhabitants with food and growth (e.g., Ps. 145:9, 15–16; Matt. 5:44–45; Acts 14:16–17).

God's common grace allows time for the unregenerate to repent and be saved. Apart from salvation, every person is morally depraved and lives in willful spiritual darkness. This total depravity encompasses every aspect of who we are, beginning in our heart/mind/soul/spirit and flowing out of our physical being.

Common grace is also visible in our personal and societal relationships (Gen. 4:17, 19, 26, 5:4; Rom. 13:4). And, despite how depraved and degenerate the world has become, we see common grace extended to all mankind in that God is still restraining evil. Because God has given every person an inward sense of right and wrong, we are not as wicked as we could be (Rom. 2:14–15). The Lord is gracious and compassionate; Slow to anger and great in mercy. The Lord is good to all, And His mercies are over all His works (Psalm 145:8–9, NASB).

Another evidence of common grace is our ability to create through the arts and, germane to our discussion, make discoveries through technology and science. God's common grace allows the unregenerate physician to learn how to practice medicine,

[xvi] For a deeper, concise treatment of Common Grace, I recommend the booklet in the Critical Issues in Biblical Counseling series, Common Grace by Heath Lambert. Shepherd Press, Wapwallopen, PA.

the researcher to have exciting and necessary breakthroughs, and the technician to invent the internet. However, common grace does not guarantee that all the findings of the unregenerate physician or researcher are correct. Because their minds are morally insensitive, their thoughts are futile, they are dull in understanding, and their heart is hard (Eph. 4:17–18), they cannot understand spiritually discerned things, and they suppress the truth in unrighteousness (Rom. 1:18–23). "Who is doing the science may very well influence what scientific questions are asked, which, of course, relates to what conclusions are reached."[127] Therefore, research can be driven by a political or ideological agenda that produces results or conclusions contrary to the Bible. While not all researchers can be painted with a broad brush, there is no doubt that recent research has led to the normalization of many aberrant, ungodly behaviors and belief systems. Although societal and mental health problems have multiplied, many of the same people are proposing "solutions" to the issues they have created. We can see the unraveling of our society as a result.

But what about Christian scientists or researchers and their discoveries? Because the theory of evolution is a cornerstone of modern biology and medicine, many Christian researchers integrate their faith with evolutionary science in various ways. They may view scientific discoveries as part of God's common grace, which provides valuable insights into His creation. They believe they can contribute to understanding the natural world by participating in bio-evolutionary research.[128]

Common grace plays a significant role in the debates between biblical counselors and those counseling under the banner of Christian counseling, such as Clinically-Informed Biblical Counselors (CIBC) or Redemptive Counselors (RC). These Christian integrated counselors argue that effective and faithful counseling must incorporate and endorse extrabiblical psychological insights and methods derived from clinical counseling, which they believe are revealed through common grace. Their argument centers on the idea that integrating psychological principles with biblical truths will address the mental and emotional issues resulting from trauma more holistically and effectively. Some even assert that it is an ethical obligation to integrate secular counseling tools and techniques if they help the person feel and function better, viewing this as part of loving one's neighbor.[129] However, Historical Biblical Counselors (HBC) counter that while common grace exists, it must be subordinate to Scripture, and integrating secular psychology risks undermining the sufficiency of God's Word and introducing conflicting worldviews. For example, even if psychological insights are part of common grace, they are fallible and often tainted by worldviews (e.g., humanism, naturalism) that conflict with biblical anthropology.

Historic biblical counselors agree that common grace allows for beneficial scientific discoveries. Still, the secular worldview is incompatible with Scripture, and their theories often conflict with biblical teachings, leading to a compromised approach to counseling. There is too much emphasis on human wisdom and secular concepts, replacing or overshadowing the Bible's wisdom and guidance. Charles Spurgeon warned against the infiltration of liberal theology and secular ideas into Christian practice, viewing it as a "downgrade" that compromises the integrity of biblical faith and practice.[xvii]

I believe our integrated counterparts genuinely want to help people who are facing the aftereffects of a short-term horrific incident, like witnessing a shooting, experiencing a one-time sexual or physical assault, or long-term suffering such as sex trafficking. They see the same problems that often develop because of catastrophic events that we see, such as feelings of depression, fear and anxiety, self-hatred, substance abuse, despair, and the difficulties the person has in handling their anger and self-destructive desires. It might be clear that the afflicted person struggles with a chronic sense of guilt or responsibility, has difficulty trusting people or feeling intimate, and lives with deep hopelessness or despair. Our counseling friends may see the same issues related to experiencing calamity as we do, but we see them through vastly different lenses. They see them as disorders, mental health issues, and diagnoses from the DSM-5TR. This approach may lead those suffering from the effects of severe mistreatment or affliction to believe they are somehow "broken" and that they will struggle for the rest of their lives with the terrible physical and emotional struggles of post-traumatic distress. Biblical counselors see the effects of catastrophic events through biblical lenses. We recognize that even the issues associated with severe suffering are, as Paul says in 1 Corinthians 10:13, "common to man."

By understanding human nature through the lens of biblical anthropology, we gain valuable insights into the complexities of suffering. Next, we will explore how these insights inform a biblical model of care, providing practical guidance for counselors.

Consider and Apply

1. How does your belief in the dual nature of humans (material and immaterial) created in the image of God influence your approach to counseling those who have experienced catastrophic suffering? How does this

[xvii] For a brief yet comprehensive treatment of this topic, I recommend the reader watch the video by Pastor Austin Collins, located at http://fbcjax.com/first-thoughts/psychological-charlatans-and-common-grace/

understanding shape your counseling methods and goals, ensuring you address the person's spiritual and physical aspects?

2. How can you ensure that your counseling ministry addresses the spiritual root causes of suffering-related issues rather than merely focusing on physical symptoms? Consider specific strategies for using biblical principles that address the heart and soul of your counselees.
3. Can you maintain a commitment to the sufficiency of Scripture while recognizing the role of general revelation and common grace in understanding human suffering? How will you use insights from the natural world and scientific discoveries to support, rather than replace, biblical counseling principles?
4. Consider how you can engage with differing perspectives in your counseling practice without compromising Scripture's authority and sufficiency.

CHAPTER 4

A Biblical Model of Care

Building on our understanding of biblical anthropology, this chapter introduces a comprehensive model of care for catastrophic event survivors. We will explore the foundational principles of biblical counseling and how they can be applied to support those in need.

At the 2022 Annual Conference of the Association of Certified Biblical Counselors, Dale Johnson reminded attendees that secular theories and practices cannot be wrapped in the Scriptures and called biblical counseling.[130] As biblical counselors, our counsel must originate and flow from the Word of God. This will allow us to approach a suffering saint in truth and with love as a fellow sufferer rather than a clinician who approaches only the emotions (Matt. 22:37–38). We can engage with them and their problems empathetically and humbly. We have an incredible opportunity to provide an alternative to the mishmash of theories and ideas the secular and integrated counseling world has to offer.

Foundations of Biblical Counseling: Key Principles

A Biblical View of the Heart

The theology of the heart is vital in biblical counseling. The word *heart* occurs across different translations more than 1,000 times! In Scripture, *heart* is usually used more comprehensively than we tend to use the term culturally. The Bible has much to say about man's heart, often highlighting its spiritual and moral significance. When the Bible refers to the heart, the emphasis is not solely on emotion but on the immaterial or inner person. It includes, among other things, the mind, the soul, the will, the conscience, thoughts, beliefs, and desires.[xviii] Here are a few key verses that illustrate that point:

- Jeremiah 17:9: *"The heart is deceitful above all things and beyond cure. Who can understand it?"* This verse emphasizes the inherent deceitfulness and complexity of the human heart in unregenerate man.
- Proverbs 4:23: *"Above all else, guard your heart, for everything you do flows from it."* This verse reminds us of the importance of protecting our hearts, as our thoughts, beliefs, desires, and actions proceed from it.
- Matthew 5:8: *"Blessed are the pure in heart, for they will see God."* Jesus highlights the value of a pure heart in experiencing God's presence.
- Psalm 51:10: *"Create in me a clean heart, O God. Renew a right spirit within me."* This is a prayer for inner transformation and renewal.

Louis Berkoff refers to the heart as "the central organ of the soul,"[131] and Strong's Greek Lexicon defines the heart this way,

> [Heart]Denotes the center of all physical and spiritual life; the vigor and sense of physical life: the center and seat of spiritual life: the soul or mind, as it is the fountain and seat of the thoughts, passions, desires, appetites, affections, purposes, endeavors: of the understanding, the faculty and seat of the intelligence: of the will and character: of the soul so far as it is affected and stirred in a bad way or good, or of the soul as the seat of the sensibilities, affections, emotions, desires, appetites, passions.[xix]

The Jewish perspective of the heart has more to do with "intent, purpose, and passion. Therefore, thinking and reasoning of the mind were closely associated with the heart's intentions or perspectives leading to actions."[132] The Hebrew word, *lêb* is used over five hundred times for the word "heart" in the Old Testament. Its overall usage encompasses the inner man, mind, will, heart, and understanding, all working in concert.[xx]

[xviii] Strongs Concordance, "καρδία/kardía" found at Blue Letter Bible https://www.blueletterbible.org/lexicon/g2588/kjv/tr/0-1/. Accessed 3/30/2023

[xix] Strong's Greek Lexicon (KJV)"G2588 - kardia -," Blue Letter Bible, accessed March 16, 2019. https://www.blueletterbible.org//lang/lexicon/lexicon.cfm?Strongs=g2588&t=kjv

[xx] Strongs Concordance, "לֵב/ **lêb**," STRONGS H3820 https://www.blueletterbible.org/lexicon/h3820/kjv/wlc/0-1/. Accessed 4/4/2023.

The Effects of the Fall on the Heart

"The Fall produced in humans a state of depravity."[133] Adam and Eve were created sinless, with the desire to worship God. Since the fall, human desires have been perverted by sin. Our hearts (mind, affections, and will) have become desperately sick and wicked, according to Jeremiah 17:9. Every intent of fallen humankind's thoughts has become "only evil continually" (Gen. 6:5). In our unregenerate state, the heart is not basically good but seriously flawed and utterly corrupt, and without the grace of God will remain so. Since Adam, all men and women are sinners by nature and by choice; thus, it would be accurate to describe humankind as basically depraved, not basically good. Sin has wholly affected, damaged, and distorted the heart's desires.

John Bunyan, the Reformed Baptist pastor known for writing *Pilgrim's Progress*, wrote in the 1680s, "Sin and corruption would bubble out of my heart as naturally as water bubbles out of a fountain."[134] Author Paul David Tripp describes the effects of the sinful heart, "Something is wrong with my inner self that fundamentally affects the way I operate as a human being."[135] Tripp is speaking of the heart. He says, "The first thing sin produces is rebellion. This is more than breaking a few rules; it is a fundamental flaw in my character. It is not something I learned; I was born with it."[136] Biblical counselor Pam Gannon explains, "We might be convinced that our abuse is our greatest problem in life and that it defines who we are, but in reality, our greatest problem is what's going on in our own heart. Our hearts can deceive us, so we have to be extremely careful of what we choose to own as truth."[137]

Jeremiah 17:9 clearly shows how genuinely sick and deceptive the unregenerate heart is. There is no other thing about a human being that is referred to as desperately wicked as the heart. The Lord Jesus Christ clearly understood the deceptive nature of the heart. In Matthew 15:11, 18–20, and Mark 7:21–23, He says evil thoughts, murders, adulteries, fornications, thefts, false witness, slanders, deeds of coveting and wickedness, deceit, sensuality, envy, pride, and foolishness proceed from the heart. When sequenced with Proverbs 27:19, Luke 6:45, Ezekiel 11:19–20, and 36:26, we begin to understand the complexity of the heart and its impact on our lives.

No aspect of us is untouched or unperverted by the sinfulness and wickedness that lurks within the heart: our intellect is affected (2 Cor. 4:4), we have a reprobate mind (Rom. 1:28), and our understanding is darkened (Eph. 4:18). Our emotions also are degraded and defiled (Rom. 1:22, 24, 26; Titus 1:15), and our will is enslaved to sin and stands in opposition to God (Rom. 1:20; 7:20). The thoughts, beliefs, and desires of the sinful heart are the catalyst for the physical, emotional, and sexual abuse that comprises the trauma our counselees suffer. Unregenerate victims and those who inflict trauma upon them share a common problem with the rest of unredeemed humanity: original sin that separates them from a Holy God.

Sally: A Case Study in Catastrophic Suffering- The Heart

Sally and Abigail continued to meet several times a week. As a part of biblical counseling, Abigail asked Sally to take time each day to pray, read Scripture, and do biblical and practical assignments that would help her grow and change. Work on Sally's identity continued, and while she faithfully completed her homework, it was evident that progress was impeded because of her spiritual condition. Because Abigail wasn't confident Sally was indeed a Christian, she approached their time together as evangelistic as well as to help Sally with the fruit issues in her life. A major focus was on the heart, as the Bible describes it.

Sally was reading Psalm 139 but was unable to reconcile what God's Word said about her being 'wonderfully made' when she had been told for most of her life that she was trash and other horrible things. Because Abigail wanted her to begin to think biblically, they turned to Proverbs 27:19, and after Sally read the verse, she explained that the heart is like a mirror, showing us what is inside. As they conversed, Abigail explained that the heart is the inner person and encompasses everything about Sally that we know is there but cannot be seen. She used the examples of soul, conscience, mind, will, emotions, thoughts, beliefs, and desires. After reading Mark 7:14–23, Sally had a breakthrough. She understood that the things she struggled with were, in one way or another, coming from within her heart, not entirely from outside her. Finally, they looked at Jeremiah 17:9, which says that the heart is deceptive and desperately wicked and beyond our natural ability to understand it or how it works.

Abigail explained to Sally that her heart is the motivator for what she thinks, believes, and desires, and those motivations lead to her behavior and feelings, like running to drugs, lying, or hiding. Abigail explained that the heart is inherently sinful and separates her from God and that her current struggles (addiction, despair) are fruits of a heart affected by both sins against her and her own responses to the catastrophic suffering she has endured.

Abigail drew a tree and had Sally write all the "fruit" of her life on the tree. The tree was covered in sinful fruit, and at this point, Sally expressed that she thought she was hopeless. Abigail drew a heart at the base of the tree where the roots are and explained that Sally's feelings of worthlessness and mistrust in God are heart-rooted lies, not brain disorders. She countered Sally's lies with Scripture, flipping to Ezekiel 36:26 and asking Sally to read it. As she read the powerful words of God, 'I will give you a new heart with new and right desires,' which emphasizes God's promise of a new heart, Abigail pointed out that in this paradigm, secular fixes (e.g., thought-stopping) for spiritual renewal, don't align with the need for transformative power (1 Pet.1:15–16). She asked Sally if she thought she had the power to change herself, and Sally admitted she did not. Abigail gently reminded Sally of what she learned long ago in Sunday School: salvation through Christ is the prerequisite for heart transformation. Sally needs a new heart because she currently has a heart of stone. Abigail pointed to the verses in Ezekiel and told Sally that only God could replace her heart of stone with a heart of flesh.

A tiny spark of hope lit Sally's eyes.

The Need for Redemption in Christ

Because of the sinful condition of the heart, we all need redemption and regeneration. David, King of Israel, is known as a man after God's own heart (1 Sam. 13:14; Acts 13:22). He also committed adultery and murder (2 Sam. 11). Psalm 51:1–7 reveals that David recognized he was in sin. He knew his sin had separated him from God. It was not just the sins regarding Bathsheba and the murder of her husband, Uriah, but David recognizes he was "born a sinner" (Ps. 51:5). David understood that through the disobedience of Adam, he was an object of God's wrath because in Adam all sinned. He understood God's righteous judgment and that there would be judgment for his sin. In Psalm 51, David asks for pardon for his sins and redemption and salvation.

Now, as you can imagine, there can be many difficulties in approaching someone with the gospel who has been victimized and is traumatized. As you begin to interact with them, be aware that they may not want anything to do with God because they are suffering deeply, and their suffering has helped them draw conclusions about God that may not be true. Some may recoil at the thought of following God since He allowed them to be abused despite their pleas for His help or if they experienced something horrific they believe God could have prevented. Others may wonder about God's existence and justice and battle doubt and anger. People who have endured long-term abuse or trauma will struggle intensely with the selfless love of God, especially the One who allowed them to suffer so profoundly or for so many years of their lives.

Sally: A Case Study in Catastrophic Suffering- Resistance

The light in Sally's eyes quickly faded. Her posture stiffened, and she angrily told Abigail she 'didn't want this salvation stuff.' She went on yelling how God didn't save her from Billy or what she suffered in the woods, on the streets, or any other time. Sally used the term 'churchies' for people who worked in the rescue missions and soup kitchens she frequented. She told Abigail how they treated her when she came in desperate for food or warmth. Sally said she experienced nothing but judgment coming from those there to help. One lady even prayed over her for demonic deliverance from her wicked ways of prostitution instead of prayers for safety, hope, or peace. Sally did not trust God and had no plans to start trusting Him now.

Abigail responded with compassion and acknowledged that Sally's pain was real. She assured her she was not going to force anything. She asked what Sally was thinking about and out tumbled her beliefs: God is mad at me. God doesn't care about me. I'm too messed up to be bothered with. Pointing to Proverbs 27:19, Abigail reminded Sally that her heart was speaking what she believed inside because of the hurt and devastation she had experienced. She reiterated that she would go slowly but reminded Sally that Scripture says we've all sinned (Rom. 3:23). Sin separates us from God (Rom. 6:23). Only Christ can bridge that gap (Rom. 5:8). This was not news to Sally. Still, she adamantly proclaimed she was not ready to make such a decision.

The Survivor's New Identity in Christ

The Christian has a new identity, and his or her ability to grasp what it means to be "in Christ" will be critical to their ability to move forward and process the wounds of their soul. It becomes the foundation for the person's most basic understanding of their new identity, a new creation according to 2 Corinthians 5:17. Assist them in developing a new understanding of who they are. It is likely that a person who was abused does not understand their *Imago Dei* or that they have been crowned with glory and majesty (Ps. 8:4–5), so one of the first things to focus on is their creation in the image and likeness of God (Gen. 1:26–28). That means every person has been "fearfully and wonderfully made" (Ps. 139:14) and bears great dignity as a bearer of God's image despite anything that has been done to them. Grudem says, "… when the creator of the universe wanted to create something 'in his image,' something *more like himself* than all the rest of creation, he made us. This realization will give us a profound sense of dignity and significance as we reflect on the excellence of all the rest of God's creation…"[138]

As I counsel people who have suffered sexual trauma, it becomes clear that understanding and adopting their identity in Christ is among the most critical components in the process for them. Most of my counselees who were sexually abused or trafficked have built their identity upon lies. Sadly, as children, they were enculturated by their parents or other people in their lives to think of themselves as failures, unlovable, incapable, or incompetent, in addition to being dirty, unwanted, and hopeless. Nicewander and Brookins explain, "Sexual abuse, especially in childhood, attacks our identity, saturating the very core of our soul with lies."[139] Those who have suffered abuse since childhood feel as though their experiences are the final word on their identity. They cannot discount their sexual assault history as being a part of who they are. Their "self" has been mired in abuse and degradation. Therefore, as much time as is needed should be taken to help them develop a biblical view of their position and identity in Christ (Ephesians 1).[140]

For someone who has lived their life convinced they are permanently defiled, the message that Jesus has cleansed us and made us holy and blameless in God's sight is uncomfortable. There may be resistance and disbelief, but don't be discouraged; gently persist. And, might I suggest, don't just *tell* them these things, *show* them! Let the Bible speak for itself! Begin by showing them Ephesians 1:4–5, and have *them* read that in Christ, they have been spiritually adopted into the family of God and are His beloved son or daughter. Cross-reference verses to show them that in Christ, they have a permanent and eternal relationship with God, a relationship in which they will never be abandoned or cast out again. Point out the shocking words and phrases God uses to describe those who are His in Ephesians 1. Give them time to meditate on what God says about His children. He says the Christian is redeemed and forgiven, made righteous, a new creation, God's workmanship, reconciled to God, a saint, chosen, holy, and beloved, a child of light, not darkness (which is especially meaningful to some who have been prostituted), as well as being pure, blameless, above reproach, the glory of God, and in the righteousness of God.

Sally: A Case Study in Catastrophic Suffering- Resistance (continued)

Each time they met, Sally was stiff and tightened her jaw, clenching and unclenching her hands throughout the session. When, in due course of the session, Abigail tenderly and compassionately asked what she was thinking, Sally invariably responded with some version of, "I'm trash, garbage, useless, stained forever. God's mad, or He doesn't care. I'm not worth saving." She was rude and unkind to Abigail, seemingly daring her to "fire" her from biblical counseling. Abigail would remind her that while she cared deeply for her and wanted to help, Sally was not allowed to be cruel or to sin against her with her words. She gently reminded Sally that her words reflected the thoughts and beliefs in her wounded heart, shaped by what others did.

As she had done each of the last several meetings, she opened her Bible to Ephesians 1:4–5, slid it toward Sally, and asked her to read it. This time, she instructed Sally to read it aloud and put the word "me" instead of the pronoun in the text. Sally read, 'Even before He made the world, God loved me and chose me in Christ to be holy and without fault in His eyes. God decided in advance to adopt me into His own family by bringing me to Himself through Jesus Christ.'

Sally's brow furrowed as she read, her voice faltering. "Holy? Without fault? That's not me—I've done too much; I am too ruined." Abigail assured her that even though it may feel impossible, God's words are true even when we doubt. She turned to Colossians 1:22 and had Sally read it, also replacing the pronouns with "me" and "I." Abigail guided Sally as she read: 'He has reconciled me to himself through the death of Christ… so I am holy and blameless as I stand before him without a single fault.' *Sally shook her head in disbelief and again said she didn't feel it and couldn't believe it was true about her. Abigail reminded Sally that this statement could be true about her. She could be in Christ—God's daughter, adopted forever (Rom. 8:15).*

Abigail gently persisted, assuring Sally she understood how uncomfortable it might be because it was so different from what she knew. She took a piece of paper and asked Sally to write out each word from Ephesians 1 and Colossians 1:22, saying who she is and who she could be in Christ. In the following sessions, they continued to compile statements drawn from various passages of the Bible until they created a chart highlighting the biblical truths about Sally's identity and relationship with God in Christ.

Statement	**Bible Verse**	**Scripture Reference**
I can be a co-heir with Christ	"In him we have obtained an inheritance, having been predestined according to the purpose of him who works all things according to the counsel of his will."	Ephesians 1:11
I ~~can be~~ AM fearfully and wonderfully made	"I praise you because I am fearfully and wonderfully made; your works are wonderful, I know that full well."	Psalm 139:14

Statement	Bible Verse	Scripture Reference
I can be a new creation in Christ	"Therefore, if anyone is in Christ, he is a new creation. The old has passed away; behold, the new has come."	2 Corinthians 5:17
I can be adopted into the family of God	"In love he predestined us for adoption to sonship through Jesus Christ, in accordance with his pleasure and will."	Ephesians 1:4-5
I can have a permanent relationship with God	"And you also were included in Christ when you heard the message of truth, the gospel of your salvation. When you believed, you were marked in him with a seal, the promised Holy Spirit."	Ephesians 1:13
I can be redeemed	"In him we have redemption through his blood, the forgiveness of our trespasses, according to the riches of his grace."	Ephesians 1:7
I can be forgiven	"In him we have redemption through his blood, the forgiveness of our trespasses, according to the riches of his grace."	Ephesians 1:7
I can be made righteous	"And to put on the new self, created after the likeness of God in true righteousness and holiness."	Ephesians 4:24
I ~~can be~~ AM God's workmanship	"For we are his workmanship, created in Christ Jesus for good works, which God prepared beforehand, that we should walk in them."	Ephesians 2:10
I can be chosen	"Even as he chose us in him before the foundation of the world, that we should be holy and blameless before him."	Ephesians 1:4

Statement	Bible Verse	Scripture Reference
I can be holy and beloved	"To the saints who are in Ephesus, and are faithful in Christ Jesus."	Ephesians 1:1
I can be a child of light	"For at one time you were darkness, but now you are light in the Lord. Walk as children of light."	Ephesians 5:8
I can be made pure	"Husbands, love your wives, as Christ loved the church and gave himself up for her, that he might sanctify her, having cleansed her by the washing of water with the word."	Ephesians 5:25-26
I can be blameless	"Even as he chose us in him before the foundation of the world, that we should be holy and blameless before him."	Ephesians 1:4
I can be above reproach	"And you, who once were alienated and hostile in mind, doing evil deeds, he has now reconciled in his body of flesh by his death, in order to present you holy and blameless and above reproach before him."	Colossians 1:21-22
I can be the glory of God and in the righteousness of God	"And to put on the new self, created after the likeness of God in true righteousness and holiness."	Ephesians 4:24
I can be reconciled to God	"All this is from God, who through Christ reconciled us to himself and gave us the ministry of reconciliation."	2 Corinthians 5:18
I can be a saint	"To the saints who are in Ephesus, and are faithful in Christ Jesus."	Ephesians 1:1

These statements and corresponding Bible verses highlight the biblical truths about Sally's identity and relationship with God in Christ. This will provide a strong foundation for understanding her worth and position in Christ in salvation. Once a person comes to faith in Christ and then believes how God sees them in Christ, they are free! They can experience freedom in their relationship with God, others, and themselves.

Every person's identity problem is solved by belonging to God in Christ and acknowledging that God accepts us. Our identity in Christ goes deeper and is more secure and stable than any identity we were given as a woman, man, sister, brother, daughter, son, mother, father, or anything else, but we must believe and embrace it.

Often, a counselee will talk about having low self-esteem as part of what they have endured and express a desire to raise it. Lou Priolo made an excellent point when he said, "As a Christian, you should have as your objective [sic] not a 'good' or 'positive' self-image, but rather an accurate self-image based on biblically correct perceptions and evaluations."[141] Our goal is to help them view themselves through the lens of Scripture and accept what is true about themselves according to the unchangeable standard of God's Word rather than their self-evaluation. David Powlison provides further essential insight into identity after devastating harm. He says to the survivor, "What happened to you is not the last word on who you are and where your life is going. It's a significant part of your story, but it's not the *most significant* part of your story. It's only one part of the new story of your life that Jesus is writing."[142]

Consider and Apply

1. What are the key components of a biblical model of care for trauma survivors?
2. How can you help your counselees understand and embrace their new identity in Christ?
3. What practical steps can you take to integrate spiritual care with practical support in your counseling ministry?

CHAPTER 5

Redefining Trauma-Related Terms

Language shapes our understanding of reality, and this is especially true when it comes to trauma. This chapter will examine common psychological terms and diagnoses, offering a biblical reframing that provides a more accurate and hopeful perspective. By aligning our language with Scripture, we can help counselees see their experiences through the lens of God's truth.

In a previous chapter, you read about the secular belief systems that consider the effects of trauma to be mental health issues, so a counselee will likely come with one or more psychological diagnoses related to their catastrophic suffering.

Secular Diagnosis and Psychological Descriptions

The chart below contains the most common labels, descriptions, symptoms, and behaviors.

Secular Diagnosis	***Psychological Description***[143]
PTSD	**Primary Description:** PTSD is a mental health condition triggered by experiencing or witnessing a traumatic event. **Symptoms include** flashbacks, nightmares, severe anxiety, and uncontrollable thoughts about the event. Intrusive memories, avoidance of reminders, negative changes in thinking and mood, and changes in physical and emotional reactions. **Primary Behaviors:** flashbacks, nightmares, hypervigilance, irritability

Dissociative Identity Disorder	**Primary Description:** dissociative disorders involve a disconnection between thoughts. **Symptoms include** memory loss (amnesia), a sense of being detached from oneself (depersonalization), perception of people and things as unreal (derealization), identity confusion or multiple identities (DID) **Primary Behaviors:** memory loss (amnesia), sense of being detached from oneself (depersonalization)
Borderline Personality Disorder	**Primary Description:** BPD is a mental health disorder characterized by pervasive instability in moods, behavior, self-image, and functioning. These symptoms often result in impulsive actions and problems in relationships. **Symptoms include** intense fear of abandonment, unstable and intense relationships, distorted self-image, impulsivity in potentially self-damaging activities, recurrent suicidal behavior or self-harm, emotional instability, chronic feelings of emptiness, inappropriate, intense anger, transient, stress-related paranoia or dissociation**. Primary Behaviors:** frantic efforts to avoid real or imagined abandonment, alternating between idealization and devaluation in relationships, impulsive behaviors such as spending sprees, unsafe sex, substance abuse, self-harming behaviors, frequent mood swings
Reactive Attachment Disorder (RAD)	**Primary Description:** RAD is a condition in which a child does not form healthy emotional bonds with their caregivers, often due to severe neglect or abuse. It is characterized by difficulties in forming secure attachments**. Symptoms include** unexplained withdrawal, fear, sadness, or irritability, lack of response to comfort, failure to smile, watching others closely but not engaging in social interaction, failure to reach out when picked up, no interest in playing interactive games. **Primary Behaviors:** avoidance of eye contact and physical touch, expressing fear or anger through tantrums, seeking control over their environment, difficulty forming meaningful connections

Major Depressive Disorder (MDD)	**Primary Description:** MDD is characterized by a persistent feeling of sadness and loss of interest in activities. It affects how you feel. **Symptoms include** persistent sadness or low mood, loss of interest in activities, changes in appetite and sleep, fatigue, feelings of worthlessness or guilt, difficulty concentrating, and suicidal thoughts. **Primary Behaviors:** persistent sadness or low mood, loss of interest in activities
Generalized Anxiety Disorder (GAD)	**Primary Description:** GAD involves excessive worry about various aspects of daily life. Symptoms include persistent worrying**. Symptoms Include** persistent worrying, overthinking, difficulty handling uncertainty, indecisiveness, inability to relax, difficulty concentrating, fatigue, muscle tension, and sleep disturbances. **Primary Behaviors:** persistent worrying, overthinking,
Adjustment Disorders	**Primary Description:** Adjustment disorders are emotional or behavioral responses to a significant stressor or life change. **Symptoms Include** sadness and hopelessness, anxiety, irritability, withdrawal, reckless behavior, difficulty concentrating, and changes in sleep and appetite. **Primary Behaviors:** sadness and hopelessness.
Substance Use Disorders	**Primary Description:** Substance use disorders are characterized by an inability to control the use of substances like alcohol. **Symptoms Include** compulsive use, loss of control, neglecting responsibilities, risky behavior, secrecy and isolation, financial problems, tolerance, and withdrawal symptoms. **Primary Behaviors:** compulsive use, loss of control, neglecting responsibilities, risky behavior, secrecy and isolation, financial problems, tolerance and withdrawal symptoms
Panic Disorder	**Primary Description:** Panic disorder is marked by recurrent panic attacks. **Symptoms include** sudden and repeated panic attacks, intense fear or discomfort, physical symptoms (racing heart, sweating, trembling), fear of losing control or dying, and avoidance of situations where panic attacks have occurred. **Primary Behaviors:** Sudden and repeated panic attacks.

Words matter and the language used to describe what a person is going through determines how they understand and respond to it. Mark Shaw says,

> The world's system of secular counseling is not more kind or loving than God. By relabeling or ignoring sin, secular counseling attempts to take the moral sting away from the bible's language for the very same thoughts and behaviors. This is a massive problem. Remember that words are signs that point in a direction. They give meaning. In a fallen world, that meaning will either be true and point in the direction of God, or it will be false and point away from him.[144]

Psychological terminology points suffering people away from God and medicalizes human experience. They are directed toward solutions that have no power to help them because they are void of spiritual power.

Reframing Psychological Terms Biblically

To be clear, it is not the place of the biblical counselor to tell a counselee they have or don't have a diagnosis given to them by a licensed professional. We also do not instruct or suggest that a counselee stop taking any medications. Our work is done in the counselee's spiritual or immaterial being, so we reframe their concerns biblically. Biblically redefining the psychological terms or labels they have been given will demystify what they have been through and give them hope that they can overcome their problems.

Ask the counselee if they want to know how the Bible understands their experiences, and then show them that the Bible is rich with descriptions of trauma and its effects. More importantly, God's Word provides insights into their actual problems and real solutions. Scripture speaks to a person's labels, symptoms, descriptions, and behaviors, but in a different way than secular terminology does.

Psalm 10 is frequently used in biblical counseling to aid and comfort a person who has endured various kinds of abusive behaviors. When I have walked counselees through this Psalm, it is evident they can relate to the emotion of the psalmist, and his words resonate with their experiences. They find God meeting them where they are spiritually and emotionally in their confusion and torment. Often, this Psalm becomes the cry of their aching heart.

Within Psalm 10, the hurting person finds spiritual clarity for the cultural and psychological constructs contained in the words *abuse and trauma.* Sometimes, these labels or secular diagnoses are used to legitimize sinful thinking, beliefs, reactions, and responses. We aim to help them see the affliction and their reactions through biblical eyes. We do this by redefining terms or labels they have been given in previous treatments. For example, depression is sorrow without hope. Anxiety is fear; triggers are provocations or temptations to sin or to react in a manner that may or may not be sinful. There is deep comfort in realizing that the Bible explains that abuse is one person subjecting another to sinful, selfish, oppressive, and destructive behaviors. There is no hope in labeling someone a narcissist or an abuser, as these labels and their accompanying behaviors are often said by those in the secular realm to be unchangeable. There is more hope when the victim understands that someone who claims to love or care about them has been scheming to deceive, humiliate, oppress, violate, or harm them or another image bearer of God through physical or sexual mistreatment or to weaken and denigrate them by using various sinful manipulations of the mind and soul or by speaking words that are demeaning and destructive. Biblically reframing secular constructs and diagnoses is often very beneficial for the suffering person. It helps them see their problems and circumstances through new eyes, often the eyes of hope. There is HOPE in defining things biblically because then there are answers.

Secular Label	***Biblical Description***
PTSD	Distress, fear, severe anxiety, and runaway thoughts. Remembering painful events (flashbacks) and nightmares
Dissociative Identity Disorder	False fixed beliefs and perceptions, delusions, not living in the present reality, madness ("an impairing reaction to circumstances, environments, and/or traumatic experiences that rest outside of our faith's ability to bear them"), fleshly responses to pain (avoidance). A form of self-dependence.
Borderline Personality Disorder	Anger and aggression, resentment, bitterness, anxiety, lack of self-control, fear, idolatry, self-harming, and distorted identity
Reactive Attachment Disorder (RAD)	Self-focused behaviors, aggression or anger, lack of self-control, feelings of abandonment, fear, sorrow without hope, anxiety, and fleshly responses to pain (avoidance)

Major Depressive Disorder (MDD)	Sorrow without hope, melancholy, sadness, crushed in spirit, despair, guilt, shame, self-pity, jealousy, resentment, discontent, self-centered, fleshly responses to pain (avoidance), unrealized wants and desires, despair over losses.
Generalized Anxiety Disorder (GAD)	Fear, worry, anxiety, ruminating thoughts (meditation), restlessness, inability to concentrate, lack of faith in God's love or care, self-protection, and self-sufficiency.
Adjustment Disorders	Sadness, hopelessness, fear, worry, anxiety, anger, frustration, isolation, impulsiveness, irresponsibility, self-worship, double-mindedness.
Substance Use Disorders	Idolatry, misplaced worship, lack of self-control, selfishness, irresponsibility, sorrow without hope, bondage (enslavement to sin), drunkard, fleshly responses to pain, avoidance, escapism.
Panic Disorder	Intense fear, lack of self-control, lack of faith in God's love or care.

Other terms the biblical counselor may have to redefine biblically are

Secular Term	***Biblical Description***
Attitude	The spirit of one's heart or thoughts
Can't forgive self	Unbelief, insufficient confidence in God's Word
Co-dependent	Idolatry; fear of man
Complaining	Murmuring; disputing; discontent
Compulsive disorder	Life-dominating sin; bondage to sin; guilt
Dysfunctional	Sinning through ongoing conflict, strife, miscommunication, or other divisive malicious behaviors
Ego	Pride

Emotional problem	Thinking problem (the emotions are working fine)
Frustrated	Angry; interference blocks selfish goal; disappointed; cast down discouraged.
Grief	Sorrow, mourning
Grudge	Refusal to forgive
In denial	Self-deceived, deceitful heart
Insane/unstable	Double-minded
Insecure	Fearful
Mental health	Spiritual health
Mistake	Sin
Need	Desire
Overwhelmed	Fainthearted
Oppositional Defiant Disorder (ODD)	Rebellion toward God's authority; anger
Self-esteem	Lover of self
Self-image	Self-judgment
Self-pity	Resentful; discontented; self-centered
Suicide	Self-murder

Biblical language places the Scriptures in the center of care for the counselee. It helps them understand that their experiences are not foreign to God and that He provides the solutions to their suffering in His Word. Some suggest that referring to one's painful experiences as "suffering" rather than "trauma" minimizes their pain, but that's not true at all. In fact, the word "suffering" comes from the words *evil* and *to suffer*. As each verse below reveals, trauma is a form of suffering evil, trouble, distress, affliction, hardship, or pain: 2 Chron. 36:15–16; Rom. 7:5; 8:18;

2 Cor. 1:5–6; Gal. 5:24; Phil. 3:10; Col. 1:24; 2 Tim. 3:11; Heb. 2:9–10; 10:32; James 5:10; 1 Pet. 1:11; 4:13; 5:1; 5:9.

How God's People Cried Out

In the Scriptures, we read how God's people cried out to Him in distress. As you look at portions of Psalms and laments from David, Asaph, Job, Jeremiah, and Solomon, it is clear that God's people also suffered horrific and painful experiences. Our biblical ancestors are not wooden, unfeeling, robotic beings; the Scriptures reveal that some responded well, and others' faith and hope wavered amid confusing and painful experiences. This may encourage the counselee who thinks they should not have feelings or emotions about what they have been through. Here are some examples from the Bible:

"Why, O Lord, do you stand far away? Why do you hide yourself in times of trouble?" (Ps. 10:1) Here, the psalmist feels abandoned and struggles to understand why God seems distant during periods of suffering and injustice. Those whose affliction is long-term may think God has abandoned them.

"Why do you hide your face? Why do you forget our affliction and our oppression?" (Ps. 44:24). The psalmist struggles to understand why God appears to be intentionally absent during periods of affliction and oppression. He pleads for God's presence and intervention even though he also recounts God's history of faithfulness. This Psalm highlights the tension between faith and the experience of suffering, something wounded people grapple with.

"Look to the right and see; there is none who takes notice of me; no refuge remains to me; no one cares for my soul" (Ps. 142:4). Here, the psalmist writes of the feeling of being utterly alone and without anyone to help or care for him in his time of need. This sentiment highlights the depth of his despair and the stark reality of his isolation. Feeling and believing they are alone in their misery is a common misbelief of someone in the midst of affliction and suffering. While validating the counselee's feelings of loneliness is important, it is equally important to challenge any misbeliefs about God's care and presence. Communicate that even when human support is lacking, God's Word assures us that He is always with us and cares deeply for our souls, even in the darkest times. (Ps. 34:18, Heb. 13:5).

"My spirit is broken, my days are extinct; the graveyard is ready for me" (Job 17:1). This verse captures the depth of Job's anguish. He is physically and emotionally exhausted. He feels that his life is nearing its end, and he is overwhelmed by his suffering. Job is grappling with the weight of his afflictions and the seeming absence of hope. Those who endure extended seasons of misery will relate to Job's cry.

"Behold, I cry out, 'Violence!' but I am not answered; I call for help, but there is no justice" (Job 19:7). Job cries out against the violence and wrongs he is experiencing but feels that his pleas for help and justice are unheard. Job has a profound sense of abandonment by God and struggles to understand why he is suffering without any apparent response or intervention from Him. The Book of Job's theme of divine silence in the face of human suffering is a central issue. More than almost any other issue, this will resonate with those who have suffered injustice and cried out to God for help in the midst of their catastrophic affliction.

"My heart is in anguish within me, the terrors of death have fallen upon me. Fear and trembling come upon me, and horror overwhelms me" (Ps. 55:4–5). David is experiencing intense fear and anxiety. He is in deep emotional turmoil. As he grapples with intense fear, he also seeks refuge in God. A fearful counselee will resonate with David's cries.

"In the day of my trouble I seek the Lord; in the night my hand is stretched out without wearying; my soul refuses to be comforted" (Ps. 77:2). The psalmist appears to be experiencing intense anguish and is continually seeking comfort and relief from God, yet he finds none.

"My eye will never again see good" (Job 7:7). *"So I am allotted months of emptiness, and nights of misery are apportioned to me…When I say, 'My bed will comfort me… then you scare me with dreams and terrify me with visions"* (Job 7:3, 13–14). In these verses, we see Job's profound anguish and the unrelenting nature of his suffering. He is experiencing a profound sense of hopelessness and the intensity of his physical and emotional torment. Those experiencing prolonged physical suffering due to medical trauma or any other reason will relate to Job's cries.

The words of Solomon will resonate with those enduring times of poverty and persecution (cf. Ps. 107:4–9). Solomon noted: *"Again I saw all the oppressions that are done under the sun. And behold, the tears of the oppressed, and they had no one to comfort them! On the side of their oppressors there was power, and there was no one to comfort them" (*Eccl. 4:1*).* These verses highlight the imbalance of power, where powerful people leave the oppressed without any source of relief or support. Oppressed people, such as victims of child sexual assault and some in domestic abuse situations, have experienced crying out for help and relief, and they have been ignored. They believe no one will help them.

The Bible does not shy away from depicting the intense pain and suffering that individuals can experience. In the New Testament, we read that Hebrew children were murdered in front of their mothers in an attempt to kill Jesus. *"A voice was heard in Ramah, weeping and loud lamentation, Rachel weeping for her children; she refused to be comforted, because they are no more"* (Matthew 2:18, ESV). After being betrayed by one of His disciples, Jesus was arrested, beaten, spit on, tortured, and crucified (Matt. 26:50–56; 27:26–33; Mark 14:43–50; 15:15–41; Luke 22:47–54, 63–65; 23:26–49; John 18:12–14; 19:1–3,16–37). Identifying with Christ's suffering can be a source of comfort and strength. Jesus, who was sinless, experienced the ultimate trauma and understands the depth of human pain. Hebrews 4:15–16 reminds us that we have a High Priest who can sympathize with our weaknesses and invites us to approach God's throne of grace confidently.

In the unfolding story of the early Christian church, following Christ was not an easy way of life for the new Christians. Jesus' apostles were imprisoned, beaten, and executed (Acts 5:17–18, 40; 7:59–60; 12:1–4; 2 Cor. 11:24–25; 2 Tim. 4:6–8). Christ-followers who refused to renounce their faith in Jesus were imprisoned, fed to the lions, and used for sport in the Colosseum. Those who avoided capture witnessed the persecution that befell their friends and families. They lost their homes, families, livelihoods, and reputations. Regarding what Paul and his companions faced in Asia, he said, *"For we were so utterly burdened beyond our strength that we despaired of life itself"* (2 Cor. 1:8). This suggests that the danger was extreme and life-threatening.

In Romans 8:18–39 Paul writes about suffering in a fallen world:

> [8:18] *For I consider that our* ***present sufferings*** *cannot even be com-*
> *pared to the glory that will be revealed to us.* [8:19] *For the creation*
> *eagerly waits for the revelation of the sons of God.* [8:20] *For the creation*
> *was subjected to* ***futility (frailty)****—not willingly but because of God*
> *who subjected it—in hope* [8:21] *that the creation itself will also be set*
> *free from the* ***bondage of decay*** *into the glorious freedom of God's*
> *children.* [8:22] *For we know that* ***the whole creation groans and suf-***
> ***fers*** *together until now.* [8:23] *Not only this, but we ourselves also, who*
> *have the firstfruits of the Spirit,* ***groan inwardly*** *as we eagerly await*
> *our adoption, the redemption of our bodies.*[8:24] *For in hope we were*
> *saved. Now hope that is seen is not hope, because who hopes for what*
> *he sees?* [8:25] *But if we hope for what we do not see, we eagerly wait for*
> *it with endurance.*
>
> [8:26] In the same way, the Spirit helps us in our ***weakness****, for we do*
> *not know how we should pray, but the Spirit himself intercedes for us*
> *with inexpressible groanings.* [8:27] *And he who searches our hearts knows*
> *the mind of the Spirit, because the Spirit intercedes on behalf of the*
> *saints according to God's will.* [8:28] *And we know that all things work*

together for good for those who love God, who are called according to his purpose, 8:29 because those whom he foreknew he also predestined to be conformed to the image of his Son, that his Son would be the firstborn among many brothers and sisters. 8:30 And those he predestined, he also called; and those he called, he also justified; and those he justified, he also glorified.

8:31 What then shall we say about these things? If God is for us, who can be against us? 8:32 Indeed, he who did not spare his own Son, but gave him up for us all—how will he not also, along with him, freely give us all things? 8:33 Who will bring any charge against God's elect? It is God who justifies. 8:34 Who is the one who will condemn? Christ is the one who died (and more than that, he was raised), who is at the right hand of God, and who also is interceding for us. 8:35 Who will separate us from the love of Christ? Will ***trouble, or distress, or persecution, or famine, or nakedness, or danger, or sword?*** *8:36 As it is written, "For your sake* ***we encounter death all day long;*** *we were* ***considered as sheep to be slaughtered."*** *8:37 No, in all these things we have complete victory through him who loved us! 8:38 For I am convinced that neither death, nor life, nor angels, nor heavenly rulers, nor things that are present, nor things to come, nor powers, 8:39 nor height, nor depth, nor anything else in creation will be able to separate us from the love of God in Christ Jesus our Lord.*

While suffering is not this passage's primary thesis statement, it does acknowledge present sufferings. Look at the highlighted words above. Paul uses groaning, suffering, decay, trouble, distress, persecution, bondage, and danger. These are all words we would associate with suffering trauma and its effects.

Think about what Paul says in 2 Corinthians 1:3–7:

Blessed *be* the God and Father of our Lord Jesus Christ, the Father of mercies and God of all comfort, who comforts us in all our **affliction** so that we will be able to comfort those who are in **any affliction** with the comfort with which we ourselves are comforted by God.

> Just as the sufferings of Christ are ours in abundance, so is our comfort through Christ. But if we are **afflicted**, it is for your comfort and salvation; or if we are comforted, it is for your comfort, which is effective in the patient enduring of the same **sufferings which we also suffer**; and our hope for you is firmly grounded, knowing that as you are sharers of **our sufferings**, so also you are *sharers* of our comfort.

Notice the language- affliction and suffering. Paul is talking about the crushing pressures of his ministry life. He identifies his endless suffering, being delivered over to death, troubles, hardships, and distresses; enduring beatings, imprisonments, and riots; hard work, sleepless nights, hunger, thirst; dishonor, bad reports, being sorrowful and poor; being severely flogged, exposed to death repeatedly, being scourged five times, beaten with rods three times, pelted with stones, three times shipwrecked, out in the open sea for a day and night, homeless, in danger from rivers, from bandits, from countrymen, and Gentiles; in danger in the city, and the country, at sea; and in danger from false believers, was cold and naked. In addition to all his extraordinary suffering and, yes, trauma, he had everyday concerns about the spiritual health of the churches (2 Cor. 11: 21–28).

And yet Paul says,

> *No temptation (trial) has overtaken you but such as is common to man; and God is faithful, who will not allow you to be tempted beyond what you are able, but with the temptation (trial) will provide the way of escape also, so that you will be able to endure it.* 1 Corinthians 10:13 [xxi]

Suffering and affliction come in all forms (James 1:2). Our problems are varied and diverse. While the world leads us to believe that our sufferings or afflictions are unusual or unique, the truth is that no matter how tempted suffering people may be to believe that their situations are different or abnormal, we are to teach sufferers to think carefully and biblically about them and to realize that God says our afflictions are common to man (2 Cor. 1:3–7; 4:7–11; 6:5–10; 11:23–27; Gal. 6:17; Phil. 3:10; Col. 1:24).

[xxi] "Peirasmos πειρασμός," *Strong's G3986*, in *Thayer's Greek Lexicon*, electronic database (Blue Letter Bible, 2002, 2003, 2006, 2011), https://www.blueletterbible.org/lexicon/g3986/kjv/tr/0-1/. Strong indicates that this Greek word, used to describe adversity, affliction, or trouble, is sent by God to test or prove one's character, faith, and holiness (Luke 22:28; Acts 20:19; James 1:2; 1 Peter 1:6).

Trauma is normal. Affliction, hardship, and suffering are normal and should be expected because we live in a fallen world with fallen people. There is a tendency (even among Christians) to embrace an unbiblical and idyllic mindset in which we wrongly believe that this world is a great place and suffering is unusual; this is not true. Trauma is also not a modern problem. Our ancient ancestors also suffered from unbelievably painful experiences. Thankfully, our loving Father has left us a Book to read how His people cried out to Him in their distress.

When a person is enduring the effects of catastrophic suffering, they often experience responses in the inner man that are internally wrenching and create much anxiety (Job 9:16–31). The biblical counselor will help the counselee understand that because they are an embodied soul, what affects them physically affects them spiritually, and what affects them spiritually affects them physically. This is clearly revealed in the language of many of the Psalms. For example, counselees describe a churning stomach that accompanies post-incident response or a gnawing internal feeling of anxiety that causes them to question everything (Ps. 6:2; 31:9). A person who has endured evil and hardship may live with much fear.

Consider undertaking a study of fear in the Bible. You'll find that a variety of Hebrew words directly refer to what it is like to experience the kind of fear described by those who've experienced this kind of ruthlessness. *"Egypt was glad when they departed: for the fear of them fell upon them"* (Ps. 105:38). Strong's defines "the fear of them" as *feelings of dread, alarm, fear(ing) a specific thing, and having great fear, or terror.*[xxii]

King David cried out, *"My heart shudders within me, the terrors of death sweep over me. Fear and trembling come upon me, and horror has overwhelmed me"* (Ps. 55:4–5, CSB). This entire verse contains verbiage revealing that David is writhing in fear, terror, and horror. The comparable New Testament root word is '*fobos*' – from which we get the word phobia, which means *(to be put in fear); alarm or fright: to be exceedingly afraid, or full of terror.*[xxiii] In Psalm 56:3–4, the psalmist expresses fear of his enemies and those who seek to harm him.

In addition to experiencing various aspects of fear, suffering caused our Old Testament ancestors to lose faith or gain faith, doubt or hope, trust or flounder. Job 3 is an example of this point. In verse 3, Job wished never to have been born. He then asks why he didn't die at birth (Job 3:11), and in verses 20–21, Job complains that he wants to die, but God will not take him. As we read through the subsequent chapters of this book, we see that Job has lost faith because he does not

---

[xxii] Trembling with dread: Lexicon: Strong's H6343 - *paḥaḏ*

[xxiii] Phobos

understand; he has lost hope because even death seems to elude him, and his faith begins to flounder. We could find verses, passages, and chapters in Job that display each aspect of suffering. In no other book in the Bible do we see traumatic suffering as in Job. We also learn from Job that suffering will cause people to look to God for help or comfort or harden their hearts in anger. Pain and misery cause people to evaluate what is truly important to them (Phil. 3:7–10), and some say that, in hindsight, going through a trial time helps them to evaluate their priorities.

The post-trauma distress a person experiences can promote self-centeredness and self-pity (Ps. 25:16–17). They look at others who seem to have it so much better than they do and wonder, why them and not me? Why must I suffer? This attitude can even be true of Christians, especially if those who prosper are unbelievers. They wrongly think that because they are Christians, they are entitled to relief and prosperity, perhaps "because of all I do for God" (see Psalm 73). They feel sorry for themselves and sit in a pile of self-pity, waiting for things to change and begin to go their way.

The affliction causes a person to isolate, like a solitary bird perched on a rooftop (Ps. 102:7). Veterans who experience post-combat distress express feeling alone and isolated, separated from others who cannot relate to or understand what they lived through in combat.

"My soul is bereft of peace; I have forgotten what happiness is; so I say, 'My endurance has perished; so has my hope from the Lord'" (Lam. 3:17–18). Many commentators, such as Matthew Henry, interpret these verses as expressing the prophet's deep despair and loss of peace due to the severe afflictions the Hebrews were facing. A suffering survivor can resonate with Jeremiah's feelings of being utterly cut off from any sense of well-being or prosperity. There is often deep emotional and spiritual turmoil experienced by the afflicted person who feels abandoned and without hope, provoking a time of intense spiritual crisis. Biblical counseling can lead the person to faith and reliance on God's mercy.

"Panic and pitfall have come upon us, devastation and destruction; my eyes flow with rivers of tears…" (Lam. 3:47–48a). The imagery in these verses, "terror and pitfalls" and "ruin and destruction," illustrates the intense and multifaceted nature of the suffering and captures the fear, danger, and profound sadness that a person who experiences such devastation endures. The imagery also underscores the extent of the physical and emotional wreckage left by experiencing a calamity. The vivid imagery of "streams of tears" communicates profound grief and unending sorrow, highlighting the depths of overwhelming emotion the suffering person displays.

From what we've looked at so far, it's easy to understand why suffering, affliction, and distress can cause a person to wonder if God loves them. Even the psalmist cried out, *"My God, my God, why have You forsaken me? Far from my deliverance are the words of my groaning. O my God, I cry by day, but You do not answer; And by night, but I have no rest"* (Ps. 22:1–2). Many afflicted people will communicate this experience without using these exact words. They lay awake in their beds, crying out to God for deliverance. They are tormented by their memories and their pain in the night, and they cannot see God through the pain of their circumstances. Their internal pain causes them to wonder if God has forgotten about them or hears their cries (Ps. 27:7–9). Some become angry or frustrated with God. They have been praying for months and years, and their circumstances are not changing. These people speak of the ceiling that their prayers appear to bounce off, never making it to the throne of God.

This kind of affliction causes them to wonder if God is punishing them or is unhappy with them (Ps. 51:11). They wonder if they have somehow displeased God with their actions and caused Him to look upon them with anger and visit trouble upon them. This is particularly true of war veterans. The reality is that killing is a part of warfare, and even when it is done as a part of service to one's country, the soldier can experience these thoughts and fears. Like David in the Psalms, after his sin with Bathsheba, they confess and repent of all the sins they can remember, but they cannot overcome their feelings of being punished for what they are enduring.

Suffering causes us to feel sorrowful and sometimes to sorrow without hope (Ps. 22:1–2). Prolonged suffering can bring the ultimate suffering, sorrow without hope, which is often labeled as clinical depression. This is the ultimate defeat, as all efforts have been exhausted, and there is nothing else to be done, yet the problem remains. They believe the situation is never going to change.

"I have been forgotten like one who is dead; I have become like a broken vessel" (Ps. 31:12). The comparison to being "dead" highlights the depth of his emotional pain and the extent to which he feels cut off from human connection. The broken pottery metaphor conveys David's feelings of being irreparably damaged, which is a common misbelief of those who have experienced catastrophic suffering. *"My heart throbs; my strength fails me, and the light of my eyes—it also has gone from me… For I am ready to fall, and my pain is ever before me"* (Ps. 38:10, 17). This dark and haunting language helps to communicate the intensity of the person who has lost all hope for the future. Biblically, we could describe such a person as being crushed and in despair.

The despair causes them to have a downcast spirit and to wonder if they will ever be "ok" again (Ps. 42:5–6; Lam 3:20). Much like Naomi, they wonder what the future holds and if things will ever be "normal" again (Ruth 1; Ps. 35). And as their circumstances remain unchanged, they grumble and complain to God about them. And some, in their confusion, anger, and distress, shake their fist in anger and rage at God, whom they know could change things with a word but does not.

As you can see, nothing about the biblical terminology for affliction is minimized. The Bible is full of narratives of people who have endured all kinds of suffering, and the responsibility of the biblical counselor is to learn from the Bible the experience of trauma and how to help those who have experienced it by applying its timeless truths to the hearts and lives of the afflicted individual.

Reframing problems biblically is part of helping the afflicted person develop a theological perspective on what they have endured. They will be distressed; sin does that, and they likely have already been searching for answers. Many will have already been to the secular world – willingly or unwillingly, looking for help. They will have been through the treatments the world has to offer, and yet they are still miserable. Biblically, we can show them there *is* help, healing, and hope to be found in Christ. Unlike psychotherapy, the Bible contains eternal truth that not only remedies the mind but resolves the issues of the devastation of the soul that people who have experienced horrific events endure.

By redefining trauma-related terms biblically, we can offer a more hopeful and accurate understanding of suffering. In the next chapter, we will delve into foundational counseling principles that can guide our interactions with those who have lived through calamity and tragedy. These principles will help us build trust, offer genuine empathy, and address difficult questions with biblical wisdom.

Consider and Apply

1. How can you effectively reframe psychological terms and diagnoses in biblical language?
2. What common psychological terms do you encounter, and how can you redefine them biblically?
3. How can you help your counselees see their experiences through the lens of Scripture?

CHAPTER 6

Foundational Counseling Principles

Effective counseling requires more than just knowledge; it demands a compassionate and empathetic approach. This chapter will outline foundational principles for biblical counseling, emphasizing the importance of hope and authenticity and addressing difficult questions. Building trust and offering genuine support can create a place for the counselee to experience healing and transformation.

The Bible offers specific counsel on how to endure catastrophic suffering and other difficult experiences. We help our counselees understand that their responses to what they have experienced are not, as the DSM label says, post-traumatic stress disorder. Extreme responses to physical and sexual abuse and terror are *normal* when one experiences such soul-crushing and distressful events. Their responses may be normal human responses to very abnormal situations, even if they are not necessarily godly or righteous. This is not to say that all responses to extreme hurt are sinful; some are habitual and have been learned over time. The counselee may not be aware they are responding poorly; it is simply all they know to do. The biblical counselor must be cautious and gently probe the counselee to gain understanding and insight. However, regardless of why an afflicted person responds the way they do, their actions sometimes cause additional problems in their lives, including adding to the harm and suffering they and those around them are experiencing. They want the pain to stop, and this is why they come for help.

Begin with Hope

While the history of mankind and the suffering and hardship that accompanied the fall is indeed dismal, the Christian has been given a message of hope. Even in the immediate aftermath of the fall, while Adam and Eve trembled with fear in the bushes and God pronounced curses on all of creation (Gen. 3:7–8, 14–19), God already had a plan to restore mankind and creation through the incarnation, life, death, and resurrection of Jesus Christ, the God-man who willingly came to earth, took on human nature, and lived among us as a man (Gen. 3:15; Rom. 5:8–9). That plan is displayed from Genesis to Revelation, where redemption is made known to everyone who reads the Bible and internalizes its truths. Jesus Christ experienced living in this fallen world before dying on the cross for our redemption. This is the origin of hope for the distressed sufferer. Even though temporarily their hopes were crushed by their circumstances, in Christ, they can experience the one hope that can never be destroyed: *"In this is love, not that we loved God, but that he loved us, and sent his Son to be the propitiation for our sins"* (1 John 4:10). The good news is that Jesus Christ came to redeem sinners and to set humanity free from the penalty of sin and death (Rom. 5:8–9).

The words in the Bible, written under the inspiration of the Holy Spirit, are not intended for "religious" people in "religious" contexts; they are words for sinners separated from God and for the actual troubles and literal failings all people have, for all the things that prompt the Son's self-sacrificing love. What they have been through can lead to life transformation. Eventually, you will encourage them to focus on what God has done, is doing, and will do for them. You will show them that He has a purpose and a plan for all that has befallen them: to bring them to Christ and grow their faith (Rom. 8:28–29). Even enduring the torment of something as horrific as sex trafficking can be the vehicle through which salvation and spiritual growth are attained.

There is something deeply refreshing in saying that what is broken cannot be fixed up as good as new and requires rebirth. It is good for the sufferer to hear that while the pain from what hurts so badly may not be taken away, God offers healing and comfort and is attentive to their pain (Ps. 147:3). God is present and can help them through the hard, accurate reckoning of what happened. And they can learn reasons to live that are better by far than merely feeling better. For the believer, suffering holds purpose, refining faith, drawing them to Christ (Rom 8:28; 1 Pet. 1:6–7), while for the unbeliever, it's meaningless, a futile echo of a broken world (Eccl. 1:2). This hope turns anger to trust, bitterness to forgiveness, rooted in God's good plan.

Correct anthropology, their new identity, and the answer to the problems plaguing the soul are found in Christ. While the history of mankind and the suffering and misery that has accompanied the fall is indeed dismal, mankind has been given a message of redemption. Because of what God did through Jesus Christ, humans can experience genuine hope and change. Through the person and power of the

Holy Spirit, the counselee can learn and realize the greater reality of God's love, power, and redemption. They can experience joy in the Lord as His Spirit uses the Word to encourage and enable them to live for Him. However, freedom in Christ does not mean the end of pain or that everything works out the way the sufferer thinks it should. In Christ, freedom means hope amid difficulties and pain and a realization that while there are consequences for the actions a person takes, God continues to work in them.

Practical Steps for Counselors

Distress is a fact of life, and while it is true that horrific experiences can be the catalyst to a downward emotional spiral, it doesn't have to go in that direction. Communicate that there is hope in learning and believing that what they are suffering, or their miserable experience, does not have to define them or determine their future. Biblically framing the struggle provides hope and comfort because the distressed person will find the Scriptures full of tragic loss, suffering, and pain. Jesus understands the burden of the soul experiencing PTS. Jesus Christ experienced unbelievable suffering, and He can empathize with the affliction and pain of a person with post-incident distress (Heb. 4:15).

The late David Powlison said in this extended quote,

> God does meet us in our need. He enters our plight in person. He shares in our troubles. Suffering is the crucible in which Christ shows himself. Suffering is the crucible where faith awakens. Suffering is the crucible where love becomes wise. We learn faith and love when life goes wrong. A person who faces grievous evil must do a hard reckoning to come out wise and not corrupt. Hope results when something good emerges from an encounter with great evil. God's grace is always at work for good in a world of evils. Hope results when we help the sufferer recognize that Christ faced, engaged, and walked through grievous evils. He did it first and best. He did it for us. He promises to do it with us and in us. He does what he promises. There is hope.[145]

There is hope in knowing that change is possible because feelings and responses are not a disease. Daniel Berger remarks, "Traumatic events have a long-term, negative influence when a person clings to a wrong worldview, looks for hope in the wrong place, or disassociates from reality." There are aspects of dealing with post-traumatic distress and complex suffering that can appear overwhelming. It can seem like it is too much for biblical counseling, and sadly, some say relying on the Scriptures is too simplistic of an approach for such complicated problems. We must take heart. In Christ, the Christian is fully equipped to come alongside such a person to counsel, comfort, console, and calm.

Sometimes, a person in a crisis has difficulty functioning. The church body can offer to help with everyday tasks like cooking, cleaning, caring for the kids, running errands, and so forth. The principles of Galatians 6:2–5 are essential here. The counselee struggling to cope will benefit from having others come alongside them to help bear their load for a while. Still, they must be encouraged to do things independently because getting the counselee back into regular routines is essential. Offer to help when tasks seem overwhelming. They should be encouraged to structure their time, keep as constructively busy as possible without missing rest or sleep, spend time with others who care about them, and verify they are doing so. The counselee may also feel incapable of making decisions. It is helpful for them to make as many daily decisions as possible since this will increase their feeling of control over life's daily events. Be gently directive, depending on the severity of their responses to the traumatic event. Don't smother them with attention or hover; give some measure of space, but stay within reach. Allow them some private time, and don't pressure them to do things they might not be ready to do.

Provide counsel on important life decisions or changes they may want to make. Sometimes, a person in a significant life crisis will want to make huge decisions that will alter their life; however, this is not generally advisable. This includes deciding on a new place to live, finding a new job or career, breaking up with a significant other, or quitting school. Encourage the affected person to take the time to recover and get some perspective on what happened before making any major life changes.

The impact of catastrophe can be lessened through some common-sense actions that the counselor can suggest. First, encourage the affected person to take care of themselves physically, including eating regular, healthy meals, even if they don't feel like eating; getting plenty of rest to give their body a chance to recover from the emotional and physical toll the trauma has taken; and avoiding the use of alcohol or drugs. Periods of strenuous exercise alternating with periods of relaxation can help alleviate some physical reactions.

Hope in Christ enables the sufferer to have a realistic view of themselves. Their terrible circumstances, which test their faith and what their faith is in - Christ or something else- can lead them to find true and lasting hope and recovery from even the worst of catastrophic suffering. Faith and hope in Christ open the door to practical solutions based on the Word. The hurting person finds true peace, freedom, and a sound mind in His Word. God wastes nothing. He uses all things for good. "*Behold, I am doing a new thing; now it springs forth, do you not perceive it? I will make a way in the wilderness and rivers in the desert*" (Isa. 43:19, ESV). This verse is rooted in God's message to the people of Israel during their exile and suffering. It is a powerful message of hope and renewal. God declares He is doing something new that signifies a new beginning already underway, and He is challenging them to recognize that He is at work. Even in times of difficulty and devastation, even when things appear hopeless (represented by the imagery of the wilderness and desert), God is actively working; He is guiding and providing help and hope where there seems to be none.

Be Authentic

You want to be authentic when talking with someone who has experienced cataclysmic suffering and pain. It gives them hope that you will be "real" with them. As you build a relationship with them, the counselee finds hope in having someone listen to what they have experienced and how it has affected them. Communicate that you care about them, are interested in them, and how they are doing. Spend time with them and let them know you are there to care for them. Initially, what matters most to a hurting person is your presence, not any immediate words of advice or Scripture you may offer, so be a good listener. Spend 95% of your time listening and 5% talking. Provide a listening ear and allow them to share what happened, how they feel, and what they are experiencing. All people want to be heard. It is very hope-giving for the person to know someone will just listen to them.

As you listen to their story, don't tell them, "I know how you feel," if you haven't lived through the same kind of experience. It is perfectly fine, and even preferable, to admit you haven't gone through their experience! Let them know you don't know what it's like to endure that kind of suffering; you can only imagine how difficult it must be. Instead, ask the person to share in what ways what they endured has affected them and how they feel in the present. Initially, you will hear many feeling-oriented statements, which is okay in the early stages of the counseling relationship. Eventually, you will help them operate by faith, not feelings.

When you do speak or respond, point them to the truth. Talking about their experiences might be very emotional for them and may raise fear and anxiety levels. Assure them they are safe (*if* that is the case) and offer to pray for them. Initially, they may not want you to pray, but if they consent, keep the prayer short and to the point. Call out to God, asking for His help and presence in times of trouble.

Express *your* confidence in the fact that God will hear and respond. Be careful to avoid offering platitudes and clichés ("It could have been worse" or "Count your lucky stars") or glibly quoting Bible verses such as Romans 8:28–29, Philippians 4:4–9, and 1 Thessalonians 5:16–18. These are essential verses, but at this moment, offering them might come across as dismissive, insensitive, and minimizing their suffering. They might misunderstand your intention and perceive you are reducing their horrific experience to a common occurrence that a Bible verse can quickly remedy.

You might consider praying the Psalms, such as 34:4, 7, 8, 18, and 19, which express the faithfulness of God to those who seek Him. It is comforting to hear that the Lord is good and that He blesses those who take refuge in Him. Your counselee will benefit from hearing how God delivers those who seek Him from all their fears, that He encamps around them, is close to the brokenhearted, saves those crushed in spirit, and delivers them from all their afflictions. This is incredibly encouraging to someone suffering from the fears that accompany traumatic memories and experiences.

Be aware that those who have endured terrible experiences are often lost and angry. They may not want anything to do with God. They do not want to hear that Jesus Christ is in the business of bringing freedom to those in bondage. One survivor of long-term trauma says this:

> Our past experiences shape how we interpret nearly everything around us… Oftentimes, these experiences also define our perceptions of who God is, as well as what our purpose is on this planet. Those who have been raised in the church may not realize how greatly their understanding of Jesus and salvation differs from the understanding of those who have never been anything but hurt by the world.[146]

Addressing Difficult Questions

When counseling those who have been badly harmed, it is wise to initially be cautious and careful when speaking about the hope found in Christ. The victim will likely have many difficult questions, and it will be necessary to answer complex questions about God and their suffering. They may ask

- Why did God allow this to happen to me?
- Is God the author of evil?

- Is God punishing me for something?
- Where was God when I needed help?
- Why does God allow evil to exist?
- How can a loving God permit such suffering?
- Does God care about me or my pain?
- Can I ever trust God again after this?
- What purpose can there be for my suffering?
- Why do bad things happen to good people?
- How can I find peace and healing in my life?

Sally: A Case Study in Catastrophic Suffering- Why?

Sally does not believe God cares for her and wonders why He allowed her to be trafficked and abused and why He allowed her baby to be aborted against her will. Sally was seen by medical providers who could and should have recognized she was being trafficked and offered help, but they never asked. Sally feels forsaken by God and believes He has treated her unjustly. More than once, Sally asked, "Where was He?" "Why didn't He protect me?" "Why won't He protect me now?"

Sue Nicewander says,

> With every fiber of her spirit, she cries out for an explanation for the injustice and evil she has suffered. "Why, God? Why?" She's angry and afraid to be known by God or anyone else because she feels so ashamed nothing erases the taunting, cruel voices that tell her it's all her fault and that she'll never measure up. [She] feels dirty and damaged, but she can't bring herself to talk to God about it. She doesn't trust God.[147]

Biblical counselors must take the time to address their counselees' concerns about God's character and their experiences. Trusting God is a must for the counselee to recover, yet often, it is what they push back on the hardest. They don't have a biblical perspective on their suffering, and the biblical counselor must help them develop one by slowly teaching them theological truths.

Demonstrate from the Scriptures that God is both all-good and all-powerful (Ps. 145:9; Rev. 19:6). It can be incredibly challenging to reconcile the idea of God's goodness with the reality of what the counselee has experienced; however, the attributes of God are deeply relevant to the counselee's ability to understand and navigate their suffering. God *is* holy and pure, and His nature *is* entirely good.

The existence of evil and suffering does not negate these attributes. He is not the author of wickedness or evil, nor does he cause or promote it (James 1:13). He did not cause the sin committed against them or that they witnessed, and He did not take pleasure in it.

One explanation for the evil that befell them is related to the free will God gave mankind. Free will is a gift from God that allows us to choose right or wrong (Gen. 2:16–17; Deut. 30:19). This freedom is essential for genuine love and relationship with God. However, free will also means that people can choose to do evil, leading to misery. God does not cause or desire evil and affliction; He hates it even though He allows it to exist. This tension, in which both prosperity and adversity come from God, reminds us that God is not the author of evil but ordains its existence in the world (Eccl. 7:14; Isa. 45:7). It encourages us to recognize God's hand in all circumstances, understanding that He is sovereign over both the good and the difficult times. Ultimately, God uses calamity and evil for His sovereign purposes (Ps. 5:4–6; 11:6; Isa. 45:7; 1 John 4:8). He uses all things for His glory (Rom. 11:36). These truths are difficult to comprehend and unsettling to contemplate but are essential for the counselee to accept.

Some people do not believe God understands what they have endured. They struggle to see God as being present in their woes and sorrows. For many, God is an ethereal being who they wrongly believe cannot relate to them or their experiences. The counselor must open the Scriptures and show them that Jesus intimately knows what it is like to suffer and be betrayed by those he loved (Matt. 26:14–16; Mark 14:10). He knows what it is like to be distressed and alone in need (Matt. 26:56; Mark 14:50). In Matthew 26:37, we read that on the night He was betrayed, after the Passover meal, they went to the Garden of Gethsemane. The disciples went with Him to the garden, and Jesus told them to sit and wait while He went to pray. He took Peter, James, and John to where He prayed. As soon as Jesus was alone with His closest disciples, He told them He was *"deeply grieved, to the point of death."* We think about the physical torment that He was about to endure. We understand that Jesus was troubled or full of anguish, but I suspect you and I have no earthly clue what He suffered in the Garden of Gethsemane. Jesus knew He would die on the cross, but not before He experienced the wrath of His Father and drank from the cup that was filled with the divine judgment against the sin of the world (Isa. 51:17). For the first and only time since before time began, the Father turned His face away from the Son. The parallel account in Mark 14:33 can further expand our understanding. The word used there for "distressed" indicates that Jesus experienced a feeling of horror and astonishment.

He was in the grip of terror, something that may resonate with a person who has experienced some form of catastrophic suffering.

Jesus experienced human emotion. He felt as though He could not physically survive the burden of sorrow that He was carrying in the Garden. Jesus clearly was in an agony of soul that was almost unbearable. His distress was so overwhelming that the capillaries in His body burst and mixed with his perspiration, causing Him to literally sweat great drops of blood, as Luke's gospel notes. He experienced anguish at a level some of us cannot possibly imagine. His distress was so intense that God sent an angel to strengthen him!

Jesus displayed extreme responses to abuse and terror— responses that, while intense in depth— are normal human responses to very abnormal situations. In Psalm 38:10, the psalmist says that because of the discipline of the Lord, his heart throbs, and his strength fails because of what he endured (Psalm 38:17; 69:12). This is similar to what Jesus said in Matthew 26:37! Jesus "*fell on His face and prayed*" that the cup would pass from Him. While Jesus was in the grip of intense agony, His closest disciples were nearby and likely able to hear everything He said. They fell asleep even though Jesus pleaded with them to be watchful, stay awake, and pray. God told Jesus "No "when he prayed for the cup to pass Him by (Matt. 26:39, 42, 44). One of the men He shepherded, Judas, who lived and traveled with Him for three years, ultimately betrayed Him. When Jesus was arrested, they all left him. They all ran away (Mark 14:50–52). Peter, one of the closest in His inner circle, denied knowing who Jesus was! Added to the anguish Christ experienced was being betrayed by those he loved.

Jesus endured evil—he was humiliated, beaten, mocked, slapped, punched, brutalized, whipped with a Roman flagrum,[148] stripped naked, and crucified. He was hung on a cross, which was not only the greatest humiliation for a Jew but also the most barbaric form of torture the Romans could devise (Isa. 52:14; Matt. 27:27–31). This after the skin and muscles were torn from His body through the flogging He received. Those walking by mocked and scorned and taunted Him (John 19:23). *I am poured out like water, And all my bones are out of joint; My heart is like wax; It is melted within me* (Ps. 22:14). Jesus Christ empathizes with the affliction and suffering a victim experiences.

Through His own torment, He understands and offers a way forward—a path to healing that begins with trusting His presence in our pain. Hope rooted in His sacrifice equips us to face the deepest wounds. Building on these foundational principles, His empathy, God's sovereignty, and biblical truth, we turn in the following chapters to explore responses to fear, anxiety, grief, loss, guilt, and shame.

By applying Scripture to these struggles, we can offer practical counsel and lasting hope to those in need.

Consider and Apply

1. Reflect on your own experiences or those of others you know. How have responses to calamitous suffering manifested, and how have they impacted daily life and relationships?
2. How does this chapter's biblical examples and teachings resonate with your understanding of suffering and God's role? What new insights have you gained?
3. In what ways can you build trust and authenticity in your counseling relationships? How can you ensure you are genuinely present and empathetic with those you counsel?
4. How can you prepare to address the difficult questions about God and suffering that counselees may have? What biblical truths can you rely on to provide comfort and guidance?

CHAPTER 7

Biblical Responses to Post-Event Fear and Anxiety

The effects of catastrophic suffering manifest in various ways, often leading to fear, anxiety, grief, and guilt. This chapter will explore biblical responses to these specific problems and provide practical steps for overcoming them. By grounding our approach in Scripture, we can offer genuine hope and healing to those who have experienced deep suffering.

Understanding Fear and Anxiety

PTSD is considered an anxiety disorder by the American Psychological Association (APA), and the World Health Organization (WHO) recognizes C-PTSD under the broader group of "Disorders Specifically Associated with Stress," alongside PTSD and a few other disorders. However, post-trauma responses are not at their root an organic or medical problem; therefore, they do not meet the medical threshold for disease. PTSD does not originate as "a pathological condition of a part, organ, or system of an organism."[149] However, complicating physical problems resulting from long-term lack of sleep, fear, and anxiety may develop and require medical intervention.[xxiv] How does the biblical counselor help the trauma survivor who is afraid, worried, and anxious from their experiences?

[xxiv] When a counselee is experiencing physical problems, they should always be referred to a physician for a medical exam including blood work to rule out any biological cause for what they are experiencing. When biological causes (outer man) are eliminated as the source of the problem, the focus turns to spiritual (inner man) causes.

Your counselee may talk about the strong and intense emotions they experience, including feelings of fear and anxiety, anger, numbness, and sadness. They may have disturbing visual memories, thoughts, and perceptions. Sometimes, there is an urgent need to escape and a desire to get up and run.

When a person is in what they perceive to be imminent danger, the brain sends messages to the body, specifically the endocrine system, that cause hormones to be released that are designed to prepare us physically to deal with real danger, even when none exists. This is the experience of anxiety, which is experienced leading up to a dangerous, stressful, or threatening situation, which may be real or imagined. It is an apprehension that triggers a dread of something that seems to be impending. It is based on "what if." Anxious living brings physical exhaustion from the strain of constantly being on high alert. It may be comforting to the counselee to hear that the body responds to anxious thoughts as God designed it to function. They might also experience "body memories," which are "a sensory recollection of traumatic experiences related to pain, discomfort, tension, and arousal."[xxv]

Body memories can be provoked by everyday occurrences, such as a particular smell or sound, recalling something that happened, a nightmare, or a touch that causes them to respond physically as though the event is happening again. The counselee might talk about having recurrent nightmares, flashbacks, and intense distress when something reminds them of the horrific event, making it feel as if the incident had just happened. Then, they become apprehensive that it actually would happen again. In the hands of a skilled biblical counselor, the vivid memories of the past (flashbacks) can be transformed into a call for Christ.[150] For example, Timothy Lane's booklet on PTSD uses Psalm 27 to reveal that the Scripture has much to say on this vital topic.[151] Psalm 27, written by King David, provides a glimpse into his life when he was running from Saul. While we cannot say that David experienced post-trauma stress or anxiety, this Psalm reveals that he suffered hardship, suffering, and horrible events that were not isolated from God's mercies. The Psalm ultimately points the reader to Jesus, who understands what the sufferer is going through and sympathizes with them in their weaknesses. Lane remarks that when people have experienced severe harm, they question God's goodness. He says, "[God] is always moving toward you, and he understands your questions and doubts."[152]

Extreme fear, often labeled as panic attacks, is also prevalent in those who are fearful and anxious. Panic results when fear, worry, and anxiety come together and

[xxv] Because several medical conditions can cause a person to be fearful and anxious, rule out the outer man as the cause of how they are feeling. Instruct them to get a medical checkup to ensure there are no biological causes for their feelings of anxiety. Once it's determined that their body is not the culprit, you can confidently address the inner man as the origin of the fear.

overwhelm a person's thoughts. Panic is fear that is so life-dominating that the counselee will describe being unable to control it or their reactions to it. Commonly, those who experience panic attacks have learned to fear the feeling of fear itself, and the fear of the fear spirals out of control. Their physical distress is real, and they will describe feeling like they are short of breath or feeling smothered, or like they are choking. They may be dizzy, feel faint, sweat profusely, have a rapid heartbeat or heart palpitations, and tremble or shake.

Practical Steps to Overcome Fear and Anxiety

Many with extreme fear have become accustomed to functioning on a system that is continually overloaded with stressful messages that keep the body in a constant state of arousal or panic. The person experiences an ongoing, intense fight or flight response, and it frightens them; it is sometimes physically painful, and there is a lack of understanding of what is happening to them. It often leads to associating feelings of extreme fear and panic with a specific object or place. They, of course, want to avoid those feelings, so they begin to avoid the association of things that provoke the extreme fear response (commonly referred to as "triggers"). Responding by avoidance only reinforces the wrong thinking the person has going on in their heart. It creates a self-fulfilling prophecy that "if I go here or talk to that person, I am going to have a panic attack," when that is not necessarily true. The counselee becomes reclusive or avoids being alone, depending on what provokes that feeling of extreme fear and everything that goes with it. The result is thinking and focusing in a faulty way and learning to fear the fear. They might allow fear to control them, sometimes leading to periods in which the counselee stares straight ahead and is unresponsive to commands or questions (catatonia). They appear to check out from reality (dissociate) as a form of self-protection, having a loss of memory and confusion after the event. Over time, it becomes easier to disassociate from emotionally painful or traumatic events rather than deal with them, making this a difficult habit to break. On its face, these two coping responses might appear to be good, but biblically, the counselee needs a different perspective on these responses to fear and anxiety. Disassociation and catatonia are forms of self-dependence that promise the hope of escaping from pain and hardship that they cannot deliver. They are false refuges, running to self instead of God, who alone is our stronghold (Ps. 46:1). Avoidance and dissociation flee pain but find no peace, unlike Christ's sure rest (John 16:33). The answer is not dissociation; it is Christ. Jesus knows this and calls us to Himself to find rest. The counselee might not want to give up what they think "works" to help them cope with life each day post-trauma. Therefore, perseverance will be necessary as the counselee may initially resist trusting God and the biblical counseling process.

This illustration of a train may help you understand how living with post-trauma anxiety feels to the counselee. Fear, panic, and anxiety are the engine running their life, and behind the engine, being pulled along by fear and anxiety are the rest of their related feelings.

Post-Trauma Fear and Anxiety

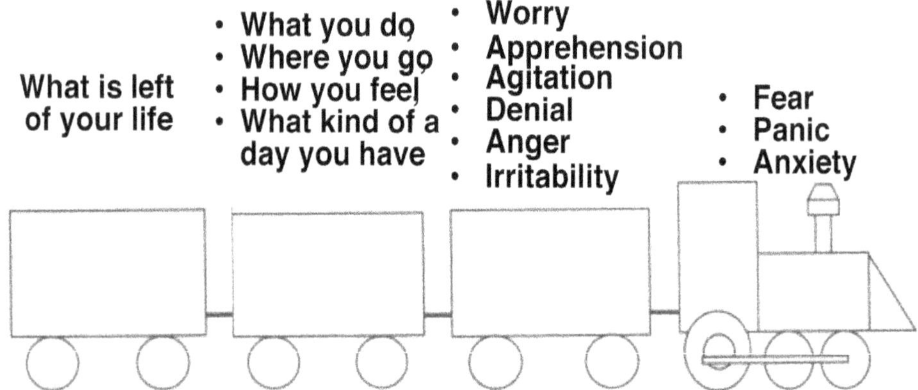

What they do, where they go, how the counselee feels, and what kind of day they have is driven by fear and anxiety. They feel powerless and out of control, as if they are on a train they cannot get off.

Everything is controlled by whether they are having a good (or bad) day with their fear and anxiety. The last car represents what is left of their life, what they can and cannot do because of their fear and anxiety, their panic attacks, and their nightmares. Their world becomes extremely small. They struggle to function every day, and eventually, they will wear out their adrenal system from continually pumping cortisol and adrenaline. The body is not made to function this way for weeks, months, or years. They will begin to experience other health issues due to a weakened immune response and eventually physical collapse.

Recognize the person may be rightfully fearful based on what they have experienced. While helping someone with post-trauma symptoms, it is important for the counselor not to rush in and tell the counselee not to be fearful but to enter into the fear with them. Depending on what they have survived, they may have built strong self-protective measures as a response. Gannon and Moore reveal,

> They [self-protective measures] are comprised of things we fear we might not get, but really want, or believe we need. Things like acceptance (What if I'm rejected or ridiculed again? What if I'm unloved?) Or security/safety (What if I get hurt again?) Is it wrong to want to be loved, secure, and safe?[153]

Be careful not to convey that all fear is bad because that is false. Fear takes on different meanings and isn't always negative; it can serve a vital purpose. In one sense, a reverent awe of God—praised as the beginning of wisdom and knowledge (Ps. 111:10; Prov. 1:7), provides spiritual guidance. In another, fear is also the emotion experienced when a person is actually in a dangerous situation, as Proverbs 22:3 illustrates: *"The prudent sees the evil and hides himself, but the naive go on and are punished for it."* This is a wise response to fear. The threat of physical and sexual abuse, terror, captivity, and compromised physical health are concrete examples of both dangerous and harmful realities. Fear is understandable in such cases and is a natural response to such threats. However, in post-incident fear and anxiety, these fear responses occur when no current threat is present. The person has an identical fear response to what is *perceived* as dangerous or potentially harmful, even when no threat exists. They react to a previous or imagined situation, reflecting a state of fear and a feeling of losing emotional and spiritual control.

The counselee may be imprisoned behind bars of fear that have existed for a long time.[154] One survivor said,

> Some bars are comprised of fearful memories derived from what we suffered, fearful memories intrude, uninvited and unexpected, [sic] when something reminds us of what happened. Our disturbing memories are often vivid and seem very real, leaving us shaken to the core.[155]

The biblical counselor is to encourage the counselee to accept that the feeling of fear exists instead of denying or repressing it. However, they will need help identifying the reason for their fear and determining whether there is or is not a genuine danger. If there is no present threat, examine what potentially drives their fear and anxiety. Continue to point them to Christ, for ultimately, God brings permanent change. These are issues of the immaterial or inner person (the heart) and expose how they interpret life. Communicate to the counselee that the Scriptures address the feelings of fear, worry, anxiety, and panic experienced by those who survive catastrophic events. The Bible provides hope and help to overcome the distressing emotional responses pronounced after such events.

Since the Bible acknowledges we are single beings who are both material (body) and immaterial (heart, soul), it is essential to look *beyond* the physical symptoms of anxiety and look to the heart to determine the root of the problem (once biological causes for the symptoms are ruled out medically). The good news is that post-incident fear and anxiety, with all the accompanying feelings and emotions, is an "inner man" problem that is also experienced in the physical body. Anxiety is created in the inner self; Scripture establishes this fact. Psalm 94:19 says, *"When my anxious thoughts multiply within me, Your consolations delight my soul."* In Psalms 55:1–3, David is asking God to hear his prayers. He says, *"My thoughts trouble me, and I am distraught."* He is anxious. This is not to say the physical issues are ignored or are unimportant, but realizing that the physical symptoms are the result, not the cause, of how the counselee is living and feeling is crucial. It is natural and expected to see one affecting the other in physical and emotional responses to fear and anxiety (Gen. 2:7; Ps. 77:2–4; 88:3–5).

Identifying post-incident responses in biblical terms describes what the person is experiencing and allows the correct approach to help them with their difficulties. Because anxiety begins in the inner self, this is where the counseling starts. The Bible teaches that fearful feelings flow from what a person wants and thinks about in their heart (inner man). Thoughts and desires generated in the inner man shape what the counselee feels and does. Post-trauma anxiety originates from a fearful heart. The fearful heart includes issues we have examined previously, including an identity that is based on falsehoods, spiritual deadness, failing to live in the present reality where God resides, and having fleshly reactions to pain. Other problems are remaining in relationships full of chaos and sin, living by fluctuating emotions, and allowing futile thinking to run wild.

Consider beginning with a passage like Matthew 11:28–30, where Jesus speaks to the Jews living under the weight of Roman rule and Pharisaical legalism. The people were heavily burdened both politically and religiously by these two systems. Jesus saw their weariness and called them to Himself for rest and relief. Thoughts and feelings may burden the counselee, convincing them that they will never get over or past their terrible experience and that they are hopeless and doomed to treatments and therapy for the rest of their life. Jesus says,

> *Come to me, all of you who are weary and burdened, and I will give you rest. Take my yoke upon you and learn from me, because I am*

> *lowly and humble in heart, and you will find rest for your souls. For my yoke is easy and my burden is light.*

These verses can be the basis for building the counseling relationship with the counselee. They are likely weary and burdened from handling their circumstances alone (apart from God). The first aspect of rest Jesus provides is in the saving relationship with Him. The next element of rest comes from ceasing to find hope and help in any psychological system and embracing biblical discipleship to address the issues of the soul. These relational aspects emphasize God's sovereign grace and the transforming power found in unity with the Holy Spirit. These verses also clarify the relationship a person has with Christ in salvation. His yoke is light, and He is lowly and humble, gentle and kind. Meaning, that while the counselee will find that the path of Christian obedience requires denial of self and change in the manner of living, God's grace is ever-present to guide, direct, and correct. Jesus is a sympathetic High Priest who understands their struggles to change.

Encourage the counselee suffering from lingering memories of their experience by having them retell their story, which, depending on what they experienced, may be fragmented and contain significant gaps. Help them assemble their story cohesively and see where God is. Listen carefully and thoughtfully and ask clarifying questions as necessary. Give hope by letting the counselee know that because the anxiety is not biological (when it is not related to a medical condition), they can be confident that this is rooted in a spiritual battle and that together, you will determine if part of that battle is with sin. Because whatever is not physical is spiritual; if their problem is not medical, this is the only other option. Understand, this may be shocking to a person who has been psychologized, so make it clear that this is good news! Because Jesus died for sin, and in Him, there is victory over the responses to the sin committed against them or what they experienced.

Proverbs 20:5 says, *The purpose in a man's heart is like deep water, but a man of understanding will draw it out.* (ESV). The emotions of post-incident fear and anxiety can be a powerful diagnostic tool because they expose the thoughts and intentions of the heart. For example, when anxious, the counselee's thinking is jumbled, and they react out of habit instead of acting with purpose and intentionality (Eph. 4:31–32). To overcome any habit, sinful or otherwise, the counselee must, according to Ephesians 4:22–24, put off the old practices, be renewed in their mind or heart, and put on the new practices.

Examine the Thought Life

To biblically overcome post-trauma fear and anxiety, the counselee must begin with their thoughts. It's vital they understand that their thought life, not their mental health diagnosis, is what has a direct bearing on overcoming fear and anxiety. Help them distinguish fact from feeling (evidence from emotion) by interpreting data in the light of Scripture, not their feelings.[156] Assist the counselee in examining their thoughts and discerning the truth about themselves and their circumstances by asking a sequence of questions intended to draw out what is going on in the heart. Asking the suffering counselee questions that address what is happening in their heart amid their fear will be more beneficial than merely talking about their fears. Heart-piercing questions will help them realize that their fears and worries reveal what is most important to them. Then, help them develop the new habit of self-examination as part of their re-habituation by using questions such as these:

"Is there a real reason to be anxious, or will staying calm be more helpful for you?" This question encourages them to stop and think about their circumstances instead of reacting. Anxiety is a learned habit and, over time, becomes a usual way of life to the point where the person doesn't think about what is happening; they just react. Encourage the counselee to take the time to consider if being calm and developing a rational plan of action will be helpful, and it will teach the counselee to stop reacting and start thinking.

"What specifically are you thinking about right now?" or "What are you focusing on right now?" These questions call the counselee to pay attention to their inner dialogue. They help move them from feeling orientation to focusing on their thoughts.

"Are you thinking about things that are true and real or imagined?" Because so much fear and anxiety is based on "what if," the counselee must determine if their feelings of fear or anxiety are focused on reality or fantasy. It is common for a victim to spend time meditating on imaginary scenarios that feed their feelings. Directing them to examine the veracity of these thoughts and then tell themselves the truth will be a helpful habit to develop.

"What can you do to address the situation leading you toward panic?" Feelings of powerlessness are very common in a trauma scenario, and sufferers want to avoid all situations that may place them in jeopardy. Helping them think about realistic options to address the situation will give them confidence and a plan they can implement instead of collapsing into extreme fear or running away.

"Do you believe God is in control of this person or situation?" This is one of the most critical questions in the series. It will reveal where the counselee has placed their faith and whether they believe in God's power, might, and sovereignty.

"Are you unknowingly thinking about things contributing to how anxious, fearful, and worried you feel right now?" When they are focusing on these things, they are going to produce the bad fruit that is evident in the symptoms of panic and anxiety because the heart is not settled on and focused on glorifying God. These emotions stem from habits that have developed over the years. They have become automatic behaviors that likely operate apart from the counselee's conscious effort. Asking the counselee to examine the thoughts that may be contributing to their feelings is a good way to help them refocus on what is true and dispel lies and possibilities that lead to fear and anxiety. They tend to focus on how they feel about things rather than on what God is doing in the things He allows into their lives (Ps. 31; 1 Cor. 10:24; 13:5; Phil. 2:5–9).

"Are you unknowingly thinking thoughts that are leading you to have this physical reaction in your body?" Physical reactions are often the counselee's first clue that they are thinking unbiblically. Ask the counselee experiencing tension, fear, or panic to examine their thoughts and assist them in holding their thoughts up to theological truth, which is one way to short-circuit bodily reactions of anxiety and panic.

"What can you do to stop the panic process before it goes too far?" Counselees who experience extreme fear responses (panic attacks) are often very fearful of having a full-blown panic attack. They develop a fear of the fear that pushes them further into fear and anxiety. It becomes a circular process. Working with the counselee to develop specific biblical strategies and plans for what to think, read, pray, sing, and meditate on when they experience extreme fear enables them to establish new response patterns. Encourage them to take a couple of slow breaths without concern that they are engaging in clinical breathing therapy. God made the body to breathe, and when fear has the counselee panting, gasping, or holding their breath, a slow breath can steady them. This is not therapy; it's stewardship of the body (1 Cor. 6:19–20). The goal is not to fix them with deep breathing, but to turn their heart to the Lord. We aren't interested in tweaking their oxygen levels or manipulating their nervous system; we want to encourage the counselee to use what God has provided to stop, be still, and trust (Ps. 46:10). Fear is a spiritual wrestle (Matt. 6:25), not something to address with a technique. So, encouraging the counselee to breathe slowly and remember "the Lord is my refuge" (Ps. 46:1) will remind them that He is the one who calms their soul-crushing panic. Breathe, then run to God (Ps. 55:22).

"What's the worst thing that will happen to you if you actually have a panic attack?" This question is a very real concern to a person attempting to begin new patterns of thinking and living. Asking the counselee to think about the worst possible thing that would happen if the extreme fear takes over demystifies it for them. Often, the "what if" they have built up in their mind is much worse than the uncomfortable minutes they spend feeling extreme fear. Remind them that their body will calm down as they take deep, regular breaths and reign in the thoughts that led them to the extreme fear response (2 Cor. 10:5).

"Have you stopped thinking about God and his sovereign control over the situation?" This question is helpful after you have taught the counselee about the sovereignty of God. Calling them to examine their thinking and belief system in light of God's sovereignty helps reorient the counselee's heart.

"What are you thinking about instead of thinking about God and his sovereign control over the situation?" This follow-up clarifying question will assist the counselee in repentance and applying the biblical truths they have learned through biblical counseling.

Because the counselee is likely accustomed to emoting more than being aware of their thoughts, a thought journal is a wise project to assign them. The Thought Journal is a written log of what the counselee is thinking about, what they believe to be true, and what they desire in their heart. The Thought Journal is an invaluable tool because the thoughts, beliefs, and desires of the heart might not be immediately apparent to the counselee. Often, they will start by expressing many emotions, such as fear and anxiety, which seem to arise spontaneously without conscious effort. Feelings and emotions are metaphysical, they cannot objectively be studied because they lack physical substance. Their emotions provoke the counselee's physical responses (e.g., crying, hyperventilation, drug abuse) connected to their feelings, thoughts, perceptions, desires, will, or beliefs about reality or imagination. The counselee may think they have no control over their feelings and emotions or the actions that result from them, but this is not true. It will provide immeasurable help to the counselee to understand that their thoughts significantly influence their emotions.

The thought journal will assist the counselee in understanding that thoughts in the heart and mind provoke emotional responses. They can influence or change their feelings, emotions, and behaviors by aligning their thoughts with biblical truths. This approach emphasizes the critical need for heart change, as true transformation comes from aligning thoughts, beliefs, and desires with God's Word (Rom. 12:2; Eph. 4:23).

One method to teach a person how to examine the thoughts and beliefs of the heart is to ask themselves good questions. If the counselees can learn to ask themselves good questions, it will expose their belief system, which is essential because they act upon what they believe to be true. Asking themselves heart-level questions will reveal their desires as being God-oriented or self-oriented (Matt. 6:20–22). Self-questioning will expose any inconsistencies in what they say they believe and what they do. People tend to be selective in how they view their actions relative to their belief system. When done well, the thought journal and self-questioning will help the counselor and counselee understand the core issues of why they are experiencing feelings of anxiety or panic.

What's being exposed? Fear exposes the counselee's unbelief. Unbelief is one of the most common areas of struggle (Matt. 6:25–34; Rom. 8:28–29), and it's produced as they fret over how God could bring good out of their situation. Ultimately, anxiety exposes what a person fears, and fear exposes what they value the most (worship), and typically, what a person values most is "self." All people, but especially those who have been harmed, have a great desire for self-protection and self-gratification, and this often produces selfish, self-reliant, and self-protective behaviors. It leads to a self-centered life void of seeking how to show love to God and others (Matt. 22:36–40; 2 Tim. 3:1–5). The focus is on what they might lose, making their world grow smaller and smaller as they isolate and self-protect. The counselee must learn to reach out and give of themselves to meet others' needs instead of being self-focused.

The desire for control is also exposed. Because devastation and destruction are very much out of a person's control, there is often an enormous desire to have control over being in control, which is demonstrated in wanting to control what others say, what they do, where they go, and attempting to have absolute control over situations. The counselee will expect everyone to adjust so they feel comfortable, and they will desire absolute security, which is an illusion (Luke 9:23–25; Phil. 2:4).

Anxiety and panic can help the counselee to examine and determine where their heart has strayed from God. They can become a tool to help them understand where their faith in God is lacking and find where they have replaced their confidence in God with human fear. However, simple insight into a problem isn't enough, and neither is receiving satisfactory answers to questions that reveal the counselee's thoughts, beliefs, and desires. In addition to these things, the fearful, anxious person must renew their heart (mind, thoughts, beliefs, desires) with Scripture and then act accordingly (Eph. 4:23). Behavior changes without being transformed by the renewing of the mind (Eph. 4:23) bears little difference from the principles of cognitive behavioral therapy (CBT).

Ephesians 4:23 and other Bible verses emphasize the importance of being renewed or transformed in the spirit of your mind, which suggests a transformation beyond mere behavior modification (Rom. 12:2; Col. 3:10). Daniel Berger remarks, "Scripture establishes that anxiety is a mindset in a person's immaterial nature (the spiritual heart/mind)."[157] From a biblical counseling perspective, true and lasting change involves salvation, altering behaviors, renewing the mind, and aligning one's thoughts with biblical truths. The only way for a person to be renewed in the spirit of their mind is by the unchanging truth of God's Word. John 17:17 says people are made holy and transformed by the truth. Assist the counselee in learning and practicing spiritual disciplines such as reading the Word, memorizing Scripture, prayer, and meditation. These are activities that people struggling with fear and anxiety avoid.

The counseling and homework process will aid the counselee in seeing fear and anxiety and their responses to them as potentially sinful. Such revelations will require confession and repentance and putting a plan in place to replace their fear and anxiety with confidence in God. Repentance is vital for putting to death unbiblical fears. Repentance is not a "one-and-done" action; it is correctly understood as an ongoing activity, and it will take daily concentrated efforts to do so. As the Holy Spirit works in the counselee's heart, they will stop trying to justify or rationalize their fear and anxiety and recognize that guilt comes with sinning against God (Matt. 3:2; Mark 1:15; 1 John 4:18).

However, confessing sin and admitting guilt is not complete repentance. Too often, our counselees recognize their problems and acknowledge their sin, but nothing else happens. No other changes take place, and they return to habitual fear, worry, and anxiety. So, a change in the course of life is also necessary. Ephesians 4:24, the "put on" found in this critical passage involves an act of the will, which intentionally turns away from the anxious and fearful thoughts they are accustomed to and replaces them with true and God-honoring thoughts.

Intruding thoughts that provoke fear and anxiety are a common problem among those who have experienced horrific events. Address the counselee's fear biblically. Help them to address their heart and to develop biblical, accurate thoughts and desires to overcome their enslavement to fear (Prov. 23:7).[158] They must learn to control their thoughts and speak truth to themselves rather than listen to their unbiblical thoughts (2 Cor. 10:5). To take their thoughts captive, they must first identify what they are, which is where the thought journal will be helpful. When anxious, based on 2 Corinthians 10:3–5, the counselee can write down what is going through their mind, documenting inaccurate thoughts and perceptions, followed by accurate or biblical perceptions. Then, they can replace inaccurate thoughts with what is true from Scripture to reinforce the truth. As they replace their fearful thoughts with God's and overcome fearful thoughts with God's promises, they will overcome and practice the "put off/put on" process (Eph. 4:22–24).[159]

Consider using Psalm 56 to help the counselee bring their fears before God. Work through Psalm 56 with the counselee, or assign it as homework, and encourage them to tell God about all the fearful circumstances they have endured and residual concerns from what they experienced. Have the counselee interact with the Psalm, evaluating if the verses are similar to their feelings and determining where they differ. Have them write down what is going through their mind as they read each verse, identifying thoughts, beliefs, or desires that are inaccurate or not aligned with biblical truth. These might include fears, anxieties, hopelessness, or doubt about God's care and protection.

Psalm 56:1-2

Verse:

"Be merciful to me, my God, for my enemies are in hot pursuit; all day long they press their attack. My adversaries pursue me all day long; in their pride many are attacking me."

Inaccurate Thought:

"I am constantly under attack, and there is no escape."

Reflection Questions:

- Ask the counselee if they have felt pursued or attacked by their fears or anxieties.
- How do these verses resonate with their daily experience?
- Can they relate to feeling constantly under threat or pressure?
- How does this continuous sense of attack affect their daily life and relationship with God?

Biblical Truth:

"God is merciful and aware of my struggles. He is my refuge even when I feel pursued."

Application:

- Just as a physical refuge provides shelter from danger, trusting God means believing He will protect them from harm and guide them through difficult times.
- How have they seen God protect them recently?

Additional Verses to Study:

- Psalm 46:1
- Psalm 91:2

Psalm 56:3-4

Verse:

"When I am afraid, I put my trust in you. In God, whose word I praise—in God I trust and am not afraid. What can mere mortals do to me?"

Inaccurate Thought:

"I am alone in my suffering."

Reflection Questions:

- Ask the counselee to identify specific fears they are facing.
- How do these fears compare to the psalmist's declaration of trust in God?
- Is it essential to trust God amid fear?

Biblical Truth:

"When I am afraid, I can trust in God. He is with me, and I am not alone."

Application:

- How can the counselee begin to shift their focus from their fears to trusting in God?

Additional Verses to Study:

- Isaiah 41:10
- Deuteronomy 31:6

Psalm 56:5-7

Verse:

"All day long they twist my words; all their schemes are for my ruin. They conspire, they lurk, they watch my steps, hoping to take my life. Because of their wickedness do not let them escape; in your anger, God, bring the nations down."

Inaccurate Thought:

"People are always against me, and I have no protection."

Reflection Questions:

- Does the counselee find themselves focusing on how unfairly they've been treated?
- Are they stuck in a cycle of negative thinking about their situation?

Biblical Truth:

"God sees the schemes against me and will bring justice. He is my protector."

Application:

- Does the counselee believe in God's justice and His ability to protect and vindicate?
- How can shifting focus to God's protection and sovereignty change their perspective?
- How can this bring comfort to the counselee?

Additional Verses to Study:

- Psalm 34:17
- Romans 12:19

Psalm 56:8

Verse:

"Record my misery; list my tears on your scroll—are they not in your record?"

Inaccurate Thought:

"My pain is unnoticed and unimportant."

Application:

- Encourage the counselee to acknowledge their pain and suffering.

Biblical Truth:

"God records my misery and tears. He knows and cares about my suffering."

Reflection Questions:

- How does it feel to know that God records their misery and tears?
- Discuss God's compassion and His intimate knowledge of their suffering.
- How can this bring comfort and assurance?

Additional Verses to Study:

- Psalm 34:18
- Revelation 21:4

Psalm 56:9

Verse:

"Then my enemies will turn back when I call for help. By this I will know that God is for me."

Inaccurate Thought:

"There is no one to help me."

Reflection Questions:

- Discuss the assurance that God is for them.
- How does this truth impact their view of their current situation?

Biblical Truth:

"When I call for help, God will respond. He is for me and will turn back my enemies."

Application:

- Encourage the counselee to call out to God for help.
- How can they practically do this in their daily life?

Additional Verses to Study:

- Psalm 118:6
- Romans 8:31

Psalm 56:10-11

Verse:

"In God, whose word I praise, in the Lord, whose word I praise—in God I trust and am not afraid. What can man do to me?"

Inaccurate Thought:

"I am powerless against my fears."

Reflection Questions:

- Discuss the psalmist's confidence in God.
- How can the counselee develop a similar confidence?

Biblical Truth:

"In God, I trust and am not afraid. What can man do to me when God is my protector?"

Application:

- Encourage the counselee to praise God's word and trust in Him.
- How can they incorporate praise and trust into their response to fear?

Additional Verses to Study:

- 2 Timothy 1:7
- Psalm 27:1

Psalm 56:12-13

Verse:

"I am under vows to you, my God; I will present my thank offerings to you. For you have delivered me from death and my feet from stumbling, that I may walk before God in the light of life."

Inaccurate Thought:

"There is no hope for my future."

Reflection Questions:

- Is this true based on everything they have learned and examined in this Psalm?

Biblical Truth:

"God has delivered me and will continue to guide me. I can walk before Him in the light of life."

Application:

- Ask the counselee to reflect on how replacing the thought "There is no hope for my future" with biblical truths impacts their feelings and perspective.

Additional Verses to Study:

- Jeremiah 29:11
- John 8:12

Sally: A Case Study in Catastrophic Suffering- Fear and Anxiety

Sally, now sober at the rescue mission, still battles fear every day. One day, while she was sitting in the day room with Abigail, a door suddenly slammed loudly, mimicking a sound from her trafficking days. Sally's heart began to pound, her palms began to sweat, and she froze, her eyes darting wildly about. She wanted to bolt but stayed glued to the couch, frozen in terror. Abigail noticed Sally's response to the sound and sat beside her on the sofa. Abigail gently took Sally's hands and looked into her eyes, saying 'Sally, let's take a slow breath and turn to Christ,' modeling stewardship of the body (1 Cor. 6:19–20). 'That deep breath is God's gift to steady you; now tell me: Is there a real threat here, or can staying calm help?' Sally exhaled, whispering, 'No threat, just noise.'

Abigail pressed deeper and asked: 'What are you thinking right now?' Sally muttered, 'I'm trapped, he's coming.' Abigail nodded, 'Is that true, or imagined?' Sally hesitated, 'Imagined… it's just a door.' Abigail opened her Bible to Psalm 56:3–4: 'When I am afraid, I put my trust in You. In God I trust—what can man do to me?' She asked, 'Can you trust God here, Sally? Is He sovereign over this moment?' Sally nodded, tearfully reciting, 'I trust You.' Abigail suggested Sally journal this. She asked Sally to 'write what fear says, then what God says.' Sally scribbled: Fear: I'm trapped, helpless. Truth: God is my refuge (Ps. 46:1), He's with me (Isa. 41:10). Her breathing steadied as she replaced lies with truth and God's promises.

Focus on the Fundamentals

In addition to what has already been mentioned, learning and memorizing fundamental Bible doctrines such as the doctrines of justification, Romans 8:33, and progressive sanctification, which has been the underlying focus throughout most of this lesson, will help the counselee counter and prevent anxiety. Teach the doctrine of the perseverance of the saints and their union with Christ in Ephesians 5:32–33. It is very critical they understand the doctrine of forgiveness. However, initially discussing forgiveness with a person who has been severely hurt may cause the counselee tremendous anxiety (Ps. 103 and 1 John 1:7–9; 2:12). In addition, I recommend spending a lot of time in the Proverbs. One suggestion would be to meditate on the many promises found in Proverbs 3, particularly verses 1–26. Other suggested verses to meditate on are:

- Psalm 62:1–2 "My soul finds rest in God alone; my salvation comes from him. He alone is my rock and my salvation; he is my fortress, I will never be shaken."
- Psalm 91:1 "He who dwells in the shelter of the Most High will rest in the shadow of the Almighty."
- Psalm 94:19 "My anxiety was great within me, your consolation brought joy to my soul."
- Psalm 116:7 "Be at rest once more, O my soul, for the Lord has been good to you."
- Isaiah 40:1–2 "Comfort, comfort my people, says your God. Speak tenderly to Jerusalem, and proclaim to her that her hard service has been completed, that her sin has been paid for."
- Isaiah 66:13 "As a mother comforts her child, so will I comfort you."
- 2 Corinthians 1:3–4 "Praise be to the God and Father of our Lord Jesus Christ, the Father of compassion and the God of all comfort, who comforts us in all our troubles."
- John 14:18 "I will not leave you as orphans; I will come to you."

Fighting fear as a Christian is fundamentally about trusting a person, Jesus Christ. *Our experience of anxiety is an invitation to go deeper with Christ*; it's not just something we stop doing. Truth beckons the worrier to find rest in Christ. I hope this brings you comfort.

Consider and Apply

1. Think of three specific ways you use biblical principles to help counselees manage their fear and anxiety.
2. How do thoughts influence emotions and behaviors in trauma survivors?
3. How can you help counselees align their thoughts with biblical truths?
4. How can tools like the Thought Journal assist in this process?

CHAPTER 8

Biblical Responses to Grief and Loss

Grieving over loss is a necessary aspect of healing and an important aspect of the counseling process. The victim's sorrow is linked to embracing the sadness of their losses. Many of these losses have grieved and angered God's heart.

Biblical Examples of Grief and Loss

We can see in the Bible that the Israelites suffered harsh labor, oppression, brutal treatment, physical abuse, and the trauma of losing their children to infanticide (Ex. 1:7–14; 2:23–25). Jeremiah and Lamentations reveal Judah's grief and loss from God's judgment on their sin, with starvation and despair marking their fall (Lam. 1:1–2; 4:4–5).

In the New Testament, we see Jesus' righteous anger at the grief and loss the Pharisees brought into the lives of God's people. They lived under the burden of oppression from the Pharisees and tyranny from the Romans. While Roman tyranny brought violence and taxation, the Pharisees imposed a heavy burden of legalism on the people, enforced complex purification rituals, and excluded those they considered sinners (Matt. 12:1-14; Mark 7:1–23), which caused emotional distress for many people, as they were marginalized and ostracized from the community (Luke 7:36–50). Family members were forced to choose between public shaming or compliance (Mark 7:1–23; Luke 18:9–14; John 9:22). Jesus, a "man of sorrows" (Isa. 53:3), understands grief and loss, meeting His people in pain.

Understanding Grief

Grief is an unexpected yet common post-catastrophic suffering response and does not have to be directly related to death; it can be the loss of one or more limbs, loss of innocence, the grief of separation, or the alienation that one experiences when they have been involved in an event that no one else around them has endured. Grief emerges as a natural reaction to loss or significant change, often marked by profound sadness and sorrow that can weigh heavily on a person. When this grief goes unaddressed, the unresolved memories of those painful experiences tend to creep into daily life, disrupting it with their lingering presence.

These words may resonate with your counselee. Grief and loss related to trauma will be unique to a person, and the experience is dependent upon what they endured. Healing is a journey, so encourage the counselee to be patient and give themselves grace throughout the process. It will be beneficial for them to recognize and name their specific losses. Urge them to be open and honest with God and to expect His presence to provide peace. Naming their losses helps them acknowledge the reality of the pain and begin to work through it, which can be crucial steps in their healing.

Specific Losses Related to Intense Suffering

Some specific things a person who experienced intense suffering might grieve are things like a loss of safety. If they were physically harmed in a personal or mass trauma event, they might grieve a loss of safety because they are no longer comfortable in environments where they once felt secure. They may have previously been confident and fearless, but now they fear being in crowds, at social events, or even in the grocery store.

Victims of sexual assault and trafficking experience multiple kinds of loss, such as the loss of a part of their lives, sometimes a significant portion of their lives. They have lost control over their bodies, in some cases, lost their families and friends, and they grieve the loss of their children through abortion or if the pimp has taken or sold their child.

They have perhaps experienced a loss of trust in people they once had faith in to love or protect or be honest with them. This might be accompanied by grieving a loss of innocence, especially in cases where adults who were supposed to protect them—parents, teachers— victimized them or failed them. Betrayal cuts deep, leaving suspicion and isolation. Psalm 55:12–14 captures this pain: *hurt from a friend stings worse than an enemy's blow. Yet, God's steadfast love never fails* (Ps. 55:22).

Counseling helps them mourn this breach while turning to the One who never betrays, rebuilding trust through His unchanging character (Heb. 13:8).

Intense suffering often strips safety away. A bombing survivor or abuse victim, like Sally, grieves lost security. Once-comfortable places like grocery stores or homes now spark fear. Crowds feel threatening, and this loss isolates them, shrinking their world. However, God offers refuge. Psalm 46:1 says, *"God is our refuge and strength, a very present help in trouble."* The biblical counselor helps them mourn this loss while trusting God's protection (Prov. 18:10). Unlike fleeting self-defenses (e.g., dissociation, avoidance, hypervigilance), God's presence calms their heart, proving safety is found in Him who never leaves (Deut. 31:6).

Those who have endured severe afflictions mourn the years lost to their suffering. Trafficking survivors like Sally or an abused spouse mourn lost decades. Hopes of a joyful marriage or carefree youth vanish. Veterans miss births and holidays due to deployments. Time slips away, leaving regret. Scripture counters despair: Joel 2:25 promises, "I will restore to you the years that the swarming locust has eaten." God redeems lost seasons (Rom. 8:28). The biblical counselor guides them to lament this theft and rest in the Lord's eternal purpose (2 Cor. 6:2).

Violation robs bodily autonomy. Sexual assault or trafficking victims like Sally grieve lost control over their bodies. They had pimps who sold them, and abusers took what wasn't given. Shame festers: they blame themselves for not resisting. This loss wounds deeply. However, God redeems! The counselee is not "fixed," but reborn (2 Cor. 5:17)! Biblical counseling helps them grieve the past invasion of their body while finding honor in Christ's ownership (Isa. 43:1).

Catastrophic suffering shatters trust in those meant to protect. Sally's brother Billy, or a neglectful adult, betrays them, stealing innocence with their failure. The counselee grieves this violation, and once-safe bonds now hurt deeply (Ps. 55:12–14). The biblical counselor helps them to mourn this loss, redirecting them to trust the One who does not change (Heb. 13:8). Human betrayal fades before the love of God, rebuilding hope beyond broken trust (Ps. 146:3–5).

The physical toll of suffering afflicts the body. Constant pain or lost mobility, like Phil's limp, steals independence and alters careers or plans. Despair creeps in and threatens to make a permanent home with the counselee. Psalm 73:26 comforts the broken, *"My flesh and heart may fail, but God is the strength of my heart."* Biblical counseling helps them to lament and learn to lean on His power (2 Cor. 12:9). The counselee learns their worth isn't in ability but in belonging to God. Their grief turns to trust as they see His strength shine through weakness, not lost abilities.

Severe afflictions fracture relationships. Friends drift during trials; abuse isolates; and deployments strain bonds (veterans). Death in an incident (e.g., a fellow soldier) or an abortion deepens loss. Remorse over being spared haunts, "I could've done more," as with Grant. Loneliness grows, even amid support. Jesus wept too (John 11:35), knowing this pain. Philippians 4:7 offers *"peace… surpassing understanding."* Biblical counseling helps the counselee grieve broken friendships or lost lives, easing guilt through God's sovereignty (Rom. 8:28). The counselee realizes they are not alone; Christ is there and binds up their wounds (Ps. 147:3). Peace comes not in restored relationships but in His presence, turning isolation into communion with the God who sees and wipes away every tear (Ps. 56:8).

Processing Grief and Loss

Some survivors of disastrous incidents have much to grieve. As they face their losses, it is critical for them to process the thoughts and feelings associated with their losses within the framework of God's redemptive work. The primary goal for a Christian is to glorify God in all circumstances, even while resolving grief and loss, which involves trusting God's sovereignty, goodness, and purposes while grieving. It means honoring God through their response to grief, relying on His strength and comfort, crying out to God, and inviting Him to minister to the broken heart. Paul David Tripp encourages the grieving with this,

> Your Savior has taken the name Emmanuel or "God with us." This name reminds us that, as you came to Christ, you literally *became* the place where God dwells. You have a powerful Brother, Savior, and Friend who not only stands beside you, but resides within you. That hope will help you make it through your pain.[160]

Sufferers need not and should not face what happened to them alone. The counselor must come alongside and grieve with them. As a part of grief counseling, learning how to continue life and face the truth about what has happened to them without denying or minimizing the facts despite any temptation or pressure to deny or hide their pain is essential. Learning how to deal with life's losses within the context of God's healing requires them to face the truth, no matter how difficult that will be. While the temptation will be to deny what has happened by either running away, burying it deep inside, or attempting to numb the pain through drugs or alcohol, they must acknowledge what happened. It is normal to be afraid, but grieving is necessary.

Their ability to move forward whole and healed *depends* on acknowledging what happened, which may be the last thing they want to do because the memories may be terrifying. It takes courage to tell oneself the truth about what has been endured. It takes courage to come face to face with suffering, both the internal suffering of the soul and the external suffering it creates. Assure them that it is ok for them to be honest with themselves, and let them know that it's all right to feel their feelings (Ps. 51:6). There are things in their life that died because of what they went through, and there is nothing wrong with admitting that.

Our Empathetic Savior

Our God is empathetic, showing a deep, sinless compassion that truly understands human pain. Remind the brokenhearted person that Jesus grieved the loss of those He loved (John 11:35), and He felt the pain of suffering people around him (Matt. 14:14; Luke 7:11–15). *For we do not have a high priest who is unable to empathize with our weaknesses, but we have one who has been tempted in every way, just as we are—yet he did not sin (*Hebrews 4:15, NIV). Jesus could relate to grieving people because He also grieved. Hebrews 12:2 says that Jesus suffered. He intimately and intensely experienced grief, sorrow, loss, anguish, and pain (Ps. 22:1; Matt. 26:39). Jesus was despised and rejected by men, a man of sorrows and one acquainted with grief (Isa. 53:3). Encourage the counselee to draw near to God. Scripture says He draws near to those who draw near to Him (James 4:7–9). *God is near the brokenhearted and close to those crushed in spirit* (Ps. 34:18).

The grieving person should run to Him, but because they struggle with trusting God, they may be hesitant to do so. They may still be crying out for an explanation for the injustice and evil they have suffered, struggling with the "why" of it all. The question, "Why?" is universal and urgent. Everyone wants to know why God does what He does, and ultimately, no one can completely answer that question. In the Bible, we read about Job, who experienced enormous losses and suffering. He cried out and begged God to explain. Instead, God asked *him* questions, reminding Job that He doesn't owe anyone an explanation. Faith accepts God for who He is and asks questions without demanding answers (James 4:1–10).

Practical Steps for Healing

God does not expect a distressed person to be silent or deny their emotions but to feel and express them, to cry or weep, and to grieve the destruction they experienced. The Psalms of lament are replete with expressions of pain, fear, questions, desires, hopes, grief, sorrow, and other emotions written under the Holy Spirit's inspiration (Ps. 10, 13, 22, 31, 55–57, 73, 88; Ps. 42:3–5). The grief-stricken person can use these Psalms as a model to express their grief and perhaps even to structure their thoughts in a journaling format about what has happened to them. Walk the sufferer through the book of Lamentations to show them it is good for them to be honest about their feelings, and it will help them understand that God walks through grief, sorrow, and loss with his children.

The counselor can recommend that the counselee pray and tell Him their thoughts, feelings, and concerns. Hurting people are often fearful to tell God what they are thinking. Encourage them by reminding them that God already knows what is happening in their heart (Ps. 139: 1–12). Giving voice to the thoughts of the heart furthers a personal relationship with God. When Scripture reading and meditation are included, God "talks back," and the mind is renewed and transformed (Rom. 12:2). These two activities will provide connection and comfort and help them find consolation for their pain in God.

As they embrace God's faithfulness and cling to Him, accepting their losses and embracing healing and hope becomes easier. It will also show them that God is trustworthy, redeeming their sorrow and doing something good (Rom. 8:28–29). Point them to stories like Joseph and Daniel, who suffered losses but recognized God's sovereign purposes in what they endured (Gen. 37–50:20; Dan. 3:1–30; 6:1–28). Such stories help the counselee see that God is always at work in their grief and loss and encourages them to trust that God can heal and restore what has been broken. It involves faith that God is at work even when what He is doing cannot be seen. Help your counselee understand that learning how to heal from grief is possible. Healing begins with facing reality and remembering that God is with them. God will teach them that their grief is not meaningless. In time, they might find that talking about their experiences will help others, becoming a testimony of God's grace and power and bringing a sense of purpose and meaning to their suffering. God is purposeful, and He will teach them about Himself through their grief and loss and use their experiences to shape and grow them into Christlikeness (2 Cor. 1:3–5).

Sally: A Case Study in Catastrophic Suffering- Grief and Loss

Sally carries grief's weight beyond her trafficking scars. At 23, she mourns lost years—stolen innocence from Billy's abuse, a decade of trafficking, and abortion's ache. Day passes to church stir tears, not just fear. Abigail, her biblical counselor, found Sally staring blankly one session, lost in a memory of her childhood room before it all unraveled.

Abigail gently encouraged Sally to name her losses with God. She reminded Sally that God is near the brokenhearted (Psalm 34:18). When Abigail asked Sally what was grieving her, Sally whispered, 'Everything I could've been—family, freedom, a normal life.' Abigail nodded, 'That's honest. Let's tell Him.'

Abigail opened her Bible to Psalm 13 and began reading: 'How long, Lord? Will you forget me forever?' She handed Sally a page torn from her notebook and asked her to write her lament. She asked, 'What's died in you?' Instead of writing, Sally said: 'How long will I feel this empty hole? My childhood's gone, my baby's gone, I'm a shell.' Tears fell as she named each loss—trust in family, her body's autonomy, dreams of safety. Abigail affirmed, 'God hears this (Ps. 139:4). Jesus wept too (John 11:35).' She asked, 'Sally, can you trust He's with you in this pain?' Sally choked out, 'I want to, but why'd He let it happen? I'm too dirty—can He even want me?' Abigail echoed Job: 'God doesn't owe us why, but He promises good (Rom. 8:28). You're not too far—He came for the broken.'

Abigail turned to John 3:16 and read: 'God so loved the world, loved you, Sally, that He gave His Son. Salvation is not earned; it's His gift.' Sally sobbed, 'But I've done awful things! I sold myself, killed my baby. I don't deserve Him.' Abigail knelt beside her, 'None do. That's why Jesus died, for your sin, your grief (Isa. 53:5). He's your High Priest, tempted yet sinless (Heb. 4:15). Do you see your need for Him?' Sally nodded, trembling, 'Yes, I can't fix this alone. I need Jesus to save me.' Abigail silently prayed, 'Guide her to You, Lord.' With tears streaming down her face, Sally whispered, 'Jesus, forgive me. I need You.' Abigail gently suggested, 'Tell Him more, pray your heart.' Sally continued, 'God, I lost so much—my innocence, my baby, my hope.' Sally fell on her knees and, with loud, heaving sobs, cried, 'Save me! Oh God, save me!' Abigail rested a hand on her. 'Sally, Jesus saves you by faith, not by works, do you believe this (Eph. 2:8–9)?' Sally quietly said, 'Yes, yes I do.' Abigail said, 'Jesus has saved you, Sally, you're His. Your sins are forgiven; you're a new creation. Trust His blood, He is faithful.' As she lay on the floor quietly crying, Sally felt the first flickers of peace flood her soul, new birth's dawn (2 Cor. 5:17).

Later, when Sally was alone in her room, old fears and losses tried to creep back into her heart. She got out her journal and wrote: 'Fear says I'm lost; You say I'm found (Luke 19:10).' She remembered what Abigail told her about Joseph and turned to Genesis 50:20 and read: 'Evil meant harm, God meant good.' Weeks later, Sally wrote, 'The grief is still here, but Jesus You are closer (James 4:8).' When Sally talked about her remaining grief, Abigail affirmed that Christ bore sorrow (Isa. 53:3) and reminded Sally that He is redeeming hers. She encouraged Sally to trust Him daily. Sally nodded, 'I'm His now, I'll keep running to Him.' Sally's grief was not gone; there was still more work to be done, but her grief now bends toward hope. Sally's heart is eternally anchored in Christ.

Consider and Apply

1. How will you learn how the counselee's relationship with God has been affected by their experiences of grief and loss? In what ways have they struggled with or found comfort in their faith during these times? How does reading this section prepare you to empathize more deeply with a counselee?
2. How has the counselee's relationship with God been affected by their experiences of grief and loss? In what ways have they struggled with or found comfort in their faith during these times? How has the loss impacted their life, emotions, and relationships? What feelings and thoughts arise when they reflect on this loss? How might their experience help them minister to someone who has also experienced loss?
3. What steps has the counselee taken to acknowledge and process their grief? How have prayer, Scripture meditation, and other spiritual practices helped them in their healing journey? What can you add to the above suggestions for helping a counselee?
4. How can you help the counselee to find purpose and meaning in their pain and loss? Help them reflect on how their experiences might be used to help others or bring about personal growth and transformation.

CHAPTER 9

Biblical Responses to Guilt and Shame

From a biblical perspective, guilt is often associated with acknowledging sin or wrongdoing. It's about recognizing actions or thoughts that go against God's commandments or moral standards.

Distinguishing Guilt from Shame

As we begin to look at feelings of guilt in this section, I thought it was necessary to clearly outline the difference between guilt and shame, which we will look at in the next section. Guilt and shame are related, especially when counseling victims of physical and sexual abuse and other forms of suffering, but they are not approached the same way. Guilt and shame may stem from different heart issues, so the biblical counselor must correctly identify if the counselee is suffering from guilt, shame, or both to address the root cause of their distress correctly and provide the proper counsel.

It is often said that while guilt results from *doing something* bad, shame affects a person's sense of who they are and leads them to believe they *are* "bad." Ken Campbell says, "Guilt leads to feelings of self-condemnation. It is an unhappy feeling. We feel bad, worthless, wrong, a failure because of something we have done."[161]

The Purpose of Guilt

Dr. Robert Somerville says, "Guilt has a purpose." The purpose of guilt is to remind us that we are accountable to God (Rom. 1:20; 1 Pet. 3:16).[162] He says, "Real, true guilt is more than a feeling. It is culpability before God for breaking his standard of righteousness."[163] Daniel Berger explains,

> God has placed moral boundaries in all of us to guide and maintain proper relationships. When these moral boundaries are crossed, guilt attacks the souls of both the victim and the perpetrator. Rape, killing and violence, molestations, abuse, and abandonment go against God's nature and his desire for human relationships, and trauma often produces guilt even in the heart of the innocent victim.[164]

Guilt in the Context of Intense Suffering

In the context of intense suffering, both guilt and shame can be overwhelming. The recipients of evil might feel guilty for many reasons, both real and imagined, and there will be a close association with feelings of shame for many of the same reasons. Whether rooted in reality or not, guilt is a critical issue that must be addressed.

Real guilt is more than a feeling; it is an objective reality every human faces due to both original sin and willful sin (Gen. 3; Rom. 3:10–12, 23). So, every human being, whether afflicted by trauma or not, experiences genuine guilt that results in separation from God (Eph. 2:1). This guilt requires atonement, which is accomplished through the sacrificial death of Jesus Christ on the cross, who bore the guilt and punishment for the sins of the world (Isa. 53:5–6; 2 Cor. 5:21). The only remedy for this inherent guilt is to respond to the conviction and drawing of the Holy Spirit by repenting of sin and believing in Jesus Christ and His finished work on the cross for salvation. In this monergistic action, real guilt is imputed to Christ, and His righteousness is imputed to the person, which results in a formal declaration of justification of the believer (John 16:8; Rom. 3:24–26). Secular therapy recasts guilt as 'PTSD' or 'survivor syndrome,' medicating what biblical counselors see as a spiritual cry. Sin separates people from God, not just minds from peace. They need salvation, not medication or therapy. The Holy Spirit takes up residence within Christians and assists them in the ongoing process of sanctification. Suffering saints must understand they need forgiveness from sin to find release from guilt for their sin before, during, and after their traumatic event(s).

In biblical counseling, addressing guilt involves confession, repentance, and seeking forgiveness. Guilt is relieved by confession of actual sin that has been committed. Guilt can be a complex ball of twine to unwind, and great care must be taken not to place guilt on the counselee for victimization that occurred because of something they did wrong that played a role in their being harmed.

Case Study: Grant's Story

A man we will call Grant called in sick to his job so he could skip work and attend the Boston Marathon. He enjoyed the race until the pressure cooker bomb went off near him. The concussion of the explosion threw him to the ground, and although the shrapnel didn't hit him, he saw men and women being maimed and killed by the flying debris. He suffers from nightmares and flashbacks and lives with overwhelming guilt. He says he feels guilty for surviving the event because he didn't suffer any injury except a headache from the explosion and falling to the ground. Grant's guilt is misplaced. He feels guilty for things he is not responsible for (the explosion and surviving) and doesn't understand that his only actual guilt was lying to his boss about being sick and not going to work.

Here's a table to differentiate what Grant is guilty of and not guilty of:

Guilty Of	Not Guilty Of
Lying to his boss about being sick	The explosion at the Boston Marathon
Skipping work to attend the marathon	Surviving the explosion
Deception	Not being physically injured by the blast.
	The injuries and deaths of others
	Being a race fan
	Experiencing trauma from witnessing the event

Addressing Guilt in Biblical Counseling

In biblical counseling, it's essential to help Grant understand that his real guilt lies in the deception (lying to his boss and skipping work). His overwhelming guilt for surviving the explosion and not being injured is misplaced—many who live through something when others do not experience what is known as survivor guilt. The label describes what is felt and experienced when someone survives or escapes from a natural disaster, a hostage situation, or lives through a terrorist attack, as Grant did when he survived the Boston Marathon bombing. Psychology labels this 'trauma guilt' and prescribes drugs over faith. However, in a biblical counseling relationship, Satan's lie is exposed (Rev. 12:10). The problem is sin or unbelief, not illness, met by Christ's blood (Heb. 9:14). The biblical counselor must help the counselee understand that there is nothing they could have said or done to prevent what happened to them and others. Focusing on God's sovereignty can help such victims replace misplaced guilt. By concentrating on confession and repentance for the actual sin (deception) and understanding that he is not responsible for the horrific event or its consequences, Grant can begin to find healing and relief from his misplaced guilt and shame. If Grant resists confessing deception, the counselor should probe, 'What blocks trust in God's pardon?' (Prov. 20:5), redirecting to 'You didn't cause the bomb' (Rom. 8:28).

Victims like Grant might feel guilty for not being able to "move on" or recover quickly. Paul's experience with the "thorn in the flesh" provides a powerful biblical perspective on enduring ongoing struggles and finding strength in weakness (2 Cor. 12:7–10). We don't know the specifics of this "thorn," but it does represent something God allowed in his life to keep him humble and to show him that God's grace is sufficient to sustain and support him in his weakness. Guilt from catastrophic suffering isn't such a thorn; it's a wound God heals. The biblical counselor helps the counselee confess actual sin (e.g., Grant's deception), releasing misplaced guilt (survival) to God's sovereignty (Rom. 8:28). God's grace frees the counselee; it doesn't merely sustain them (John 8:36). Their worth rests in Christ, not a fast "recovery." The counselee will grow in understanding that God's strength redeems every struggle (Col. 1:13).

He is present with the suffering and confused person; He does not leave them to themselves. God's power is also perfected in their weakness. It allows His power to be displayed in their lives despite their feelings. The counselor should help the counselee to see that God's grace is enough for individuals, regardless of their ability to rush past pain or guilt. Remind them that moving forward is an individual process, not a race to be won. Their worth is not based on their ability to recover quickly but on their identity in Christ (Col. 1:13). *"But he said to me, 'My grace is sufficient for you, for my power is made perfect in weakness'"* (2 Corinthians 12:9, NIV).

There is a crucial relationship between sin and suffering. Discourage the counselee from confessing their experiences of suffering as sinful unless there are aspects of what happened to them that they are responsible for, which is a crucial point for the counselee to understand. Ask the counselee specific questions to help them discern for what they are and are not culpable. Some suggested questions include, "Did you violate a biblical principle or command?" "Were you rebellious to authority?" "Did you break the law?" Help them be specific and articulate precisely how they did these things if they answer in the affirmative.

Assist them in recognizing any complicating sin they committed resulting from their trials. It is appropriate to ask them if they see signs of sinful anger or bitterness in their response to their ordeal. It is also appropriate for the counselor to point out things they see while interacting with the counselee and meeting with them. Does their language reveal they have become hateful and full of rage? Are they self-medicating with drugs or alcohol to ease their pain and guilt? Do they justify their sinful responses because of what they have experienced? The biblical counselor must help them examine their heart and consider God's standards found in his Word. Teach them the purpose of guilt, which is to remind them that they are accountable to God (Rom. 1:20; 1 Pet. 3:16).

When maltreatment, neglect, or other harm has been longstanding, or the counselee has experienced a brutal or sudden calamity, they will likely struggle to recall events. The story may have significant gaps as they process guilt, and important details may be mixed up or missing entirely. Walking the counselee through the timeline of events may help them gain perspective and clarity on their situation.

Sally: A Case Study In Catastrophic Suffering- Guilt

Abigail knew that for Sally to begin addressing her feelings of guilt and shame, it was essential to help her create a timeline of her life events to provide a clear picture of her experiences and help Sally discern what she was and was not responsible for. During one of their sessions, Abigail gently introduced the idea and explained that creating a timeline would help them see everything Sally has been through and help her understand where her feelings of guilt and shame are coming from. Sally was hesitant but agreed to work on the timeline with Abigail.

Abigail handed Sally a large sheet of paper and some colored markers, and they decided to start with Sally's earliest memories. At the beginning of the timeline, Abigail encouraged her to write down positive memories, reminding her that the good times are part of her story, too. Sally took a deep breath and began writing with a green marker on the paper. She recalled playing with Billy when they were kids, climbing trees, and playing tag. She said, "Things were good back then."

As they moved forward to talking about what happened when she was 9, Sally's demeanor changed. Abigail intently listened as Sally described how Billy and his friend hurt her and said it was the beginning of the nightmare. Sally marked this significant event on the timeline, using red to signify the painful shift in her life. As she wrote, Sally said she struggled with feelings of guilt that were related to what she experienced, going all the way back to the day she went into the fort with her brother and his friend. She frequently expressed that she was responsible for all that happened to her because she went into the fort to play.

Abigail helped Sally realize several things that began to free her from her misbeliefs and misplaced guilt. First, Sally was a child who trusted her brother; this was not a sin. She was invited in there and did not scheme, disobey, or rebel in going into the clubhouse. Second, she did not tempt or seduce her brother and his friend; she was an innocent child who thought she was going to play games with them. Third, as a child, she could not consent to sexual activity, and like Tamar, she was raped (2 Sam. 13). Fourth, she did not seek out the boys she had sex with in the woods; she was manipulated and threatened into those activities. She made no profit from the use of her body; her brother and his friend did. Fifth, Sally did not seek an abortion. Her brother threatened her and forced her to go through with it and to keep silent by telling her he would slit her throat if she told anyone.

They continued to document the events of Sally's life. Moving to a new place and the times she attended school were marked in blue. When Sally talked about the kind people who took her into their homes and provided for her, Abigail encouraged her to put those on the timeline in yellow. The arrests she could recall, and her medical treatment were noted in purple.

Each event was marked on the timeline, visually representing Sally's life thus far. As they neared the present day, Sally looked at the timeline with mixed emotions. Seeing it all being laid out was overwhelming to her. Abigail told Sally she could understand how it might be so and pointed out that the timeline helps Sally know and see the truth. Sally was a victim of terrible circumstances, and the guilt and shame she felt were not entirely hers to bear. Abigail also reminded her that she was not alone in this, that they would walk this journey together, and that with God's help, Sally would find peace and healing.

My Timeline

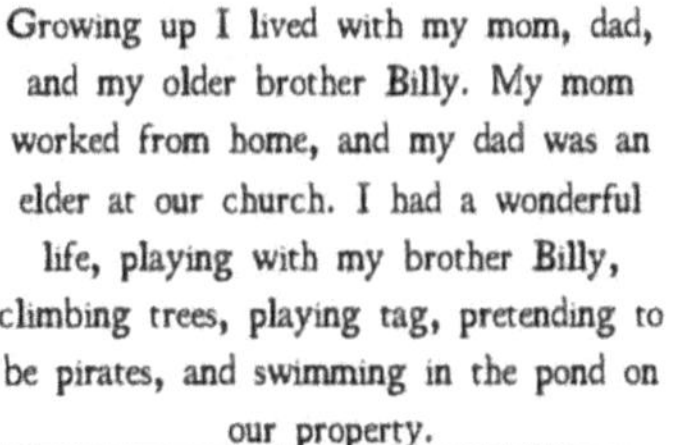

Growing up I lived with my mom, dad, and my older brother Billy. My mom worked from home, and my dad was an elder at our church. I had a wonderful life, playing with my brother Billy, climbing trees, playing tag, pretending to be pirates, and swimming in the pond on our property.

When I was 9 Billy and his best friend lured me into their clubhouse and raped me. That was the start Billy and his friend kept using me over and over.

From 9 to 13, Billy began taking me into the woods, forcing me to allow other boys to have sex with me. I started lying about every little thing. I'd hide stuff candy, coins, just because I could. I'd fight any kid who looked at me wrong. Eventually, my parents locked me in my room. It didn't matter Billy still got in.

When I was 13 I got pregnant. Billy noticed and drove me to a clinic where they did the abortion. He threatened me with a knife not to tell anyone. Afterward, the pain wouldn't stop, and I started bleeding too much. Mom found me on my bedroom floor. They asked what happened, over and over. I stayed silent because Billy's threat was stuck in my head.

When I hit 15, I ran away from home. I was picked up by a guy who said he'd help, but the next thing I knew, I was in a dank motel room. That's how prostitution started. Then I was dragged across state lines by guys who made me do porn movies and pictures. Drugs started then pills first, then needles.

From 15 to 23, I was trafficked and hauled across the country, from one town to the next. Sometimes, I was alone, and other times, I'd hook up with different guys who'd promise me safety. Drugs were my lifeline.

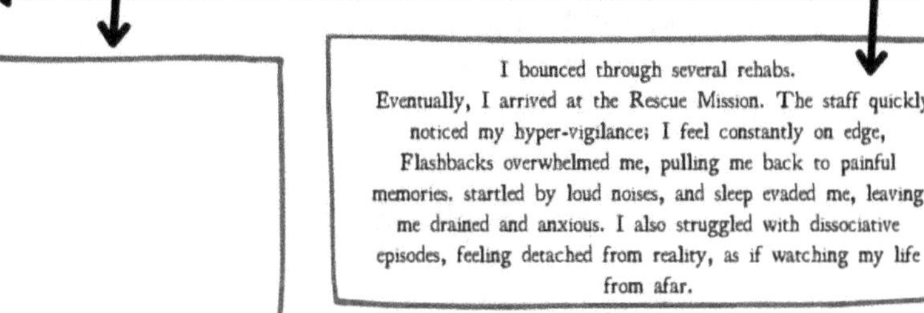

I bounced through several rehabs.
Eventually, I arrived at the Rescue Mission. The staff quickly noticed my hyper-vigilance; I feel constantly on edge, Flashbacks overwhelmed me, pulling me back to painful memories. startled by loud noises, and sleep evaded me, leaving me drained and anxious. I also struggled with dissociative episodes, feeling detached from reality, as if watching my life from afar.

Some people express feelings of guilt about how they reacted during their ordeal, such as freezing or not fighting back, as Sally said to Abigail. The counselee would benefit from an explanation reminding them that responses to horrific events are part of our human frailty and do not equal moral failure. *"For He Himself knows our form; He remembers that we are but dust"* (Psalm 103:14, LSB). This verse can assure the counselee that God understands our weaknesses and does not condemn us for them. Using the illustration of Peter's denial of Jesus can remind them that anyone can experience weakness in moments of fear (Luke 22:54–62).

Confession and Repentance

Once it is determined what they are not guilty of, the next step is to look at what they *are* guilty of, which could include things related to intentional actions or activities they were involved in that were illegal, immoral, or rebellious. They may have to acknowledge lying to their parents to get out of the house, stealing money or goods to fund an ungodly lifestyle, or participating in risky behaviors that lead to them being sexually assaulted, such as drunkenness or drug use. To be clear, the victim is not responsible for being sexually assaulted but is responsible for being under the influence.

The counselee must be willing to examine their heart and deal with their own sins of the flesh to find freedom from guilt for their sin (1 Cor. 6:9–11; Gal. 5:19–21). There is a sense of condemnation and self-blame many victims experience, along with "if only" speeches they recite to themselves every day. These thoughts lock them in a prison of their own making. "Guilt—whether valid or rooted in deception—is one central issue in PTS that must be dealt with by those who endure these experiences."[165] To help them, remind them that God knows every detail of their life; they are fully known by God now as they were in their past. Because of Christ, they are loved and accepted by Him. If they are unsaved, this can be an opportunity to help them understand their genuine guilt before God. When the counselee understands what sins they are responsible for and what they are not accountable for, taking the step of making an actual confession is beneficial.

Sally: A Case Study In Catastrophic Suffering- Guilt (Continued)

Sally's biblical counselor helped her understand that while she wasn't responsible for being raped, she allowed her fear and distrust of her parents and God to stop her from telling them what happened that first time in the clubhouse. Sally decided she was responsible for remaining silent about the sexual abuse when she was old enough to realize it was wrong. Unlike Peter's split-second decision to deny Christ out of fear—a momentary lapse driven by human frailty rather than premeditated intent—Sally chose silence for several years. She understood that fear kept her from telling her parents and that she could and should have told them she was being prostituted in the woods. Sally also recognized all the lies she told that allowed the illicit sexual encounters to continue. She admitted that not telling her parents was disobedient and rebellious, as were her actions in the home that led to her being restricted to her bedroom. In retrospect, she understood that her life would have been vastly different had she told them what had been happening to her.

Sally had guilty feelings because there were times she liked the attention she got from the boys in the woods, and there were times she enjoyed the feelings from the sexual activities. This was confusing for her, and she and Abigail discussed it at length. Abigail explained that God made her body to respond to sexual stimulation, even when it is non-consensual. Her physical response did not equal consent and accusations of this kind may be Satan accusing her conscience and attempting to keep her in bondage, which helped Sally differentiate between the sin she might have committed (if any, in terms of her responses or actions) and the sin committed against her. Sally's counselor reminded her that Romans 8:1 says there is no condemnation for those in Christ Jesus. She can take God at His word.

Sally also carried immense guilt over the abortion. Questioning Sally about what she believed her personal choice was in the matter was helpful. Having been raised in a Christian home, Sally knew abortion was wrong. They discussed her responsibility in light of the threats and coercion of her brother, and Sally recognized she was under significant threat and was vulnerable to his ongoing manipulation. Her conscience was bothered by the fact that while she did not want to have the abortion, she did walk into the procedure and allow it to be done, even though it was under duress. She continued to say in counseling that she could have told someone she didn't want to go through with it. Sally's counselor helped her recognize her guilt was real. While she was ultimately responsible before God for going through with the abortion, her culpability was not as black and white as she might initially have perceived.

Her counselor used the examples of Joseph, who was also put in a situation not of his own making and chose to honor God despite the outcome (Gen. 39), and Daniel, who, while in Babylon, chose to obey God rather than worship a false God, even under threats and coercion (Daniel 1, 3, 6) to teach Sally about the sovereignty of God and the importance of standing alone for righteousness sake in the future. Her counselor emphasized that post-abortive women often feel separated from God due to guilt, fear, and shame, and the counselor helped her itemize all the areas she believed she was guilty.

Sally also recognized that running away from home at age 15 was a decision that she made and for which she was culpable. There were periods when Sally was a willing prostitute and thief, and there were times she was sexually exploited by other men. She recognized that running away from home was the catalyst for a good number of the horrible things that happened to her over the ten years she was on the streets. Sally recognized that at many points on her journey, she had the opportunity to change course and leave the life of drug abuse and prostitution she had been living, but she chose not to because even as difficult and miserable as her life on the streets was, it seemed easier than going home to face her parents. She felt much guilt over how she treated them and the distress she thought they must feel. In this case, Sally's feelings of guilt were signposts, pointing her to the need for confession and repentance. She and her counselor combed through the details of her life, noting the things that were Sally's responsibility (sin) and those that were not.

Once the list was compiled and Sally was as confident as she could be that she remembered everything, the counselor created a visual for Sally to help her differentiate what she was guilty of and not guilty of based on her disclosure:

Guilty Of	Not Guilty Of
Lying to her parents	Being raped
Remaining silent about the abuse	Being manipulated and threatened
Disobedience and rebellion	Experiencing physical responses to abuse
Running away from home	The abortion (under duress and threat)
Participating in prostitution willingly	Being sexually exploited by others
Stealing money or goods	Enjoying attention and feelings from abuse
Drug use	The distress caused to her parents by her brother's actions
Refusing to seek help from her parents	Being a victim of her brother's manipulation

This table helped Sally clarify her actual guilt and her misplaced guilt. It is vital for her to understand that while she is responsible for specific actions, she is not to blame for the traumatic events and abuse inflicted upon her. This understanding can aid in her healing process and help her move towards confession, repentance, and, ultimately, freedom from guilt and shame.

After creating the list and the table, Sally's counselor encouraged her to take the next week to read the Scriptures, meditate on those they discussed in their counseling sessions, pray, and fast before confessing her sins at their next meeting. The counselor let Sally know that if the Lord moved in her spirit in such a way that she did not want to wait or could not wait, it was ok for her to have the confession session alone with God.

Sally confessed her sin to God in detail and then indicated she wanted to speak to her parents. Because what she had to confess to them involved exposing the sin and criminality of her brother and his friend, this was not an action to be taken quickly or without careful consideration of how to speak to her parents, who were now older and ill. These revelations would likely be a severe shock to them, and the fallout would be devastating. She also needed consultation with legal services as crimes had been committed. The meeting with her parents was temporarily set aside while they sought guidance on these issues.

Because her conscience was really burdened, Sally chose to confess to God that, at times, she enjoyed the sexual activity inflicted upon her (1 John 1:9). Hebrews 4:15–16 was very helpful to her as it reminded her that Jesus understands her struggles with sin and that His grace and mercy are available to her. She was comforted by Romans 8:1 and 2 Corinthians 5:17, which reminded her that God does not condemn her and that her identity is now found in Christ. This new identity frees her from the guilt and shame she has carried. Sally prayed Psalm 51:10, asking the Lord to help her recognize the cleansing she has in Christ by His grace and mercy. She asked God's forgiveness and found freedom from the guilt she carried. Sally also made an extensive confession to God about the abortion and all the events surrounding it (Ps. 32:5; Isa. 1:18). She prayed Psalm 51:1–2 and felt the power of David's prayer for mercy and cleansing. The Scriptures were an incredible comfort to Sally as she confessed her abortion. She said she had always felt so dirty, and the Lord's willingness to purify her from her past sin and make her white as snow enabled her to go forward in confidence as a pure and accepted child of God (Heb. 10:22).

Sally confessed to God that she had not honored, obeyed, or respected her parents (Prov. 1:8–9; Eph. 6:1–3). She confessed that she lied to them overtly and covertly. (Sally only had a rudimentary understanding of the significant consequences of the deceptions she perpetrated at this time. The counselor wanted to be sure Sally understood that her lies and deceptions were both sinful and a child's understandable response to her circumstances (Prov. 28:13). She confessed to God she had rebelled against her parents' authority while living in the home. She also confessed her fear of holding her brother accountable for all he had done to her.

False Guilt

There is another kind of guilt often experienced by those who have experienced catastrophic suffering, and this guilt does not come from unconfessed, willful disobedience but from regret over forgiven acts, sometimes referred to as false guilt. Some counselees have lived very sinful lives, and once they are in Christ, they may still experience regret and guilt over forgiven sins. The biblical counselor must make it clear that clinging to feelings of guilt over forgiven sins is wrong. For those in Christ, like Sally after confessing her abortion and rebellion (1 John 1:9), lingering feelings of being "dirty" can persist, or for Grant, surviving the marathon bombing unscathed stirs guilt despite no fault. This isn't God's conviction; it is a lie from Satan, the Accuser (Rev. 12:10), who twists forgiven sin to paralyze, or a lie from the deceitful heart (Jer. 17:9).

False guilt burdens the soul with responsibility that is not theirs to bear, often arising when they believe lies about themselves, whether from the enemy, unbiblical expectations, faulty consciences, misplaced blame for others' choices, perfectionist standards, past legalism, or what leaders like Dr. Nicolas Ellen calls a 'noisy soul'—rather than resting in God's truth (Matt. 11:28–30). Unlike actual guilt, which reflects sin against God's law and leads to repentance, false guilt accuses without cause, as when a sufferer feels culpable for unavoidable tragedy. For Sally, it whispers she's to blame for her abuse, a lie born from her pain. Others might feel guilt for failing to meet impossible standards, like perfect resistance to her abusers, or from legalistic teachings that once blamed her for their sin, distorting God's grace.

Secular therapy might label this 'trauma guilt,' medicating what the biblical counselor sees as a spiritual battle. God removes sin 'as far as east is from west' (Ps. 103:12). Sally's abortion and Grant's survival aren't theirs to bear. The biblical counselor must make it clear that clinging to feelings of guilt over forgiven sins is wrong. As Ken Campbell says, it is doubting God's declaration of forgiveness.[166] It's trading past sin for the sin of unbelief, rejecting Christ's sacrifice on the cross (Heb. 10:10). The problem is no longer the sin that has been committed; the problem is now the sin of unbelief, a failure to believe the gospel's message and that Jesus has taken away all guilt. Christ has paid their penalty, and they must be willing to rest in His sufficient sacrifice. The biblical counselor must help their counselee reject these lies by renewing their minds (Rom. 12:2). The counselor can help them identify these distortions with soul-piercing questions—"Does Scripture hold me accountable for this?"—and reframe them with truth (e.g., Ezek. 18:20—*The soul who sins shall die*). A thought journal or simple questions can help them renew their mind (Rom. 12:2), training their conscience to align with God's Word over time rather than secular diagnoses, freeing them to rest in their identity in Christ, not their past.

Encourage the counselee to meditate on Hebrews 10:23, "*hold fast the confession of our hope,*" and pray, "Lord, I believe; help my unbelief" (Mark 9:24). Proclaiming Christ's righteousness credited to them (2 Cor. 5:21) silences false accusations, while godly fellowship can reinforce this truth with encouragement (Heb. 10:24–25). For Sally, this might mean revisiting her past through Scripture's lens—her abuser's sin isn't hers (Gal. 5:1)—and leaning on believers who affirm her cleansing in Christ. Repenting of distrust in God's pardon frees them from the prison of false guilt. Sally journaled, "God says I'm clean (Isa. 1:18)," countering Satan's whispers. Repenting of distrust in God's pardon frees them from this cage. False guilt often merges with shame's "I'm worthless" lie, a snare the next section dismantles, but both fall before Christ's victory (Col. 2:14).

Consider and Apply

1. Think about a counseling situation in which the counselee expressed guilt. How did you address those feelings? Did you encourage them to seek forgiveness or try to make amends? How did the application of Scripture influence the counselee's response?
2. How important is it to understand the difference between guilt and shame? How can this help the counselee in their healing process?
3. How can the biblical principles discussed in this section help you counsel someone struggling with guilt? What steps can you take to apply these principles in your counseling ministry?
4. Reflect on God's forgiveness, as discussed in this section. How does understanding that there is no condemnation for those in Christ Jesus (Romans 8:1) change your perspective on guilt and forgiveness? How will you explain that to a suffering counselee?

The Nature of Shame

Shame is an integral part of victimization for most people. It is a moral judgment, the feeling and belief a person has that they are unacceptable because of something they did or was done to them. "Shame settles into the core of our being and, like corrosive acid, eats away at our sense of self-worth, leaving self-loathing, guilt, humiliation, and self-blame in its place. Once shame grabs hold, it is a beast so ferocious that the battle required to oust it seems impossible."[167] Psychology labels shame 'low self-esteem' and prescribes positive self-talk. The biblical counselor will help the counselee understand that they don't necessarily need positive affirmations; they need the blood of Christ to cleanse them from the stain of sin.

The shattered person is already overwhelmed with feelings of unworthiness, and so the counselor must be careful not to misinterpret feelings of shame as guilt. When providing care to those who have suffered catastrophic suffering, realize that if the counseling is focused on repentance for things that occurred that were beyond their control, this will inhibit their ability to move forward.

Shame isn't just a moment of self-consciousness; it becomes the person's identity. The counselee may require frequent reminders that their identity is rooted in Christ, not their experiences or in the shame they feel. Revisiting key Scriptures that affirm the believer's new identity in Christ and creating projects for spiritual growth that emphasize this will be key to their ability to move forward in freedom.

As you will see, sometimes a person experiences shame directly connected to something they have done. Feelings of shame are secondary to the guilt they experience for sinning against God or another person, which is why we address these two feelings and the results of experiencing catastrophic suffering separately.

Biblical Examples of Shame

Shame was first experienced in the Garden of Eden. Before eating the forbidden fruit, Adam and Eve were "naked and unashamed" (Gen. 2:25). After they ate from the forbidden tree, their eyes were opened. They realized they were naked and sought to cover themselves (Gen. 3:7). Gone was their innocence, and they interpreted their nakedness as shameful and something to be covered. Adam and Eve also attempted to hide from God, partly out of shame (Gen. 3:10).

King David's compounding sin brought him a great deal of shame that echoed far into the future of his life. David, a man of immense power, was described as 'a man after God's own heart' (1 Sam. 13:14). He was King and a warrior who should have been on the battlefield but wasn't (2 Sam. 11:1). Instead, David was on the rooftop which allowed him to view Bathsheba bathing one evening. She was the lovely young wife of Uriah, one of his generals who was off to war. After watching her bathe, David misused his authority and summoned Uriah's wife and had sex with her. The Bible does not inform us as to if Bathsheba was willing or if this encounter was by coercion or rape, but the result of this single encounter was potentially devastating for both of them. *"And the woman became pregnant; and she sent and told David, and said, "I am pregnant"* (2 Sam. 11:5, LSB).

Other than when she informed David, the Bible is silent about Bathsheba learning she was pregnant. Culturally, for Bathsheba, learning she was pregnant while her husband was off to war carried immense ramifications. Adultery would have brought her societal shame and disgrace. If Bathsheba was like any other woman in such a situation, she was likely terrified and already filled with overwhelming shame.

Had David's behavior become known, there would have been significant consequences for his actions. Adultery, especially with a married woman, would have brought him personal shame, as such sins were severely condemned in Israel. Uriah was highly regarded as one of David's mighty men, and the Bible notes he was a man of high honor and integrity (2 Sam. 11:11; 23:39). If David's abuse of power became public, and his sin against Uriah (and Bathsheba) been exposed, it would have shamed him among his military men and may have undermined the loyalty of his army to him. David wanted to keep the entire affair and resulting pregnancy hidden. He attempted to deceive Uriah into believing the child was his by arranging for him to come home from the war so Uriah would be intimate with Bathsheba (2 Sam. 11:6–13). After several attempts of this plan failed, David arranged for the death of Uriah and took Bathsheba as his wife (2 Sam. 11:14–17), keeping their secret under wraps. Scripture does not tell us that David experienced feelings of shame at what he had done. It appears he intended to move on as though nothing had happened until God sent the prophet Nathan to confront David about his sin. Nathan used a parable intended to provoke David's sense of justice, which it did. The parable and direct accusation ("You are the man!") exposed David's sins, and he at last experienced profound shame for his actions (2 Samuel 12:1–13).

Psalm 51 Application

Psalm 51 shows David's repentance from sin-driven shame and may be helpful for counselees bearing guilt for their actions. Victims, however, often carry shame for others' sins (e.g., Tamar, 2 Sam. 13), and they need a different path focused on their identity in Christ (2 Cor. 5:17). Both find hope in God's mercy tailored to their wounds. This Psalm could be a model when working with someone whose sin has disgraced them.

Psalm 51:1-2

Verse:

"Have mercy on me, O God, according to your unfailing love; according to your great compassion blot out my transgressions. Wash away all my iniquity and cleanse me from my sin." (NIV)

Discussion Points:

- **Attributes of God:** Discuss God's mercy, steadfast love, and compassion.
- **Approaching God:** These attributes help us understand God's character and why the counselee can approach God, even with deep shame.
- **Confession:** Confession of sin begins to unburden the heart of shame.

Biblical Truth:

Forgiveness: The counselee can be confident that God will forgive because it is His nature to do so.

Unburdening Shame: God's mercy and love unburden shame. Sinners confess, and victims rest in grace (1 John 1:9; Romans 8:1).

Psalm 51:3-4

Verse:

"For I know my transgressions and my sin is ever before me. Against You, you only, I have sinned and done what is evil in Your sight, so that You are justified when You speak and blameless when You judge." (NASB)

Discussion Points:

- **Facing Sin:** The counselee must face their sin in the situation.
- **Avoiding Blame-Shift:** The temptation to blame-shift and avoid accountability adds to their desire to hide.

Owning Sin: Help them own their sin, not hide (Proverbs 28:13).

Biblical Truth:

- **Ultimate Sin:** All sin is ultimately against God, even when it is against other people.
- **Clearing Conscience:** Facing sin, admitting it, and agreeing with God aids in clearing the conscience and freeing from shame.

For Sufferers:

- **Innocence:** Sufferers bear no guilt for others' evil, like Tamar (2 Samuel 13).
- **Rejecting Lies:** Counsel them to reject Satan's lies (Revelation 12:10), resting in Christ's cleansing (Romans 8:1).

Psalm 51:5

Verse:

"Behold, I was brought forth in iniquity, and in sin my mother conceived me."

Discussion Points:

- **Original Sin:** Discuss the doctrine of original sin and how it affects human nature.
- **Gospel Need:** This verse presents a natural place to discuss the need for the gospel and heart transformation.

Biblical Truth:

- **Gospel Hope:** Original sin breeds shame, so sinners and sufferers need gospel hope (Romans 5:12–17).

Psalm 51:6

Verse:

"Behold, You desire truth in the innermost being, and in the hidden part You will make me know wisdom."

Discussion Points:

- **God's Knowledge:** God knows their shame, the sinners' deceit, and the recipient's pain.
- **Truth Heals:** Truth heals both (John 8:32).

Biblical Truth:

- **Comfort:** The fact that God already knows the things that bring the most profound shame can comfort a counselee who wants to hide from Him.
- **Replacing Sin:** God desires to replace sin and deception with truthfulness and wisdom from His Word.

Psalm 51:7

Verse:

"Purify me with hyssop, and I shall be clean; Wash me, and I shall be whiter than snow."

Discussion Points:

- **Purification:** The image of purification is the gateway to explaining complete cleansing by grace through faith in Christ.

Biblical Truth:

- **Cleansing:** Cleansing frees sinners from disgrace and those disgraced from defilement (Hebrews 10:22).
- **Rejoicing:** Encourage the counselee to accept and rejoice in what Christ has done for them.

Psalm 51:8

Verse:

"Make me to hear joy and gladness, Let the bones which You have broken rejoice."

Discussion Points:

- **Downcast Hearts:** Shame-filled people have downcast hearts, illustrated by broken bones.
- **Healing:** Repentance and change in the inner man will bring healing, turning shame into rejoicing.

Biblical Truth:

- **Freedom and Joy:** This brings a life of freedom and joy.

Psalm 51:9

Verse:
"Hide Your face from my sins and blot out all my iniquities."

Discussion Points:

- **Hiding Sin:** Shame-filled people want to hide their sins from God, others, and themselves.
- **Distractions:** Both groups often attempt to hide through substance abuse or distracting activities.

Biblical Truth:

- **Crying Out:** Encourage the counselee to cry out to God as David does here.
- **Forgiveness:** God is loving and kind and will blot out the sin of the penitent petitioner.

Psalm 51:10

Verse:
"Create in me a pure heart, O God, and renew a steadfast spirit within me." (NASB)

Discussion Points:

- **New Heart:** The result of crying out to God in repentance is the gift of a new and pure heart.
- **Sanctification:** Discuss the various aspects of sanctification with the counselee.

Biblical Truth:

- **Holy Spirit:** God gives His Holy Spirit, who walks with the counselee forever and works together in progressive sanctification.

Psalm 51:11-12

Verse:

"Do not cast me away from Your presence and do not take Your Holy Spirit from me. Restore to me the joy of Your salvation, and sustain me with a willing spirit."

Discussion Points:

- **Fear of Rejection:** The counselee may fear they are unworthy of love or acceptance.
- **Sanctification Process:** Remind them that sanctification is a process and a journey that lasts a lifetime.

Biblical Truth:

- **Permanent Relationship:** Encourage focusing on the joy of their salvation and God's permanent relationship with them.

Psalm 51:13-17

Verse:

"Then I will teach transgressors Your ways, and sinners will be converted to You... The sacrifices of God are a broken spirit; A broken and a contrite heart, O God, You will not despise."

Discussion Points:

- **Using Their Story:** Encourage the counselee to use their story and personal experiences with shame and God's forgiveness to help others.
- **Transformation:** God transforms a life overwhelmed by shame into a testimony of His kindness and forgiveness.

Biblical Truth:

- **God's Glory:** Healed sinners show God's kindness to the broken, and both reflect His glory.

Encourage the counselee to consider using their story and personal experiences with shame and God's forgiveness, salvation, and sanctification to help others, demonstrating the blessing of genuine repentance and change in their lives. God transforms a life overwhelmed by shame into a testimony of His kindness and forgiveness. He specializes in taking the broken and making it new. Healed sinners show God's kindness to the broken, and both reflect His glory.

Common Misconceptions about Shame and Affliction

Just as David experienced shame due to his actions, many individuals today grapple with shame stemming from terrible things they have done. They have harmed people and live with the shame of their actions inside, too afraid to admit them or because it is not possible (due to death or because they cannot find the person) to confess and ask forgiveness for what they did. This shame can overwhelm their self-perception, relationships, and spiritual well-being.

Many people, regardless of age or gender, who have experienced sexual violations live with overwhelming shame. Whether because of rape or other molestation, they often carry an oppressive and suffocating sense of shame for what was done to them. Many express knowing they were victims, but they also believe they somehow deserved what happened to them and blame themselves.

Those who survive trauma or escape from a horrific situation also live with shame. One man experienced deep feelings of self-disgust, knowing boys and teens remained in a situation from which he was rescued. A woman expressed shame-based guilt because she knew minors were still working in the strip club she was rescued from, and she knew they were underage and being trafficked. Sally, who was raped by her brother and his friend and eventually trafficked, said she felt ashamed, guilty, and dirty. Edward Welch says, "Shame and guilt are close companions but not identical. Shame is the more common and broader of the two. In Scripture, you will find shame (nakedness, dishonor, disgrace, defilement) about ten times more than you find guilt."[168]

These feelings and emotions are on vivid display in 2 Samuel 13. King David's son, Amnon, lusted after his half-sister Tamar to the point he was physically ill and suffering. He and his cousin devised a plan to lure Tamar into his room, where he raped her despite her pleas and protests. After the rape, Amnon's "love" for Tamar became loathing. He treated her like a common prostitute and ordered her to be thrown out of his room, compounding her shame. Tamar tore the beautiful robe she wore, a symbol of her purity, put ashes on her head, and went away crying loudly as a public display of her grief and shame. The Bible does not tell us about Tamar's life after the rape other than to inform us that she withdrew from the public and lived a desolate life with her brother Absalom, suffering what one woman called "illegitimate shame (condemnation)."[169] Many survivors of sexual assault feel responsible for what happened to them. Like many other victims, both men and women, Tamar suffered because of what was done to her, not something she chose for herself. Shame is not something the survivor can just get over; shame causes a person to want to isolate and hide, creating barriers to help and healing.

Sally: A Case Study in Catastrophic Suffering- Shame

Sally carried tremendous shame for what seemed to be the totality of her life thus far. She expressed to her biblical counselor that she felt deep shame that began from the first sexual assault by Billy and his friend and continued through the sexual assaults by the other boys she was prostituted. Sally said she thought something must be fundamentally wrong with her and that she was treated this way. She felt dirty and gross because of things that were done to her and because of the things she had done.

Sally felt so ashamed because she thought she should have fought back harder or more aggressively. She thought she should have done more to stop the first assault in the clubhouse and those that followed in the woods for many years. She thought she was responsible for what happened to her. Because there were times Sally enjoyed how she felt during the sexual assaults, she believed she was complicit in her own abuse.

Sally felt ashamed of all the lies she had told her parents over the years. She felt shame for not telling them about the abuse. She believed that her deceptions contributed to the ongoing abuse and prostitution. She specifically mentioned feeling shame at the resulting issues from the abuse, such as her rebellious behaviors, acting out, and wetting the bed. She felt shame that her parents witnessed behaviors she thought were terrible and shameful.

As Sally continued to talk to her counselor, the issues became more and more weighty and her shame more evident. She was profoundly ashamed of having become pregnant and not knowing which boy was the father of the baby. The fact that there were so many boys having sex with her was reprehensible to her. She was bothered that the baby she aborted may even have been her brother's child. Her shame at having the abortion was also obvious. She spoke haltingly of the events of that terrible day, stopping frequently to sob with her face in her hands. Sally could not discuss all the details she wanted to tell her counselor because it was too painful. She did specifically mention the shame she felt in the car on the way to and from the abortion. Her brother Billy had spared her nothing as he verbally railed against her for "being stupid" and getting pregnant. She spoke of how furious he was that she was costing him money and would have to work overtime in the coming weeks to compensate for the lost time and money, which was what cemented her decision to run away at age 15. Sally understood that this decision was another "bad one," and it led to many of the subsequent hardships and abuses she experienced on the streets, including the commercial sex work, sex trafficking, pornography, and drug abuse that Sally was forced into. Overall, she had deep and abiding shame about her decisions and experiences.

Addressing Shame in Biblical Counseling

Shame can result from the gradual infliction of demeaning words and actions, such as a parent telling their child they are stupid and good for nothing. The child hears this often enough, and they begin to believe it is true. The shame is visible in their countenance and leaves them with a sense of unworthiness. They struggle to believe God would want them because they are too stupid or too bad, and they dare not seek anything from God. Open the Bible to Luke 15 and ask the person who believes they are unworthy to read the parable of the shepherd who has 100 sheep and notices one is missing. He leaves the flock to hunt for the missing sheep, and when he finds it and brings it back, he is so overjoyed that he calls all his friends and neighbors to tell them! Jesus says there will be more rejoicing in heaven over one repentant sinner than 99 people who think they are righteous. There are no expendable people in God's eyes. Jesus, the Good Shepherd, pursues them and loves those who feel unworthy. Encourage the counselee to meditate on this parable, as it highlights how God values every person He created and the joy He has when a person repents and is restored. They are so precious to Him that He died for them. If counselees resist, 'I'm too bad.' Ask questions to learn what lies they are believing

(Prov. 20:5). Remind them of the truth: 'You feel worthless, but God says you're His' (Eph. 1:6), repeating what God says about them (Rom. 8:1).

There is also a form of shame that comes because of associations a person has. There is a saying: you are known by the company you keep. Both honor and shame have to do with our connections and those with whom we spend our time. My husband and I once attended a church that ministered to young men in a medium-security facility. These "boys" had committed serious crimes, including murder, arson, and assault. Most of them were affiliated with gangs, something they were very proud of, and they often declared their intent to return to thug life when they were released. Occasionally, a young man would express interest in the gospel and ask for individual meetings for discipleship. After making a profession of faith, the shame of being associated with "church" and the Bible typically resulted in him succumbing to the pressure, and he would soon abandon his newfound faith in favor of the approval of his peers. Their incarcerated world is a microcosm of our world, which is totally upside down. How crazy is it to be shamed for abandoning sin, crime, illicit sexual relationships, and drugs for a saving relationship with Jesus Christ and living a holy life? The secular world tells us we need to embrace anything and everything except Jesus.

Many counselees didn't grow up in the church or a Christian family. They have possibly been involved in terrible things, and they experience shame because of associations in their past. For example, as a youth, I rode the school bus, and there was another student who was treated horribly every single day. Today, we would say she was bullied, but back then, she was the girl that everyone made fun of, called names, and refused to let next to them on the bus, sometimes going so far as to physically kick her and spit on her to get her to move elsewhere. It was disgraceful and disgusting. Even all these decades later, when I think of her, I am filled with a sense of shame that while I didn't participate in abusing her, I didn't do anything to stop it either.

For healing to occur and progress to be made, the person must directly address their shame. Although facing their shame may be one of the most challenging aspects of overcoming, it is also the most beneficial. When I think of that girl on the school bus, I confess my sin to God and thank Him for forgiving me, and I pray for that person, who, if she is still alive, is now an elderly woman. Had I had the opportunity to visit with her, I would tell her that the shame of her experience does not belong to her but to accept that all of the shame belongs solely to those who abused her. I would show her that Jesus was known as the friend of sinners, and He sought out people society cast out. His friends included adulterous women, thieves, the physically handicapped and abused, the blind, the lepers, and tax collectors

(Matt. 9:9–11; 11:19; Luke 5:12; 15:1–2; 17:16). The survivor in Christ gives her sin, shame, and uncleanness to Jesus and he gives her holiness, cleansing, healing, and forgiveness.

Sally: A Case Study in Catastrophic Suffering- Shame (Continued)

Over the months that Sally and her counselor met, she repeatedly heard that she was not responsible for the actions of Billy and his friends. She was a victim, not a willing participant. As a child, she had no agency to consent to sexual involvement, and what was done to her was abuse by every definition of the word. Her brother and his friends were bigger and stronger than Sally was. She was physically unable to resist their advances and abuse of her body. She was reminded that she did what she could to escape and pleaded with them to stop. There was also an ongoing emphasis in the counseling process on Sally's identity in Christ to help her understand that she is loved, forgiven, accepted, and not condemned by God and that she can be free from shame (Rom. 8:1; 2 Cor. 5:17).

When discussing Sally's shame regarding all the lies she told her parents, she was encouraged to meditate on Psalm 25:7. This verse helped her remember that because of His steadfast and unchanging love, God forgives our sins when we repent and confess them, which Sally was eager to do. She wanted to confess to God and her parents. This verse reminded her that there is nothing to earn; God's pleasure and love rest on her because of His goodness. Believing God's grace forgives her helped Sally begin to let go of the shame she felt resulting from the lies she told her parents. Because of the legality issues regarding her brother and his friend, Sally could not speak to her parents immediately, which gave her time to focus on embracing her identity in Christ. She worked diligently to remind herself that she was no longer a victim but victorious in Christ (2 Cor. 5:17).

The shame Sally felt at the large number of boys and men she had sex with both as a child and after running away from home at age 15 often tempted to overwhelm her. She was comforted by the compassion of God in Psalm 34:18. Through the counseling process, Sally described herself as brokenhearted and crushed in spirit instead of "depressed." For so long, Sally believed that she was a pariah to God, and she could not comprehend how God would want to be close to her. She clung to this verse when tempted to fall back into old ways of thinking about how God viewed her. She was reminded that despite how she sometimes felt, her suffering and pain matter to God. He has not cast her away, but He is always near her.

Sally's feelings of shame and guilt, especially regarding her past decisions and experiences, were sometimes overwhelming. She could not comprehend why a holy God would want her. Psalm 34:18 helped her understand that God will not abandon her in her moments of despair. Instead, He draws near to her, offering His love and support, which can be a source of hope and strength for Sally as she navigates her healing journey. Her counselor also focused on the promises of Isaiah 54:4, which speak to God's desire to redeem and restore His people. The promises and compassion of God in this verse were meaningful to Sally. Her shame began when she was a child and continued into her adulthood. She needed to hear that God would remove the shame and disgrace she had lived with for so long due to the actions of others and her own poor choices and replace it with honor. As she studied the rest of the passage, her identity as a new creation in Christ whose past shame does not define or determine her future was reinforced. Weeks later, Sally journaled, 'I'm His, my shame is gone' (Heb. 10:22). I am victorious in Christ, not a victim.' Sally was encouraged by her counselor to add what she was ashamed of to her confession of things she felt guilty about.

The reality is that overcoming shame can be a process that, in some cases, is revisited many times each day. Throughout this process, the counselee will benefit from reminders to embrace their identity in Christ, a key component to healing from shame. Emphasize the importance of seeing themselves as God sees them in Christ —loved and forgiven. Such a change in perspective requires the sufferer to remind themselves that they are washed clean by the blood of Christ (Heb. 9:14; 10:19–22) and stand righteous before Him (2 Cor. 5:21). Remembering one's identity as a child of God is critical in helping them overcome the shame that has been foisted upon them by whatever means. It is a choice for the tormented soul to believe they are who God says they are, which is difficult because shame continuously accumulates lies. Victimized people often think they somehow deserved what they endured; some have said God was using their abuse or calamitous incident as a form of punishment. These lies will require confrontation with the truth. For example, have the counselee read the story of the blind man in John 9:1–3. The assumption was that he was born blind because of sin. Jesus emphasized to his disciples that was not the case. His blindness was not a punishment for sin; God intended to display His glory by healing the man of his blindness. A similar situation occurs in John 15:1–15 when Jesus encounters a man who had been an invalid for thirty-eight years. Jesus is asked who sinned and if it was the man or his parents, and he replies, "Neither." He told them that man's suffering and condition allowed God's glory to be displayed in him. Examples such as these will assist the miserable person in understanding that suffering is not always a result of personal sin.

A person who has survived something horrible has experienced something unique. They are part of an exclusive group no one wants to belong to and have endured things relatively few people can relate to. This kind of isolation may also have strong tethers to shame, particularly if they were personally victimized. They wrongly believe no one else can understand their pain. They might find hope and help in the story of the woman with the issue of blood in Matthew 9:20–22, Mark 5:25–34 and Luke 8:43–48. This unfortunate woman had spent twelve years of her life afflicted with severe and, so far, incurable bleeding that made her unclean under Jewish law, bringing tremendous shame. This condition left her extraordinarily isolated as everyone, including her family, shunned her. Many traumatized counselees feel they are alone in the shame resulting from their experiences. Encourage them to reach out in faith, as this woman did, despite her fear and shame. Jesus did not turn her away; He healed her and called her "Daughter!"

A person who has been involved in substance abuse or criminal activity might believe they can never be forgiven or cleansed from their past. The parable of the prodigal son in Luke 15:11–32 may resonate with someone who spent their life participating in debauchery and dishonorable living. When the son in the parable comes to his senses and decides to return home, he prepares a speech of confession and repentance to deliver to his father and expects to be one of his father's servants. He did not know that his father watched for him every day, and when he saw his son in the distance, he ran to him and embraced him. The son did not even finish his rehearsed speech before he was returned to his father's good graces. This parable may help the person with the mindset that their past actions disqualify them from love, forgiveness, or acceptance. Anyone who repents and is saved is cleansed and restored by God's grace.

One of the most destructive lies a person with a history of wounds believes is that they are defined by what they have experienced. Many become stuck with a victim mentality, believing their past determines their future. Point this counselee towards the life of the Apostle Paul, formerly known as Saul. The Scriptures reveal that Saul was a zealous persecutor of Christians. It was said he was "ravaging the church, entering house after house, and dragging off men and women, he would put them in prison" (Acts 8:3). He was present at the stoning of Stephen and gave his approval (Acts 7:58). Later on, Saul, now called Paul, describes himself as having been "a blasphemer and persecutor and violent aggressor" (1 Tim. 1:13), sending many Christians to prison and death. While on his way to Damascus to arrest more Christians, he had a life-changing encounter with Jesus (Acts 9). Walking a person through Saul's transformation to Paul and showing them the global impact he has had through his life and writings in the New Testament may help a counselee who believes their past defines them renew their mind. Paul's new life in Christ shows that because of grace, one's identity does not have to remain defined by one's past experiences. Paul himself proclaimed, "*Therefore if anyone is in Christ, he is a new creation; the old things passed away; behold, new things have come*" (2 Corinthians 5:17, LSB).

A person who carries shame as a repercussion of their actions may express that they are unlovable because of what they have done, which causes severe internal, emotional, and spiritual pain. Peter's story in Luke 22:54–62 will minister to the soul of such a sufferer. Peter was part of Jesus' inner circle and was present in the courtyard during Jesus' trial before Caiaphas. He was standing around the fire with others, including servants and officers of the high priest. He was recognized by three people who began to question him about being one of Jesus' disciples. Feeling the pressure and fearing he too would be arrested, Peter denies he knows Jesus three times, just as Jesus told him he would do. He then goes away and "weeps bitterly." His shame mirrors sinners' self-loathing; victims echo it when falsely blamed (e.g., Tamar, 2 Sam. 13). Both heal—Peter through restoration (John 21:15–19), victims through Christ's love (Rom. 8:39).

Peter's experience of overwhelming shame can be deeply relatable to someone who believes they are unlovable because of what they have done in moments of weakness or while under duress. The weight of their shame is overwhelming, sometimes leading them to self-harm or other foolish things. Encourage the counselee by showing them that Peter's life does not end there and that his story is one of forgiveness and restoration (John 21:15–19). Jesus' post-resurrection interaction with Peter and his role as a pillar of the early church demonstrates that God can transform a person's identity and life when repentance and heart change occur.

One powerful form of shame gives a person or a group of people power over another person because it threatens them with public disgrace. This is true of the spouse facing public church discipline for unrepentant adultery, someone who has foolishly allowed themselves to be videoed in sexually compromising situations for a thrill and it's been made public, and those who have been forced or coerced into making pornography. The victims remain victims because of social humiliation. They know their videos are out there forever, and they fear public settings because they have been publicly called out and shamed by people who have seen them or know what they've done. The shame is tremendous.

The story of David and Bathsheba shows a person suffering from shame that their problem is not the judgment of others or the world. Their real problem is before God, so show them that Christ is the remedy for their shame. Shame is appropriate and reasonable when sin has been committed, leading a person to repentance and forgiveness. Jesus took their shame, and if they are in Christ, their relationship with God is secure. Encourage them to find rest in their eternal union with Jesus.

A person who has been through years of harm or multiple agonizing experiences might believe they will never heal and that they are too damaged to be used by God. Encourage them by showing them the Bible says God's power is best demonstrated in weak people (2 Cor. 12:9). The power is in the Scriptures, not your words, so show them what God's Word says. Show them that God uses people who are considered nothing in the eyes of the world. The Bible states that God used people who were destitute, persecuted, and mistreated (Heb. 11:37–38). God uses broken people to accomplish his purposes. Walk them through the lives of Abraham, Elijah, Joseph, Job, Moses, Gideon, Samson, Rahab, the Samaritan woman, Noah, Jeremiah, Jacob, David, Jonah, Naomi, Peter, and Martha, all of whom are examples of people who were broken but used by God.

Ultimately, it is a choice for a person to believe they are who God says they are, and they must believe in His forgiveness and restoration to overcome their shame. This choice must be made, as many habitual thought and belief patterns must be overcome. They must remind themselves daily of what God says about them rather than the lies their feelings tell them; then, they will sever the bonds of shame and walk in freedom.

Consider and Apply

1. Examine how shame has impacted the counselee's self-worth and identity. Discuss specific instances where they felt shame and how it has influenced their actions and relationships.
2. How do the biblical examples of David, Tamar, and others resonate with the counselee's experiences of shame? What lessons can you help the counselee draw from their stories?
3. How can you incorporate the principles of Psalm 51 into the counselee's healing journey from shame? What steps can you encourage them to seek God's forgiveness and restoration?
4. How does the counselee's understanding of their identity in Christ help them combat the lies of shame? What Scriptures can you give them to meditate on to reinforce their true identity and worth in God's eyes?

CHAPTER 10

Biblical Responses to Anger and Bitterness

Anger and Bitterness

"Anger is a reaction that incinerates marriages and disintegrates families. It energizes gossip and guns down classmates. It divides churches, turns friendship into enmity, and erupts in road rage. It is the stuff of every form of grievance and bitterness.[170] "Bitterness is defined as anger and disappointment at being treated unfairly. It is synonymous with resentment and envy."[171] The Bible says bitterness defiles many (Heb. 12:15) and results from unresolved anger. It hardens the victim's heart and allows the harm done to the counselee to become self-inflicted. It is said that bitterness is like drinking poison and expecting someone else to die.

Anger and bitterness are serious issues for many post-trauma counselees. Their reasons for anger vary, and they must be addressed as part of the biblical counseling process. Bitterness is never righteous, but the counselee's anger is either righteous or unrighteous in its origin and how it is displayed. Assisting the counselee in discerning the root and motives for their anger and bitterness is crucial to their ability to address it biblically.

Righteous and Unrighteous Anger

Unlike bitterness, anger can be righteous or unrighteous. Dr. Wayne Mack says,

> The Bible also teaches that there are times when our anger is not sinful. There are times when it's proper, righteous, and necessary to be angry. In the same passage in Ephesians 4, where we are instructed to put aside bitterness, wrath, and anger, we are told

> there is a way to be properly angry. Ephesians 4:26 commands, "Be angry, and yet do not sin." It's clear from this verse that there is a kind of anger that is not sinful. These verses do not contradict each other; they simply are teaching us how to handle two different kinds of anger – anger that is sinful and anger that is not sinful.[172]

Righteous anger aligns with God's anger. It is controlled, purposeful, and directed towards sin and injustice. It is not self-serving but focused on the harm done to others or the violation of God's standards. God's righteous anger serves a specific purpose. It is purposeful and intentional, directed towards correcting sin and injustice (Ps. 7:11). Throughout the Old Testament, God's righteous anger is displayed when His chosen people rebelled (Ex. 32:9–10; Num. 14:11–12; Deut. 9:7–8; Jer. 7:17–20). In the New Testament, Jesus' righteous anger is shown in the temple when He drove out the money changers (John 2:13–17).[173] Jesus repeatedly demonstrated righteous anger at the hypocrisy of the Pharisees, who emphasized rules and their traditions over the love of God and the people (Matt. 23:13–36; Mark 3:1–5; 7:5–15). Acts 5:1–11 further demonstrates God's righteous anger. The immediate judgment of Ananias and Sapphira for their hypocrisy and deceit sent a strong warning to the early church.

Unrighteous Anger and Bitterness

God never displays unrighteous anger. In a person who has experienced devastating harm, unrighteous anger is complex and multifaceted. It is often related to bitterness and shares many of the same characteristics, such as being self-centered and uncontrolled. Both unrighteous anger and bitterness can be deeply rooted in the personal hurt, pain, betrayal, injustice, or perceived wrongs that occur in catastrophic events. Both may also lead to sinful behaviors and attitudes, often resulting in self-destructive actions and the destruction of relationships.

Understanding Anger and Bitterness in Suffering

Understanding the nature of anger is crucial, especially when dealing with those who have been grievously harmed. Catastrophic suffering, whether due to an isolated incident such as being in a horrific car accident or long-term, as in child abuse or neglect, trafficking, or other forms of abuse, involves pain that is a direct result of sin and sometimes, the counselee feels responsible for the actions of others and is angry at themselves, thinking, "If only I would not have said or done (blank), he or she wouldn't have done (blank)." These thoughts can become obsessive, and the person replays events repeatedly, feeling increasingly angry that they didn't respond differently. Bitterness sets in when the person does not resolve these feelings and allows them to fester.

Specific Examples of Anger and Bitterness in Catastrophic Suffering

Child Sexual Abuse or Neglect

Survivors of child sexual abuse or neglect may express anger at those who did not protect them. The reasons adults do not come to the defense and rescue of abused and neglected children are varied and complex, and care should be taken to help the counselee understand them to the degree they can be ascertained. The counselee is angry at the person who violated them, and God is, too. Some anger in a victim can be a natural, righteous, and healthy response. Psalm 127:3 clearly states that God values children. They are the most vulnerable among us and must be cherished and protected. A victim's anger may be both righteous and unrighteous in such situations. When it is for the same righteous reasons as God's anger, the initial anger is not sinful but flows from a desire for justice. However, this anger can fester and become bitter if it is not addressed and resolved. It can lead to a chronic state of resentment and emotional turmoil. Scriptures like Psalm 7:11 describe God as a righteous judge who is angry with the wicked daily, suggesting that anger can be a response to injustices. It is crucial to address both anger and bitterness in the healing process to prevent long-term emotional and spiritual damage.

Human Trafficking

Those who have been trafficked are angry at their pimps and traffickers; they are angry at those who bought their bodies. One former prostitute describes her rage:

> I was bleeding and sweating. I was angry and full of rage. I felt so much rage for every man who had raped me, who had requested vile acts of me, who did what they wanted even when I said "no" because it was somehow okay to violate a prostitute. The anger I felt for every objectification, for each time I was sold as a commodity, for each act that nullified my humanity, for every human being would use my body as a shell without thought of the degrading

> pain they instilled in me, overtook me. It wasn't just rage about my own predicament, either. I felt rage for every one of my friends who had been murdered by men paying for sex, whose bodies had been discarded like yesterday's trash. Rage filled the deepest part of my being.[174]

Their anger is justified, as profiting off the sale of people for sex is abhorrent to God and a profound moral evil. It violates the dignity of people made in the image of God by reducing them to objects to be used for selfish and ungodly purposes (Matt. 22:39; 1 Cor. 6:15–16, 18–20; 1 Tim. 1:9–10). If not addressed, deep-seated anger can evolve into bitterness. Bitterness can take root and grow, leading to a hardened heart and a pervasive sense of resentment. As part of the counseling process, the counselee must learn and accept the fact that God is angry about their victimization and will one day bring justice (Matt. 18:5–6; Rom. 1:18; 12:17–20; Gal. 6:7–8; 2 Thess. 1:6–9). God is faithful, and those afflicted can learn how to be angry without sinning in their anger (Eph. 4:26b–31), and they can learn to overcome evil with good.

Those who have been victims of labor trafficking often feel a deep sense of anger because they were trapped in a situation with no means of escape or improvement. Mondago, a young man from rural Nigeria, was lured to the United States with the promise of a construction job that would allow him to support his family back home. However, upon arrival, his passport was confiscated, and he was coerced into working in agricultural fields under brutal conditions. He received minimal wages and lived under the constant threat of violence by his captors. His days were filled with grueling, backbreaking labor, and any attempt to escape was met with harsh punishment. This exploitation persisted for several years, trapping him in a cycle of abuse and despair. Now free, Mondago is angry at those who deceived and enslaved him. He feels a deep sense of betrayal from the false hope he was given, which, instead of financial freedom, led to years of suffering and exploitation. His frustration extends to the lack of timely intervention from authorities. Mondago's anger towards those who deceived and enslaved him is in line with God's anger towards injustice and mistreatment. The Bible clearly condemns deceit and the oppression of the vulnerable (Prov. 14:1; Isa. 10:1–2; Jer. 22:3; Zech. 7:10). His anger is a response to feeling betrayed by the false hope he was given; it is a natural response to the violation of trust. However, if left unresolved, his anger and sense of betrayal can easily turn into resentment, bitterness, or even vindictiveness, seeking to repay evil for evil, eventually consuming his thoughts and emotions. The deceit and exploitation he suffered go against God's support for truth and justice, as stated in Proverbs 12:22, but the resulting anger must still be resolved in a manner that glorifies God.

Soldiers and War

Soldiers who experienced the effects of war are angry at what they have seen and participated in and the effects the war had on their bodies, souls, marriages, and families. Sgt. First Class Frank Smith and Staff Sergeant Phil Brown returned home to a life they did not recognize. Those in their small town greeted them with "Thank you for your service!" unaware of the deep burdens they carried.

The men carried the physical scars from the shrapnel, and Phil now walked with a limp, but the profound spiritual burden they carried outweighed their physical pain. Their anger at the loss of life, the horror at the actions they took in service to their country, and their disgust at the final result of the conflict simmered just below the surface (Eccl. 9:18; Isa. 1:7). They struggled with feelings of overwhelming guilt, questioning the morality of the killing and destruction they were involved in.

Their anger extended beyond their inner battles, affecting their marriages and children. Their wives, who took on all the responsibilities of mom, dad, and provider in their absence, now balked at the teachings of Ephesians 5, setting up consistent daily conflict in the home that often led to yelling and screaming. Their children, who saw their dads as protectors four short years ago, didn't need them now. The men felt unnecessary and like a burden, adding to their anger and bitterness. They learned the children complained to their wives that dad had changed, that he wasn't the happy, friendly, loving dad who left but was now angry, sullen, and prone to outbursts of rage that frightened them. The kids avoided their dads, adding to their anger and grief.

God's anger is at the sin in the world that has resulted in all their suffering and pain (Isa. 63:10). God is a God of peace and reconciliation, yet He has ordained and allowed war throughout history (Deut. 9:4–5; Josh. 6). His anger is not against the soldiers but against the sin that has brought about such suffering, pain, and moral confusion. Their physical and spiritual scars manifest the world's brokenness, which grieves God (Gen. 6:5–6; Ps. 5:4–6). The complicated family dynamics and upending of the biblical roles in the home and marriage do not please God and must be addressed biblically by each family member in a biblical counseling context (Eph 5:22–25; 6:1–4; Col. 3:18–21).

Sally: A Case Study in Catastrophic Suffering- Anger and Bitterness

Sally's past was a furnace of rage. Raped at 9 by her brother Billy and his friend in a makeshift fort, she was later trafficked by Billy into prostitution. "He sold me like trash," she told her counselor, Abigail, her voice trembling with fury. She burned with anger at Billy for silencing her with threats—coercing an abortion at 15—and at the men who paid to use her, deaf to her pleas. "I'd see their faces at night," she said, "and want them dead." Self-directed anger gnawed too: "If I'd fought harder, maybe it wouldn't have happened." Bitterness took root, a poison she drank daily, resenting even God. "Where were You?" she'd cry, fists clenched, echoing Jonah's despair (Jonah 4:3).

Abigail recognized Sally's anger had righteous roots—God hates such evil (Ps. 7:11; Matt. 18:6)—but it had twisted into unrighteous rage and bitterness (Heb. 12:15). "Your anger at sin aligns with God's," Abigail said, "but vengeance and self-blame don't." She pointed to Ephesians 4:26: "Be angry, and do not sin." Abigail asked, "What do you want that you're not getting?" Sally snapped, "Justice. My life back." "Who's denying you?" "Billy. Those men. God." Probing deeper—"How does this affect your trust in Him?"—Sally admitted, "I blame Him for letting it happen."

Abigail shared Psalm 37:4: "Delight in the Lord, and He'll give you your heart's desires." Sally scoffed, "He didn't protect me." Abigail replied, "He's angry too—He'll bring justice (Rom. 12:19). Can you trust Him with your rage?"

Later in her room, Sally began journaling, praying Psalm 4:4—"Tremble, and do not sin"—and confessed, "God, I hate them. Help me let go." Matthew 6:14–15 pierced her: forgiveness wasn't for Billy but for her freedom. Weeks later, she said, "I'm still angry, but it's not consuming me." Bitterness faded as she rested in God's vengeance, not hers (2 Thess. 1:6–9).

A Biblical Perspective on Anger and Bitterness

Many sufferers are angry at what they have endured, and it is essential to understand that not all of their anger is wrong. God is angry at sin and sinners. For example, Proverbs 6:16–19 lists things God detests, many of which occur in victimization.

There are six things that the Lord hates, seven that are an abomination to Him:

Haughty eyes - the proud and arrogant attitude of the oppressor or the abuser is often present in someone who believes they have a right to dominate, objectify, oppress, or harm another person for their own pleasure. God hates their pride and that it devalues a person created in His image and likeness (Gen. 1:27; Ps. 10:2–3; Prov. 8:13; 16:5).

17 A lying tongue - refers to the deception that invariably occurs in trauma caused by oppression or abuse. Those who harm others will lie and instruct their victims to lie to cover up their actions and to avoid accountability. God hates lying because He is the truth (John 14:6), and because it goes against His principles of justice and righteousness (Ps. 101:7; Prov. 12:22; 19:5).

And hands that shed innocent blood- Because humans are made in His image and likeness, taking an innocent life is a grave injustice. God detests any actions that harm innocent people because He is a just God (Isa. 61:8). This is a common theme throughout the Bible, reflecting His commitment to justice and protection of the innocent and vulnerable, many of whom are helpless children (Ps. 106:38; Isa. 59:7).

18 A heart that devises wicked plans – severe suffering often results when someone plans harm against another person or group. Whether it is setting off a pressure cooker bomb at a race, abusing a spouse, paying a person for sex, or shooting up a school, their evil actions are intentional and premeditated (Ps. 10:2; 22:11; Prov. 12:2; Mic. 2:1). God hates this because, in part, it is the opposite of His love for righteousness and lovingkindness.

Feet that run rapidly to evil- This phrase indicates that the perpetrator eagerly seeks out and engages in evil deeds without hesitation. One who willfully and even enthusiastically runs toward sin, sin that often leads to the harm and degradation of others, angers God (Isa. 59:7; Rom. 3:15; Prov. 1:16). God hates the intentionality of running away from what is holy, righteous, and good (Ps. 5:4–6; Rom. 1:28–32).

19 A false witness who declares lies- this is very common in abuse situations of all kinds. Any person who knowingly denies or minimizes the wicked treatment of another is a false witness who declares lies. In some situations, friends and family choose to protect the perpetrator(s) out of fear of exposure, fear of being harmed themselves, or fear of the consequences (legal or financial) if they speak the truth. Sadly, our judicial system also adds to this problem (Ex. 23:1). God despises lying lips in part because of the additional harm it causes to the victim(s) (Prov. 19:5) and because He declares He is the God of truth (John 14:6).

And one who spreads strife among brothers- Significant conflict and division can occur when something traumatic happens in a family unit. God values relationships and encourages His people to be peacemakers (Ps. 82:3–4; Rom 12:18), and He is angered by the various forms of injustice and oppression listed in Proverbs 6.

God is also angered at the victim's unrighteous responses. For example, bitterness can breed self-righteousness, and the afflicted person can adopt an attitude of judgment and spiritual superiority towards those who hurt them. Combined with vengeful speech that is malicious, deceptive, or hateful, it reveals the bitterness in the wounded heart. If bitterness persists, the affected person might fantasize about how to seek revenge and may even devise plans for assault or murder. They may initially believe there is nothing wrong with how they are thinking, but the counselor must help them see that God hates their thoughts, beliefs, desires, and plans born out of a bitter heart as much as He hates what was done to them.

Anger at God

Underneath the confusion and anger at their suffering and misery, the counselee may be angry at God for allowing disaster to befall them. Judgments about God and their circumstances fuel their rage. "How could You let this happen, God? You could have prevented it, but You didn't. Where were You when I was crying out?"

They grapple with pain and injustice, and that God didn't remove them from their situation faster or prevent it from happening. While it is understandable to wonder "why," the counselee should be encouraged to examine the heart behind these questions to determine if they are accusing God of wrongdoing or blaming Him for the sin committed against them. Ed Welch says, "Anger typically begins in a way that imitates God – it makes judgments about right and wrong. But [sic] it can quickly turn into a stance against him."[175]

Biblical Example: Jonah

Jonah is one biblical example of unrighteous anger towards God because He sent the Old Testament prophet to the city of Nineveh to urge them to repent of their wickedness. Jonah wanted God to destroy the Ninevites because they were the cruel enemies of the Israelites. Jonah, hoping to prevent God's mercy toward people he hates, initially disobeys God. After God disciplines Jonah for his disobedience, he goes to Nineveh and delivers the message of repentance, and the people respond. Jonah becomes angry that God did not destroy them but showed compassion and mercy. His anger and bitterness at God's kindness brought him to the place where he experienced depression (Jonah 4:3).

Jonah's responses and resulting feelings of depression are representatives of what happens when anger is allowed to control a person, and when it becomes the main characteristic of their life (Prov. 16:32; 19:19; 22:24; 25:28). Like Jonah, the counselee may continually meditate on the wrongs done to them, which may lead to bitterness. Sinful anger and bitterness are the seedbed for several other issues that are often present in afflicted people, such as self-harming behaviors, drug and alcohol abuse, and violence.

Counseling Anger and Bitterness

Express understanding to a distressed, angry counselee and seek to understand the source of their anger before providing counsel to repent (Prov. 18:13, 17; 20:5). It is helpful to see anger as both a natural reaction to the sin committed against them and their struggle with sin. Take the time necessary to gain involvement with this counselee and convey an understanding that the affliction and misery resulting from the sin of others can lead to intense anger. When anger results from personal harm, work with the counselee by following basic biblical counseling principles to learn what aspects of their anger are righteous or unrighteous.

Proverbs 4:23 (NASB) states: *"Watch over your heart with all diligence, for from it flow the springs of life."* Sinful anger indicates that something is wrong at the heart level, so unless the counselee is acting out in ways that make them a danger to themselves or others, begin by dealing with the heart of the problem. You will likely find the counselee's anger comprises the individual components we have already looked at in this book. Identity, fear, guilt, shame, hurt, grief, and distrust are all feeding the anger and bitterness the suffering person is experiencing. Individually addressing them will go a long way toward helping the counselee repent at the heart level.

What the counselee does with their anger must also be investigated. Do they yell, scream, rage, throw objects, hit or break things? Such behaviors (fruit) are unacceptable and must be confronted by the counselor and repented by the counselee. Again, because these actions are the visible evidence of what is going on in the counselee's heart, resist the urge only to address the fruit of the angry heart and go after the roots of the problem growing in the heart. Examine the Scriptures with the counselee and use effective questions to help them see the hidden thoughts, beliefs, and desires that enable them to recognize and justify their unrighteous anger and bitterness. Some suggested questions are:

- **"What do you want that you are not getting? What are you desiring that seems out of reach because of your suffering?"**
  This question will help the counselee identify unmet needs, wants, or desires that may fuel their anger and bitterness.
  Scripture focus: Psalm 37:4 and Phil 4:19.
  Suggestion for follow-up question(s): "How does this unmet expectation or desire affect your relationship with God?" "How does it affect your relationship with the person or persons who are denying you what you want?"

- **"What are you getting that you don't want? How does it conflict with what you think/believe God desires for you?"**
  This question will help the counselee identify specific things that may provoke them to sinful anger and the bitterness they cling to.
  Scripture focus: 2 Cor. 12:9; Ps. 55:22.
  Suggestion for follow-up question(s): "How do you see God working in these circumstances?" "Are you fighting against God's sovereign will?"

- **"Which of your perceived rights is being violated? What do you think/believe has been unjustly taken from you or violated by your experiences, and how does this understanding align with biblical justice or God's sovereignty?"**
  This question will help the counselee identify if injustice has actually been committed against them or if what they claim as a "right" is not something they are entitled to, according to Scripture.
  Scripture focus: Mic. 6:8; Prov. 3:5–6.
  Suggestion for follow-up question(s): "Does your belief system align with God's Word?" "What do you think biblical justice looks like in your situation?"

- **"What do you believe you are being denied? How does this challenge your understanding of God's goodness?"**
  This question will help the counselee identify their unmet desires and expectations, some of which may be realistic and some based on entitlement, resentment, or bitterness.
  Scripture focus: Ps. 37:4; Phil 4:19.
  Suggestions for follow-up question(s): "Do your responses align with how the Bible instructs you to handle unmet expectations?" "Do you see any entitlement, resentment, or bitterness patterns in your life?" "Can you trust in God's goodness despite these perceived denials?"

- **"Who do you believe is denying you these perceived rights? Who or what do you hold responsible for these denials, and how does this affect your trust in God or your relationship with them?"**
  This question will help the counselee identify who they believe is responsible for their plight: God or others. It will help them consider their trust in God and His faithfulness and sovereignty.
  Scripture focus: Prov. 3:5–6; James 1:19–20.

Suggestions for follow-up question(s): "Upon self-examination, do you see patterns of entitlement, resentment, or bitterness in your heart?" "How can you bring these feelings before God and seek His help to transform them?" "How do you reconcile your perceived denials with the promises found in Scripture?"

- **"Who do you think is responsible for your anger/situation?"**
  This question will help the counselee realize who or what they hold accountable for their anger or trauma. Follow-up question(s): "How does this influence your spiritual walk or view of forgiveness?" "How does this affect your relationship with God?"
  Scripture focus: Matt. 6:14–15; Rom. 12:19.
  Suggestions for follow-up question(s): "Do you find forgiving those you hold responsible difficult?" "How does this align with biblical teachings on forgiveness?"

- **"What do you believe would make you happy? How does this align with or differ from the joy described in Scripture?"**
  This question will help the counselee explore their understanding of happiness and how it influences their ability to find contentment in light of their anger and trauma.
  Scripture focus: John 15:11; Phil 4:11–13.
  Suggestion for follow-up question(s): "What do you believe God wants you to learn or how He wants you to respond in your search for happiness, considering your situation?" "How has your search for happiness impacted your faith, prayer life, or trust in God's plan for you, especially considering your experiences?"

- **"Do you believe you are entitled to be angry and bitter? Do you see your anger or bitterness as a justified response, and how does this belief mesh with biblical teachings on anger, righteousness, and sin?"**
  This question will help the counselee examine their belief system regarding their anger and bitterness and how they justify these feelings and beliefs. It will help them understand if their belief system is biblical.
  Scripture focus: Col. 3:8; Eph. 4:26–27.
  Suggestions for follow-up question(s): "Can you list how your belief that your anger or bitterness is justified impacted your faith?" "How do you think God views your anger or bitterness and your justification of it?"

- **"On what foundation are you building your 'right' to be angry? Is it based on human justice, personal pain, or something else? How does this align with God's justice and mercy, as Scripture describes?"**
  This question will help the counselee understand how their perception of justice and their pain influences their justifications for anger and bitterness and how they can seek God's guidance in dealing with it.
  Scriptural focus: James 2:13; Matt. 5:7.
  Suggested follow-up question(s): "How does the foundation of your anger and bitterness influence your spiritual walk positively or negatively?" "How does your view of justice and personal pain affect your ability to forgive?"

- **"Do you believe you are entitled to specific responses or outcomes because of what you've been through? How does this sense of entitlement align with the biblical teaching of God's grace and our stewardship of our lives?"**
  This question will help the counselee understand the sense of entitlement they have developed and gain God's perspective on their belief system.
  Scriptural focus: Rom. 12:3; Phil 2:3–4.
  Suggested follow-up question(s): "How specifically has your sense of entitlement impacted your faith, prayer life, or trust in God's plan for you, especially considering your experiences?" Will you seek God's help in repenting of your sense of entitlement, even when you feel justified in your expectations?"

- **"Can your 'rights' be supported by Scripture? Do your 'rights' reflect more of a human understanding of justice and fairness than a biblical one? What does the Bible say about our rights versus our responsibilities?"**
  This question will help the counselee gain insight into the root of their feelings of entitlement and how these feelings align with or diverge from biblical teachings.
  Scriptural focus: Phil. 2:5–7; Rom. 12:10.
  Suggested follow-up question(s): "In what specific ways can you emulate Christ's humility and servanthood in your own life, despite your anger and trauma?" "What practical steps can you take to prioritize seeking God's justice and mercy and fulfill your responsibilities as a Christian, even when you're struggling with feelings of injustice?"

- **Is it the other person's fault you are angry and bitter? While someone's actions might have contributed to your current emotions, how does personal responsibility for your reactions fit into this? Ephesians 4:26–27 talks about not letting anger lead to sin; how does that apply here?"**
  This question will help the counselee recognize that their angry or bitter reaction to another person reflects their own heart condition and understand that they cannot shift the blame for their anger or bitterness onto someone else. While another person's actions can indeed be a provocation for anger, the responsibility for how the counselee responds belongs to them.
  Scriptural focus: Rom. 12:18; Prov. 29:11.
  Suggested follow-up question(s): "Do you understand that while the other person might have sinned against you, what you do with your anger is a matter of your personal stewardship?" "Will you acknowledge that while you can't control others, you can control your responses?" "Do you understand that God expects you to do so?"

- **"Is it possible for you to be angry and not sin? The Bible differentiates between righteous and sinful anger. Ephesians 4:26 says, 'Be angry and do not sin.' How might you discern between the two in your life, and what steps can you take to ensure your anger leads to righteousness rather than sin, such as bitterness?"**
  This question will help the counselee check the heart-level motivation behind their anger and discern if it is to defend the oppressed, uphold truth, correct wrongdoing (righteous), or if it is driven by personal pride, revenge, or a desire to control others (unrighteous).
  Scriptural focus: Eccl. 7:9; Ps. 37:8.
  Suggested follow-up question(s): "Are you willing to think of three specific ways to apply Ephesians 4:26 to your situation?" "Are you willing to measure your anger against biblical principles to discern if it reflects God's love, justice, or mercy?"

Stuffing Anger

Anger becomes sinful when internalized, leading to inner turmoil, emotional distress, and bitterness. Ephesians 4:26–27 instructs the Christian this way, *"In your anger do not sin: "Do not let the sun go down while you are still angry, and do not give the devil a foothold."* The counselee may think that not outwardly expressing their anger demonstrates self-control and that they are righteous for avoiding sinful outbursts. While there is undoubtedly some virtue in not demonstrating explosive anger, it is not as virtuous as they may think. The counselee may believe that internalizing their anger is the godly way to manage it and to avoid conflict, and to the degree that they are not actively seeking conflict, they are correct. However, overall, internalized anger is no more righteous than explosive anger. A person who has been abused or harmed might think it is sinful to allow themselves to feel or express anger. They wrongly believe that being a patient or godly person means ignoring their feelings, which is not what the Scriptures intend.

Assist the counselee in discerning if they are misinterpreting scriptural teachings on anger and self-control. For example, James 1:19–20 can be misunderstood to mean that internalizing anger is the same as being slow to anger, and that is not accurate. The biblical call to be slow to anger is about having a measured and patient response and being wise in how and when to reveal anger. It does not imply a person should stuff their anger instead of showing it.

Someone who has struggled with explosive anger in the past might think stuffing their anger means they are demonstrating self-control, which brings the issue back to the heart. Self-control is a fruit of the Spirit (Gal. 5:22–23) and cannot be manufactured in the flesh by avoiding conflict and restraining oneself from expressing one's thoughts, beliefs, and desires. Self-control is developed when the heart is submitted to God's Word and will and the working and conviction of the Holy Spirit. For a person who has experienced trauma, this is risky and frightening. They are often accustomed to suppressing all their feelings because it creates a false sense of security and safety. Internalizing their emotions has worked for them in the past. They may be very reluctant to attempt to implement new, biblical patterns of behavior out of fear of "ruining" the new relationships they are forming or "failing" biblical counseling.

Assist the counselee in learning how to bring their internalized anger to God. They must acknowledge it before God and ask His help to learn how to express it in ways that honor Him. The Psalms are an excellent way to demonstrate that God understands human emotions like anger. Assure them God understands the emotions He gave them, and allow the Scriptures to speak for themselves.

Have the counselee consider Psalm 4:4–5 *Tremble, and do not sin; Ponder in your heart upon your bed, and be still. Selah. Offer the sacrifices of righteousness, and trust in Yahweh* (LSB). Trembling is a reaction or a response to strong emotions, which the angry person has plenty of. These verses encourage acknowledging emotions like anger but not allowing them to lead to sin. The recommended course of action is considering a righteous response and not acting until they do. The key is to respond, to take action, not allow the anger to fester.

Also, Psalm 73:21–22: *When my heart was embittered and I was pierced within, then I was senseless and ignorant; I was like an animal before You* (LSB). Some versions of verse 22 use the phrase, *"I was a brute beast before you"* indicating that their expressed anger was irrational or violent, which may resonate with a trauma survivor who has changed from angry outbursts to suppressing their anger out of fear that they will displease God. These two verses can help the counselee whose anger has turned bitter in their soul realize that the Psalms deeply connect with human experiences. This connection may help them move from internalizing their anger to a place of willingness to bring it into the light and acknowledge it, which is the first step towards dealing with it biblically.

The biblical counselor can utilize the thought journal and the questions previously suggested in this section on anger to help the counselee who internalizes their anger begin to process what is at the heart of the matter and then resolve conflicts with others and God.

There can be a godly and righteous response to the anger the victim experiences. The following process is adapted from Wayne Mack's biblical procedure for helping people deal with their anger constructively instead of destructively.[176] First, counselees should ask themselves what is happening around them when they are experiencing anger. Asking the Lord to help them see the situation accurately amid their sinful anger will help them be honest about what is going on in their hearts (Eph. 4:26). Self-examination is essential to getting to the heart of the issue (Ps. 139:23–24). It helps the counselee discern if their emotions are honoring God and recognize areas needing repentance and change.

Second, they can learn to interpret what is happening through a biblical grid rather than leaning on their own understanding (Prov. 3:5–6), emphasizing the importance of using Scripture as the counselee's authority for how to process and respond to anger. This step also stresses the importance of taking their thoughts captive and renewing the mind, which will help the counselee to align their thoughts with God's truth to find healing (Rom. 12:2; 2 Cor. 10:1–5; Phil. 4:8). Additionally, impart the vital part prayer plays in this process. Prayer emphasizes that genuine change comes from God and that He must be actively involved in the process of healing (Ps. 147:3).

Third, they must examine their heart regarding how they are tempted at the moment. The suffering counselee has likely developed patterns of thinking and behavior that have become habitual. Ongoing self-examination helps them identify these sinful thoughts, beliefs, and desires of the heart that lead to problematic actions. Are they tempted to pout or sulk, run away or quit, be malicious, punish someone, get revenge, or retaliate? They must then ask themselves how these thoughts, beliefs, and desires align with Scripture. Regardless of their circumstances, they must determine the biblical response and implement God-honoring reactions to their situation.

Fourth, when confronted by unpleasant, potentially irritating circumstances, teach the counselee how to take authority over their emotions and recall the biblical truths they desire to implement. Remind the counselee that the changes they are making begin in the heart and that diligent application of biblical principles will lead to lasting change (Col. 3:10). There will be victories, and sometimes they will fall back into sin and react out of their fleshly desires when they are not actively choosing to live by the Spirit (Rom. 7:15–20; Gal. 5:16–17). Emphasize the biblical truths instructing God's people to live and respond when things provoke them to anger. Use Scriptures like Ephesians 4:26, *"In your anger do not sin: Do not let the sun go down while you are still angry,"* to emphasize that while anger itself is not sinful, it is essential to respond to it in a way that honors God. Encourage them to memorize bible verses such as James 1:19–20 and Colossians 3:18, which they can recall when tempted to respond in anger. Help them to develop spiritual disciplines such as daily Scripture reading, prayer and fasting, regularly attending church, and becoming an active part of the church community. Self-control is a fruit of the Holy Spirit, as is renewing one's mind with Scripture, so encourage the counselee to do all these things under submission to the power of the Holy Spirit (Gal. 5:22–23).

The fifth step is for the counselee to determine if they are willing to obey God and please Him or if they will please themselves. On what is their heart focused? Self-examination helps them to identify areas where they may be tempted to live for themselves rather than obey and honor God. Are they willing to make intentional choices that reflect a commitment to live by biblical principles rather than the flesh? When they sin, are they willing to confess to God and those they sinned against in their anger and seek forgiveness? Because this involves humbling themselves before God and others, it reveals a heart that desires to be in the right relationship with others and before God.

Enacting the counsel provided here will help the counselee to realize their unrighteous anger and bitterness. They will need gentle, biblical confrontation with direction to repent, change, and forgive. Anger must be confessed and put off, and bitterness must be dealt with and uprooted so the counselee can find freedom and honor God. The only way to overcome bitterness and unresolved anger is to forgive.

Confession and Healing

As the counselee works through the sin committed against them, they must also be willing to deal with their own sin by confessing their thoughts and behaviors against God and their body. The Scriptures and the principles taught in biblical counseling will help them learn how to think, believe, and desire things that glorify God, which will contribute to the lifelong changes they desire.

Consider and Apply

1. How does the counselee's anger align with the biblical definitions of righteous and unrighteous anger? Can they identify specific instances where their anger was directed towards sin and injustice (righteous) versus when it was self-centered and uncontrolled (unrighteous)?
2. Have the counselee reflect on Ephesians 4:26–27 and Psalm 7:11. How do these verses guide their understanding of anger and its proper expression? What steps can they take to ensure their anger aligns with God's standards?
3. In what ways has the counselee allowed their anger to lead to sinful behaviors or attitudes? How can they confess these sins to God and seek His forgiveness, as instructed in 1 John 1:9?
4. Make a plan for how they will incorporate spiritual disciplines (prayer, meditation and memorization of Scripture, and involvement in a church community) to address the anger resulting from their ordeal. Create a plan with specific actions they will take to replace self-harming behaviors with biblical responses.

CHAPTER 11

Biblical Responses to Self-Harm

Understanding Self-Harm

Self-harming behaviors have been around since ancient Bible times. 1 Kings 18:28 describes idol worshipers who slash themselves with swords and spears as was their custom until their blood flowed. It was found in ancient Greece and the Middle Ages when it was popular for religious people to self-flagellate. They would whip themselves with cords or chains as part of a religious ritual—yet God declares such acts futile, for 'the sacrifices of pagans are offered to demons, not to God' (1 Cor. 10:20), and He calls us to worship in spirit and truth (John 4:24).

In the late 19th century, two American doctors reported that women all over Europe were puncturing themselves with sewing needles. They were embedding these needles under their skin. In fact, this practice was common enough that European doctors had developed a name for the women who practiced this form of self-torture. They were called needle girls. They were considered to be hysterical and attention-seeking. This behavior—of embedding objects under the skin—has not been talked about much in the present, but it continues with teens embedding glass, needles, and pins under their skin.

In the early 2000s, we began to see an emerging problem: a dramatic increase in self-harming behaviors. Onset typically occurs around age 13 or 14, with males and females performing self-harming behaviors. However, boys tend to hit or burn themselves, and girls tend to cut themselves with razor blades, knives, pins, and fingernails.

Self-harming behaviors are prevalent in people who report emotional distress, such as depression and anxiety, and among those who have a poor ability to manage their emotions or keep them in check. Self-harming is one method a post-event sufferer might use in an attempt to find relief from the confusing mix of feelings and emotions they experience, including guilt, shame, and anger. Cutting, burning, hair pulling, and other self-injurious behaviors are unhealthy attempts to transform their emotional pain into physical pain. This faulty coping mechanism becomes a sinful habit, seeking relief or control apart from God (1 Cor. 6:19–20).

People tend to let their feelings guide their actions in the moment (even when they deny having any feelings at all), yet Scripture calls us to take every thought captive (2 Cor. 10:5) and trust that God's peace surpasses fleeting emotions (Phil. 4:7).

Cutting, burning, hair pulling, head banging, eyeball pressing, biting

Traumatic episode, abuse, neglect, etc.

Inability to resolve pain biblically, anger, rage, frustration, guilt, self hate, self blame

UNBIBLICAL THOUGHTS AND BELIEFS

Unbiblical beliefs about self:

"I am to blame"

"I am too stupid"

"It is all my fault"

"It will never change"

"I deserve..."

"I am bad, evil, worthless..."

"No one will listen to me"

"I can't cope"

"I can't handle it"

"How could I do this?"

"I am so angry"

"No words can express how I feel"

These thoughts lead the person to self-mutilate

Self-mutilation (self-injury, self-harm) can be defined as an attempt to intentionally cause harm to one's own body. The injury is usually severe enough to cause tissue damage to some degree – from superficial scarring to permanent major disfigurement such as amputation.

They cut or self-mutilate believing it:

Puts them in control (pride)
Punish themselves
Expresses anger over pain they have endured (rebellion against God)
Will help them to "feel" through the numbing pain (denial) of a past experience
Will relieve the pain of anger, sadness, loneliness, shame, guilt
Will make them feel "alive"
Will help them release all the pain inside

Self-mutilation brings temporary relief, a sense of regained control, satisfaction, emotional relief, a calm and peaceful feeling afterward.

Relief is short lived and guilt, shame and fear at their actions are experienced. The realization that the same circumstances are still there leads to a cycle of repetition with the goal being relief.

Understanding the Heart of Self-Harm: Motives and Misconceptions

Individuals who engage in self-harm often do so for various reasons, including:

- Emotional Release: Self-harm can provide a temporary release of pent-up emotions, such as anger, sadness, or frustration.
- Numbness: Some individuals self-harm to feel something when they are otherwise emotionally numb or disconnected.
- Control: Self-harm can give a sense of control over one's body and emotions, especially when other aspects of life feel uncontrollable.
- Punishment: Self-harm may be used as a form of self-punishment for perceived failures or guilt.
- Communication: It can be a way to express distress or seek help when verbal communication feels impossible.

A person who self-harms has an overall focus on self – on their pain, their loss, their feelings, their wants, their desires. Because this behavior is so compulsive, distraction techniques, mindfulness, and other external attempts to stop hurting themselves are rarely long-lasting, bringing a sense of hopelessness to the self-injurer as they come to (wrongly) believe nothing can help them. Their thoughts, beliefs, feelings, emotions, and desires must be examined in light of Scripture. In other words, the root cause for the behavior must be identified for genuine healing to occur.

Sally: A Case Study in Catastrophic Suffering- Self-Harm (continued)

When Sally arrived at the Mission, the staff assumed her lack of eyelashes or eyebrows and the large bald spots on her head were likely due to malnutrition and drug use. During her intake physical, dozens of scars were noted on her arms and up and down the length of her legs. Her extremities also bore numerous burn marks from cigarettes and lighters. When she was asked, Sally admitted she pulled out her lashes and eyebrows, and the scars on her body were from her repeatedly cutting herself and picking off the scabs.

She described her self-harming behaviors as "not a big deal." Sally denied that her self-harming behaviors were attempts to end her own life. While she had attempted suicide before, she steadfastly maintained, like others who self-harm, that she did not cut or burn herself in an attempt to die or to kill herself. She said she was very intentional about where and how deep she cut herself so as not to cut into a major vein or artery.

Distinguishing Self-Harm from Suicide: A Biblical Clarification

Self-harming and suicidal behaviors differ in several important ways. Non-suicidal self-harm is more prevalent than suicidal self-harm. It is less medically severe and causes less lethal damage compared with suicide attempts. It involves different methods of self-harm, like cutting and burning, rather than something involving firearms, hanging, or poisoning. However, more and more data is indicating that self-harm may be an especially important risk factor for suicidal behavior.

Forms of Self-Injury: Physical Manifestations of Inner Turmoil

Forms of self-injury or self-mutilation include but are not limited to:

- Cutting- The body with a razor blade, pin, needle, or other sharp object. They score, mark, and/or cut their skin until they bleed.
- Burning- with a cigarette or by heating another object and pressing it on the skin. It leaves a wound, and often, the scab is picked off to form a scar.
- Hair pulling – creating bald spots all over the head, pulling out eyelashes or eyebrows.
- Eyeball pressing - using their fingers to push their eyeballs into their head. Eyeball pressing is very painful, damaging, and distorts vision. Sometimes, a child or adult who is autistic will eyeball press, headbang, or perform other self-harming behaviors as a part of their autism. Driven by sensory needs rather than heart idolatry (Jer. 17:9), this is not considered self-abuse in the biblical sense.
- Biting- biting their arms, hands, legs, lips, cheeks.
- Picking at scabs/interference with healing—Picking at the skin and scabs until they damage the skin and inflame old wounds, which can be done on cutting lines, bite wounds, and burn scabs.
- Punching oneself in the head or the thighs out of frustration, anger, or hopelessness. Some people punch themselves once or twice, but others punch themselves until they are black and blue.
- Extreme nail-biting- biting until the fingers are bloodied and there is literally no available nail to chew
- Bone breaking, an extreme form of self-harm.

- Purposeful starvation (Anorexia), drastic food reduction/severe dietary restriction- the person typically wants to disappear. Their thinking is skewed, and they believe that if they don't eat, they will just fade away.

The Heart's Deception: Self-Harm as an Idolatrous Response

Self-harm is common in those who routinely demonstrate a group of ungodly behaviors, including volatile emotions, impulsivity, a tremendous fear of abandonment, and a high demand for relational intimacy. Because they are often overly dependent on people, the people in their lives will say the relationship is suffocating. They are feeling-oriented rather than God-oriented and absorbed by the pain they are experiencing, leading to a lack of self-control and sinful outbursts of anger. Their life is characterized by indulging the flesh. They will often be labeled with Borderline Personality Disorder (BPD).

Sufferers of extreme sadness (depression) may also have self-harming behaviors as do those appearing to have "low self-esteem" (biblically understood as pride). Self-deprecation often masks a demand for worth apart from God (Phil. 2:3), fueling self-focus. While such a person may say self-deprecating things, the reality is that they think very highly of themselves and use manipulation to gain the attention they believe they deserve. Their entire focus is on themselves, which violates Scriptures such as Philippians 2:3–4 and Matthew 22:39. They do not consider others more important than themselves. Life is all about them.

Another problem with self-harming as a symptom is anxiety – Sally is an anxious woman. During her biblical counseling sessions, Abigail noted she was fidgeting and unconsciously twirled her hair around her finger and pulling it out. She claimed she was not aware of it while she was doing it. Like others who self-injure, Sally demonstrated impulsive behavior and poor self-control overall. During biblical counseling sessions, she would run her fingers up and down her arms in a scratching motion. She wore long sleeves and couldn't scratch herself, but the motion was there. She struggles with severe anxiety, tends toward disordered eating, feelings of depression, and living in her emotions. Sally told Abigail she hurts herself because it is the only thing that allows her to feel anything at all. However, this contradicts all the other feeling-oriented language she uses.

Overall, self-injury is a person's attempt to cope with or relieve painful or hard-to-express feelings apart from God. It is an unbiblical method of dealing with indescribable pain and loneliness—the heart's deception (Jer. 17:9; Heb 3:13) drives this—God calls us to 'cast our cares on Him' (1 Pet 5:7), not harm ourselves

(1 Cor. 6:19–20). Understanding that self-injury is always associated with a more significant problem is imperative. It is a clue that something else is happening in that person's heart.

It should not be surprising that self-injurers commonly report they feel empty inside and stressed, are unable to express their feelings, and say they are lonely, not understood by others, and fearful of intimate relationships and adult responsibilities. What provokes self-harm varies—whether one devastating event or repeated traumas—but it's the unbiblical heart response (e.g., guilt, rage) that turns pain inward. The inability to biblically resolve pain, anger, rage, frustration, guilt, self-hate, and self-blame creates a toxic stew of raw emotion. The person struggles to externalize the pain, guilt, rage, frustration, self-hatred, or self-blame so it is internalized.

While they may experience a short-term feeling of relief or control, it solves nothing and only leads to further complications and harm. They also may self-injure as a form of punishing themselves. As in Sally's case, the person has deep feelings of shame and guilt. They believe they are responsible for what happened to them or others and that they should be punished. There may also be unbiblical thoughts and beliefs about themselves related to their identity.

Self-injury can also be one way the counselee attempts to cope with anger towards God for their catastrophic suffering. They may believe God is responsible for the sin committed against them, that God has caused their pain, and that He has betrayed or abandoned them. They do not understand that they are questioning God's goodness and sovereignty and accusing God of doing evil. The counselor can guide them to lament biblically (Ps. 13), turning rage into trust in His goodness (Rom. 8:28).

Those who practice self-harming behaviors express that doing things like cutting or burning themselves helps them to "feel" something. They declare that the catastrophe they endured has numbed them, and they can't feel anything emotionally. This paradox—claiming numbness yet seeking relief—reveals deception (Jer 17:9). The heart believes self-harm 'works,' masking the deeper lie that God's comfort isn't enough (Ps 34:18). They say they are emotionally numb, yet they find relief through self-injury, which highlights the role of the inner man, their faulty belief system, and the deception that leads them to seek relief in sinful, fleshly ways. The person is deceived and believes that self-harm is the way to cope with what has happened to them. Self-mutilation—driven by wrong thoughts, beliefs, and desires—may bring temporary relief, a sense of regained control, satisfaction, emotional relief, and a calm, peaceful feeling afterward. Still, relief is short-lived, and they experience guilt, shame, and fear at their actions. There is also the inescapable reality that the same circumstances and situations are still there, leading to a cycle/repetition with the goal of relief not actually being attained.

The biblical counseling process must include helping the counselee to see how their actions are rooted in deception. 'The heart is deceitful above all things' (Jer. 17:9)—and begins with the gospel: Christ died for our sins (Rom. 5:8), offering forgiveness and a new heart (Ezek. 36:26). Counselors must then lead them to repent—turning from self-harm to God (Acts. 3:19), confessing their sin (1 John 1:9), and seeking His strength (Ps. 32:5). This unfolds in stages: first, assess the behavior's scope (Prov. 20:5); second, expose heart lies with Scripture (Heb 4:12); third, replace sin with godly habits (Eph. 4:22–24), all rooted in God's grace (Titus 2:11–12).

The counselee must understand that their desire to find relief and control through self-injury is a sinful method to find relief from the shame, guilt, and other pain they carry. Because they are replacing God and His ways with their own, it is idolatrous. Self-harm is idolatrous because it elevates human control over God's sufficiency (Col. 3:5), trusting fleshly relief instead of His healing (Ps. 147:3). Counselors must also address the suffering fueling self-harm—sins against them (Ps. 82:3–4)—helping them see God's justice (Ps. 9:7–8) and comfort (2 Cor. 1:3–4), not their own punishment. Beyond stopping self-harm, biblical counselors guide them to God's hope and His promise of joy (Ps. 147:3; Rom. 15:13), replacing despair with trust (Ps. 34:18). The biblical counselor should also enlist godly community, whether it is in church, small group, Bible study, or other individual discipleship; bring in someone who can help biblically bear their burdens (Gal. 6:2). They can encourage confession and prayer and be a presence in their life (James 5:16).

They have sinful thoughts, beliefs, and desires that need to be examined in light of Scripture and addressed biblically. Still, they also have developed a strong attachment to a compelling behavior that provides temporary but substantial emotional relief. The counselor must help the counselee to develop alternative, practical outlets other than self-harming when strong urges arise. These are not intended to become new idols but to provide the counselee with new and righteous practices to "put on" while they are working through the issues of the heart. Suggested options are the thought journal – either written or verbal documentation of thoughts, beliefs, and desires when the counselee is tempted to self-harm. The verbal thought journal may provide more immediate help for the impulsiveness of the counselee. Physical exercise to release the energy of the emotions may also be beneficial; however, be cautious; the counselee should not compulsively exercise, trading one sinful coping behavior for another.

Other creative outlets, such as art, poetry, or music, may also help the counselee to express the emotions they believe they cannot express initially. These creative outlets could be included in the biblical counseling conversations with the counselee, describing the thoughts, beliefs, and desires of the heart that are expressed in their journaling or other outlet. These outlets—like a thought journal (Ps. 139:23–24) or prayerful exercise (1 Cor. 6:19–20)—help 'put on' righteousness (Eph. 4:24) while confronting heart lies, not replacing God with new crutches.

Counseling the Self-Injurer: Probing the Heart with Biblical Questions

The focus must remain on the heart producing the actions because that is the root of the problem. Ask heart-piercing questions to help the counselee recognize and identify the sinful thoughts and beliefs that drive their self-harming behavior. Formulate the questions carefully, avoiding those that allow for a "yes," "no," or a "grunt" for an answer. Part of the problem with a self-abuser is that they are struggling with pain they struggle to verbalize. Ask questions intended to probe thoughts and beliefs behind emotions (e.g., 'What do you believe when you feel this urge?') to reveal the heart (Prov 4:23), not just surface feelings. These are questions that will cause them to think instead of emote. It allows them to place their thoughts, beliefs, and desires into words.

Begin with basic questions about their self-harming behaviors, such as how long they have been cutting, burning, or hurting themselves and what implements they use when cutting or burning their skin. Ask specifically when they first hurt themselves and what happened before the first time they hurt themselves. (Did someone hurt or abuse them?)

What usually happens before they feel the urge to self-harm? Are specific situations, emotions, or thoughts provoking them to enact the behavior? See if they can articulate what pain they are trying to relieve and how cutting, burning, etc., helps them. Are there specific feelings of guilt, shame, or anger that you are trying to cope with? The usual response is, "It makes me feel better," or "Then I can feel something." Ask them to explain their answers, guiding them away from feeling-oriented answers and toward answers that reveal their thoughts, beliefs, and desires.

Does self-injuring provide temporary relief or a sense of control? If they think it does, the counselor should ask clarifying questions seeking to have the counselee explain the positive or godly feelings they get from cutting, hair pulling, and other self-harming behaviors. Have them articulate how long their positive feelings last and what feelings they have after the positive feelings end. What changes do they notice in their thoughts and beliefs after they self-harm?

Have they tried another method of pain relief? If so, what have they tried? What made it ineffective for them to continue? Help them recall what they think about while hurting themselves if it is a current practice. Ask them to make an effort to write down their thoughts before they next self-abuse. Overall, how has self-harming affected their daily life and relationships? Have they noticed any positive or negative changes in their behavior or mood since they started self-harming? Considering the entire cycle, do they believe this behavior is helpful?

Sally: A Case Study in Catastrophic Suffering- Self-Harm (Continued)

Sally's Thought Journal: Mapping the Hearts Lies

Abigail presented Sally with the following questions to help her with the Thought Journal homework she had assigned. Sally learned that the questions were designed to help her think and process what she was thinking about. Sally worked on the Thought Journal questions over the days between meetings with Abigail. The process was very hard for her, and several times she surrendered to her feelings and made a few small cuts in her legs with a plastic knife she took from the kitchen.

Sally presented her Thought Journal to Abigail at their next meeting. She admitted engaging in cutting her legs during the session. Although the self-harming actions revealed Sally had a long way to go in the transformation process, Abigail was encouraged that Sally confessed rather than waiting to be discovered or lying about it.

Abigail asked Sally to read the questions and her answers.

- *Q: What usually happens before you feel the urge to self-harm? Are specific situations, emotions, or thoughts provoking you to enact the behavior?*
  Sally's response: I usually feel the urge to self-harm when I'm overwhelmed with emotions like guilt, shame, and anger. Specific situations that trigger me include memories of the abuse, feeling rejected or abandoned, and when I feel like I'm losing control over my life.

- *Q: Can you articulate what pain you are trying to relieve and how cutting, burning, and so on helps you? Are there specific feelings of guilt, shame, or anger that you are trying to cope with?*

Sally's response: Cutting and burning myself helps me feel something physical instead of emotional numbness. It also feels like a way to punish myself for the guilt and shame I carry. It makes me feel like I have some control over my pain.

- *Q: Does self-injuring provide temporary relief or a sense of control?*
  Sally's response: Yes, it does. When I cut or burn myself, I feel a sense of relief and control, even if it's just for a short while.

- *Q: Can you explain the positive or godly feelings you get from cutting, hair-pulling, and other self-harming behaviors? How long do these positive feelings last, and what feelings do you have after the positive feelings end?*
  Sally's response: The positive feelings are very brief. I feel a rush of relief and control, but it doesn't last long. Afterward, I feel even worse—more guilt, shame, and anger at myself for doing it again.

- *Q: Have you tried another method of pain relief? If so, what have you tried? What made it ineffective for you to continue?*
  Sally: I've tried talking to therapists and taking medications, but nothing seems to help as immediately as self-harming. The other methods feel too slow or don't address the intensity of my emotions.

- *Q: What do you think about while you are hurting yourself if it is a current practice?*
  Sally's response: I think about how much I hate myself and how I deserve the pain. I also think about the abuse and how it feels like I'm reliving it but with some control this time.

- *Q: Overall, how has self-harming affected your daily life and relationships? Have you noticed any positive or negative changes in your behavior or mood since you started self-harming? Considering the entire cycle, do you believe this behavior is helpful?*
  Sally's response: Self-harming has made my daily life and relationships very difficult. I'm always hiding my scars and burns, and I feel ashamed around others. My mood swings are intense, and I often feel isolated and misunderstood. While it provides temporary relief, I know it's not helpful in the long run. It just makes everything worse.

Using Sally's Thought Journal and her answers to the questions, they worked together and categorized her thoughts, beliefs, and desires.

Thoughts	Beliefs	Desires
"I feel dirty when I think about what all those men have done to me."	"I am responsible for what happened to me."	"I want to feel something physical instead of emotional numbness."
"I hate myself and deserve the pain."	"I am fundamentally wrong and dirty."	"I want to punish myself for the guilt and shame I carry."
"Cutting and burning helps me feel in control."	"I am a mess and can't stay stable without medication."	"I want to have some control over my pain."
"I think about the abuse and how it feels like I'm reliving it but with some control this time."	"God has forsaken me and treated me unjustly."	"I want relief from the overwhelming emotions of guilt, shame, and anger."
"Self-harming provides temporary relief and control."	"I am not worth saving or caring for."	"I want to escape the emotional pain and numbness."
"I feel worse after self-harming—more guilt, shame, and anger at myself."	"I am a victim and not a willing participant."	"I want to be liked and accepted."
"Nothing helps as immediately as self-harming."	"I am not responsible for the actions of Billy and his friends."	"I want to hide my scars and burns from others."
"Self-harming makes my daily life and relationships very difficult."	"I am not condemned by God and can be free from shame."	"I want to stop feeling isolated and misunderstood."

Once her thoughts, beliefs, and desires were put in the chart, her responses were arranged into patterns to help Sally see the underlying heart idols or lies that she believed. These idols or lies contributed not only to her self-harming behaviors and emotional struggles but also to most of the issues Sally was dealing with as a result of her years of catastrophic suffering. Identifying these patterns enabled her biblical counselor to address and challenge her beliefs with biblical truth.

Pattern	Responses	Heart Idols or Lies
Guilt	"I deserve this."	Belief that she is responsible for the abuse and deserves punishment.
	"I think about how much I hate myself and how I deserve the pain."	Self-punishment as a way to cope with guilt.
	"Cutting and burning myself helps me feel something physical instead of the emotional numbness."	Seeking control over her pain through self-harm.
	"I feel worse after self-harming—more guilt, shame, and anger at myself for doing it again."	Cycle of guilt and self-harm reinforcing each other.
	"I feel dirty when I think about what all those men have done to me."	Internalizing the guilt and shame from the abuse.
	"I think about the abuse and how it feels like I'm reliving it but with some control this time."	Belief that she has some control over her pain through self-harm.

Pattern	Responses	Heart Idols or Lies
Shame	"I'm worthless."	Belief that she is fundamentally wrong and dirty.
	"I feel dirty when I think about what all those men have done to me."	Internalizing the shame from the abuse.
	"I hate myself and deserve the pain."	Self-hatred and belief in her own worthlessness.
	"Self-harming has made my daily life and relationships very difficult."	Feeling ashamed around others and hiding her scars and burns.
	"My mood swings are intense, and I often feel isolated and misunderstood."	Belief that she is unworthy of love and acceptance.

Pattern	**Responses**	**Heart Idols or Lies**
Guilt	"I deserve this."	Belief that she is responsible for the abuse and deserves punishment.
	"I think about how much I hate myself and how I deserve the pain."	Self-punishment as a way to cope with guilt.
	"I want to hide my scars and burns from others."	Desire to conceal her shame and avoid judgment.
Pattern	**Responses**	**Heart Idols or Lies**
Anger	"God abandoned me."	Belief that God has forsaken her and treated her unjustly.
	"Why did God allow this to happen to me?"	Questioning God's goodness and presence in her suffering.
	"Why didn't He protect me?"	Feeling abandoned and unprotected by God.
	"Why won't He protect me now?"	Ongoing anger and distrust towards God.
	"I feel like I'm losing control over my life."	Anger at her perceived lack of control and God's role in it.

Confronting Guilt, Shame, and Anger: Biblical Truths for Healing

Sally and her biblical counselor worked on her thoughts, beliefs, and desires for months, carefully addressing each lie or idol with biblical truth based on Scripture. Here's a table focusing on the pattern of guilt, including Scriptures that address Sally's heart lies or idols with biblical truth.

Pattern	Responses	Heart Idols or Lies	Scriptures	Application
Guilt	"I deserve this."	Belief that she is responsible for the abuse and deserves punishment.	1 John 1:9	If we confess our sins, He is faithful and just to forgive us our sins and to cleanse us from all unrighteousness. Sally can find forgiveness and cleansing in Christ.
	"I think about how much I hate myself and how I deserve the pain."	Self-punishment as a way to cope with guilt.	Romans 8:1	There is therefore now no condemnation for those who are in Christ Jesus. Sally can be assured that she is not condemned in Christ.
	"Cutting and burning myself helps me feel something physical instead of the emotional numbness."	Seeking control over her pain through self-harm.	Psalm 103:12	As far as the east is from the west, so far has He removed our transgressions from us. Sally can trust that God has removed her sins far from her.
	"I feel worse after self-harming—more guilt, shame, and anger at myself for doing it again."	Cycle of guilt and self-harm reinforcing each other.	Isaiah 1:18	Though your sins are like scarlet, they shall be as white as snow; though they are red like crimson, they shall become like wool. Sally can find hope in God's promise of cleansing and renewal.

Pattern	Responses	Heart Idols or Lies	Scriptures	Application
	"I feel dirty when I think about what all those men have done to me."	Internalizing the guilt and shame from the abuse.	2 Corinthians 5:17	Therefore, if anyone is in Christ, he is a new creation. The old has passed away; behold, the new has come. Sally can embrace her new identity in Christ.
	"I think about the abuse and how it feels like I'm reliving it but with some control this time."	Belief that she has some control over her pain through self-harm.	Hebrews 10:22	Let us draw near with a true heart in full assurance of faith, with our hearts sprinkled clean from an evil conscience and our bodies washed with pure water. Sally can approach God with confidence, knowing she is cleansed.

Pattern	Responses	Heart Idols or Lies	Scriptures	Application
Shame	"I'm worthless."	Belief that she is fundamentally wrong and dirty.	Isaiah 54:4	God promises to remove her shame and replace it with honor. Her past does not define her.
	"I feel dirty when I think about what all those men have done to me."	Internalizing the shame from the abuse.	Romans 10:11	Believing in Jesus protects her from ultimate shame and gives her a secure identity in Him.

Pattern	Responses	Heart Idols or Lies	Scriptures	Application
	"I hate myself and deserve the pain."	Self-hatred and belief in her own worthlessness.	Psalm 34:5	Looking to God can transform her feelings of worthlessness into a sense of dignity and joy.
	"Self-harming has made my daily life and relationships very difficult."	Feeling ashamed around others and hiding her scars and burns.	Joel 2:26	God's provision and blessings remove shame. She can trust in God's goodness and His ability to restore her life.
	"My mood swings are intense, and I often feel isolated and misunderstood."	Belief that she is unworthy of love and acceptance.	Isaiah 61:7	God promises to replace her shame with double honor and everlasting joy.
	"I want to hide my scars and burns from others."	Desire to conceal her shame and avoid judgment.	Hebrews 12:2	Focusing on Jesus, who overcame shame, can give her strength and hope to overcome her own shame.
			Psalm 25:3	Trusting in God and waiting on Him can replace her feelings of worthlessness with confidence in His faithfulness.

Pattern	Responses	Heart Idols or Lies	Scriptures	Application
Anger	"God abandoned me."	Belief that God has forsaken her and treated her unjustly.	Deuteronomy 31:6	God promises never to leave or forsake His people. Sally can trust in God's constant presence and faithfulness.
	"Why did God allow this to happen to me?"	Questioning God's goodness and presence in her suffering.	Romans 8:28	God works all things together for good for those who love Him. Sally can trust that God has a purpose even in her suffering.
	"Why didn't He protect me?"	Feeling abandoned and unprotected by God.	Psalm 46:1	God is our refuge and strength, a very present help in trouble. Sally can find comfort in God's protection and support.
	"Why won't He protect me now?"	Ongoing anger and distrust towards God.	Isaiah 41:10	God commands us not to fear, for He is with us. Sally can find assurance in God's presence and help.
	"I feel like I'm losing control over my life."	Anger at her perceived lack of control and God's role in it.	Proverbs 3:5-6	Trust in the Lord with all your heart and lean not on your own understanding. Sally can learn to trust God's plan and guidance.

The Psalms as a Voice for the Wounded Soul

Pointing the counselee to the Psalms will help them to find words for many things they have experienced. The Lord speaks for them and to them, and because He knows their struggle so intimately, He knows the afflicted person struggles to find the words to express their anger and other feelings. In His loving kindness, God provides words for them to speak.[177] As Edward Welch says, "If you read them [the Psalms], it will be like hearing your own soul speak."[178] He recommends the survivor read Psalms 4:1, 5:1–2, 6:3, 25:17–18, 63:1, and Psalm 130:1 to help them express their pain.[179]

Once the counselee's thoughts, beliefs, and desires are detailed and appropriate Scripture is identified, confession, repentance, and truth application must occur, which is commonly understood as "putting off" and "putting on." The counselor should ensure the counselee understands confession and repentance correctly rather than assuming they comprehend this important step.

Confession, Repentance, and Renewal: The Path to Transformation

As the counselee works through the sin committed against them, they also must be willing to deal with their own sin by confessing their thoughts and behaviors against God and their body. The counselee should confess their sin before God, repent (turn from their sin), and towards Christ, believing they are forgiven and cleansed (Acts 3:19; Rom. 5:8; 1 John 1:9). Then the work of living out new truth begins. The counselee will have to actively renew their mind, replacing the lies they believe with truth (Rom. 12:2; Eph. 4:23). As they are renewing their mind, they are to "put on" righteous, God-focused behaviors based on the content of what they are learning in biblical counseling. For example, suppose the counselee has the urge to self-harm. In that case, they are to examine what they are thinking, believing, and desiring at that moment, think about if their urge honors God, and then determine whether to take the course of action that honors and glorifies God, despite how they feel. They may need to enlist the help of a trusted friend or discipleship mentor in the early days of these changes. The counselee should build godly friendships and relationships in the local church so they have someone to call on in weak moments and someone who can help them remember biblical truth (Gal. 6:2; Heb. 10:24–25).

From Despair to God's Sufficiency

Self-harm is a complex and deeply rooted behavior that often stems from a combination of emotional distress, faulty beliefs, and unbiblical responses to pain and suffering. The biblical counseling process must address the heart's deception and lead the counselee to understand their actions' spiritual implications. By identifying and challenging the lies and idols that drive self-harming behaviors, counselors can guide individuals like Sally towards repentance, renewal of the mind, and the adoption of godly habits. This journey involves addressing the immediate behaviors and providing ongoing support, practical outlets, and a strong community to help bear their burdens. Ultimately, the goal is to replace despair with trust in God's sufficiency, leading to true healing and transformation.

Consider and Apply

1. How will you find and identify specific lies or idols in your counselee's heart that contribute to their self-harming behaviors, and how can you address these with biblical truth?
2. Reflect on the underlying beliefs and desires that drive the counselee's actions. Consider how Scripture can be used to confront and correct these falsehoods.
3. How can you help your counselee understand the difference between temporary relief through self-harm and lasting peace by trusting God's promises?
4. How can you ensure that your counseling approach remains focused on the heart, rather than merely addressing surface behaviors, to facilitate genuine and lasting change?
5. Reflect on the importance of heart-piercing questions and the need to continually bring the counselee back to the core issues of their thoughts, beliefs, and desires.

CHAPTER 12

Biblical Responses to Substance Abuse and Addiction

Prevalence and Impact of Trauma on Addiction

National statistics indicate that the prevalence of substance abuse and addiction is much higher in those who have experienced trauma.[180] While the statistics reveal that those in the church have a reduced rate of post-trauma addiction, the numbers are still troubling.[181] The US State Department says, "It is likely that many individuals who enter addiction treatment have experiences with sex trafficking and CSE."[182] In addition, studies suggest that up to 60% of sexually exploited women experience substance use disorders,[183] and 75% of runaway youth exploited through prostitution had a substance use issue."[184]

These sobering figures highlight a critical connection between catastrophic suffering and the turn to substances, a link biblical counselors must carefully explore. The counselee's past trauma often shapes their present struggles, driving them to seek relief or escape in ways that displace God's rightful place in their hearts. To uncover these motivations and point toward redemption, counselors can begin by asking probing questions that bridge the counselee's experiences with their current behaviors. For instance, consider asking, "What do you turn to substances for when you're feeling overwhelmed, hurt, or empty? What do you hope they will give you in those moments?" These questions invite reflection on the emotional and spiritual needs, comfort, control, or numbness that substances falsely promise to meet. Similarly, to connect their suffering to a gospel hope, ask, "How do you think your past suffering has shaped your reliance on substances? What would it look like to let God redeem that pain instead of numbing it?" Such questions reveal the heart's inclinations and plant seeds for the transformative truth that God, not substances, offers lasting healing for their wounds.

Medical Evaluation and Detoxification

Because the biblical counselor cares for the whole person, it is always wise to have the counselee be medically evaluated when there is suspicion of substance abuse. A counselee who is physically addicted to any opiate or alcohol should be referred to a detoxification program for health and safety. There are also benefits to biblical residential and non-residential programs after detox, such as those recommended by The Addiction Connection.[185] Such programs can be beneficial in positive role modeling while removing the person from the environment that fostered their habitual substance abuse. It is helpful for the repenting counselee to be surrounded by a community of people struggling with issues and addressing them similarly (Prov. 27:17).

Secular vs. Biblical Counseling Approaches

Secular "treatment" programs assist in the physical withdrawal from the substance and have an emphasis on getting the person with an addiction to cease using their drug of choice. They will also attempt to address what they perceive to be the person's most pressing presenting problems, such as homelessness (with or without children), consequences of sexual behaviors used to support their habit, physical and sexual abuse or assault, and the resulting health problems from sex trafficking.[186] Receiving "good counseling" is equated to the person's emotional state during and after the counseling process.[187] If they are feeling better emotionally, it is assumed they will no longer want to use substances, and counseling is considered successful.[188] When these are the primary motives, all too often, the addict relapses, and their sorrow deepens to hopelessness (Matt. 23:25–26)[189] because the goal of the counseling is off base. The goal of all counseling is change, but it is not limited to changing one's circumstances or feelings; it is a change of heart (Ezek. 36:26; Rom. 12:2).

Biblical counseling, by contrast, digs beneath these external symptoms to the internal realities shaping the counselee's choices. To expose the limitations of secular methods and guide the counselee toward heart-level reflection, counselors can ask targeted questions that reveal the thoughts, beliefs, and desires tied to substance use. For example, consider asking, "Can you describe a specific time when you felt the urge to use drugs or alcohol? What were you thinking, believing, feeling, or wanting right before you made that choice?" This question reveals the underlying motivations, such as seeking escape or relief, that secular methods might only temporarily ease rather than truly address. Similarly, probing the aftermath with, "How do you feel about yourself after using substances, both in the moment and later when the effects wear off?" invites the counselee to confront the fleeting nature of emotional relief and the more profound guilt or shame that persists. Such questions shift the focus from temporary feelings to the heart's condition, laying a foundation for the lasting change only the gospel can bring.

Heart-Level Change and Repentance

The goal of biblical counseling is repentance and other heart-level changes that bring about a new life that glorifies God. Fruit issues can and must be addressed; however, while they are problematic, they are not *the* problem but symptoms of the *real* problem. The problem to deal with is deeper down in the survivor's heart: what has caused them to produce such wicked fruit (Luke 6:43–45). Even if, by God's grace, the counselee becomes a Christian, their heart is affected by remnants of the flesh. Jesus said the visible sin of addiction is evidence of what is going on in the heart. Every presenting (fruit) problem has roots buried deep in the heart of idolatry, and these roots must be addressed for them to be freed. Overcoming addiction requires dealing with the heart of the matter.

To guide counselees toward this heart-level transformation, biblical counselors can pose questions that expose misplaced trust and redirect it to God. For instance, asking, "What do you believe substances can do for you that God cannot? Where do you think God falls short in meeting those needs?" cuts to the core of idolatry, revealing where substances have usurped God's role as provider and comforter. Likewise, drawing from Scripture, counselors might ask, "The Bible says our hearts produce the fruit of our lives (Luke 6:43–45). What fruit do you see in your life from using substances, and what fruit do you long to see instead?" This question anchors the counselee in biblical truth, urging them to contrast the bitter harvest of addiction with the godly fruit they could bear through repentance. These questions illuminate the heart's condition and kindle a desire for change that honors God.

Understanding Addiction as Idolatry

Tim Lane says:

> The word addiction is not in the Bible, but the concept is everywhere. The human tendency to be completely committed to the

> pursuit of destructive, self-defeating behaviors is a strong theme in Scripture. It springs from the fall of mankind and our descent into depravity. In our time, however, addiction has come to mean something more narrow. It is the standard way of talking about life-dominating struggles, especially with things that are connected with bodily appetites, such as alcohol, drugs, food, and sex. But, of course, it is not simply a biological matter. Many factors come together that may influence people toward addiction, including genetic predisposition, family dynamics, pressures from suffering, poverty, and victimization.
>
> Truly, addicts have a complex and sometimes terrible story to tell. But something more fundamental operates at the root of life-dominating struggles. Scripture tells us that the inner person (the heart) and what it craves, treasures, wants, fears, and lives for is the ultimate driver of addictive behavior.[190]

Truly, people with an addiction have a complex and often harrowing story to tell. However, as Lane emphasizes, something more fundamental operates at the root of these life-dominating struggles. Scripture reveals that the inner person, the heart, and what it craves, treasures, fears, and lives for is the ultimate driver of addictive behavior. Addiction, therefore, is not just a biological urge but a disorder of worship, a turning away from God towards false idols born out of the devastation of the fall. To help counselees grasp this, counselors can probe the heart's fears and trusts with questions like, "When you think about your life without substances, what scares you the most? What does that fear tell you about what you're trusting in?" These questions uncover where substances have become a refuge or security, exposing the idolatry beneath the craving. Similarly, asking, "Do you ever feel like God has abandoned you or doesn't care about your pain, especially when you turn to substances? Why do you think you feel that way?" reveals whether bitterness or self-reliance has displaced trust in God's goodness. Through such reflections, the counselee begins to see addiction as a misdirected worship calling for reorientation to the One who alone satisfies.

Biblical References and Understanding

The Bible provides references to what is known as addiction and its identifying behaviors (Prov. 23:20–21; 1 Cor. 6:9–11; Eph. 5:5; Col. 3:5). Biblically, addiction is better understood as devotion, surrender, slavery, obsession, or bondage to things that are used to meet a person's perceived felt needs.[191] Greed and idolatry are considered to be core components of what is understood as addiction (Gal. 5:21). Despite being created to worship God, a person's sinful lusts drive them to worship and idolize other things and displace God from his rightful place of reign on the throne of the human heart. Ed Welch remarks,

> One of the most common portrayals of the human condition, and one which captures both the in-control and out-of-control experiences of addictions, is the theme of idolatry. From this perspective, the true nature of all addictions is that we have chosen to go outside the boundaries of the kingdom of God and look for blessing in the land of idols. In turning to idols, we are saying that we desire something in creation more than we desire the Creator.[192]

When a person routinely indulges in a substance, physical dependency often follows, but the heart's enslavement typically precedes it. If the root issue, idolatry, and greed, remain unaddressed, the counselee may simply exchange one bondage for another, replacing their original addictive behaviors with whatever their recovery program overlooks. To reorient them to God's perspective, counselors can ask, "What do you think God sees when He looks at you, knowing your struggles with substances? How does that compare to what you see in yourself?" This question bridges the biblical truth of God's gracious gaze (1 Cor. 6:11) with the counselee's often distorted self-view, inviting alignment with Scripture's promise of redemption over the shame of slavery. Such reflection roots their identity in God's love, not their addiction.

Idolatry and Worship Disorder

Idolatry is manifested by the person's excessive consumption of alcohol or drugs to please self or escape the problems of life. Therefore, from a biblical perspective, addiction is a worship disorder (Matt. 13:44–52) and an issue of the heart. The Bible does not refer to the heart emotively but uses it more comprehensively, emphasizing the mind more than emotions. The heart and mind are part of a person's spiritual or immaterial part, where desires begin that bloom into habitual sinful behaviors. The counselee's desire to escape problems or seek relief from guilt, pain, or misery leads them to obey the sinful desires of the flesh and turn to drugs and alcohol instead of turning to God, becoming their go-to saviors.

To challenge this misdirected worship, counselors can invite reflection with a question like, "If you were to trust that God's love and power are enough to help you through your pain, how might that change your desire to use substances?" This question presses the counselee to confront the idol head-on, imagining a life where trust in God's sufficiency replaces reliance on fleeting escapes. By shifting their focus from created things to the Creator, this question awakens the counselees' hearts to genuine worship, guiding them toward the true treasure worth seeking (Matt. 13:44).

Sally: A Case Study in Catastrophic Suffering- Addiction

After arriving at the Mission and enduring detox for her dependence on alcohol and pills, Sally emerged into a raw, unfiltered reality. Drugs and alcohol were a reliable crutch she relied on through years of relentless sexual exploitation by Billy and his friends and the other men who bought and sold her body. Sober now, yet brittle as cracked glass, Sally sat across from Abigail, her voice a whisper, her face downcast with despair. Sally told Abigail she could still hear their voices, the men who taunted her, laughed at her, and degraded her. Every night, she craved a drink to drown them out and to attempt to wash away the filth they left on her. Her hands trembled uncontrollably, and her eyes, which were hollow and haunted, darted around the room as if searching for escape in a room with no exits. They betrayed a heart still chained to old habits and desiring the fleeting mercy of numbness. Sally insisted that her desire to drink and do drugs was not about getting high but about silencing the screams in her head. She wanted an escape from the rage she had at her brother, the pimps, the johns, and the fury she had at herself and God for letting it happen. Abigail knew beneath her fragile exterior was a deeper wound: a soul wrestling with guilt, shame, and fury, looking for peace in a bottle rather than the One who promises it (Ps. 55:22).

Unlike her self-harm (where cutting enabled her to feel), Sally's substance abuse was flight, a frantic attempt to escape guilt, shame, and the echoes of suffering. The alcohol and pills weren't just habits; they were a way to avoid the memories of all the men whose hands had seared her soul with shame. In her sessions with Abigail, the torment spilled out. Sally carried a crushing self-blame, convinced she should've fought harder, screamed louder, and somehow broken free. Beneath that lay a deeper wound: a festering resentment toward God, a belief He'd abandoned her to their cruelty, leaving her defenseless. Now, Sally believed He was too distant and too silent to care.

She told Abigail that she blamed herself for not fighting harder. She also admitted she blamed God for not stopping it. Abigail asked her what she was seeking when she craved a drink. She wanted Sally to identify what pain won't let go. Sally immediately told Abigail she was looking for peace. She felt dirty, and God was too far away. Abigail recognized the idolatry; Sally had traded God's presence for fleeting, false saviors (Col. 3:5), enthroning alcohol where Christ belonged.

Post-detox, Sally's battle wasn't just with cravings; it was with a heart still bowing to idols. She'd emerged from the Mission's detox program, her body cleansed of alcohol and pills, yet her soul clung to their fleeting comfort. Abigail knew Sally needed to see the more profound truth: her "addiction" wasn't merely a habit or survival tactic; it was idolatry, a throne she had built for false saviors over Christ (Col. 3:5). At first, Sally resisted, her defiance a shield: she'd insist it was about silencing pain, not worshiping a bottle. However, the cravings betrayed her—daily whispers promising peace she couldn't find elsewhere.

Abigail pressed gently, guiding her to face the lie. She would ask Sally to name what she sought in those urges—peace, escape, a scrubbed-clean soul—and then reflect: why turn to liquor instead of the Lord? Slowly, the realization crept in. Sally saw how she had traded God's steady presence for alcohol's hollow embrace, elevating it as her deliverer (Rom. 1:25). Abigail opened Psalm 55:22, "Cast your burden on the Lord, and He will sustain you." Sally began to grasp it: her addiction was worship misaimed, a heart chasing idols when it could rest in Him (Ps. 34:18). Confession followed (1 John 1:9), a first step toward dethroning the bottle for Christ's reign.

The Redemptive Solution

Understanding life-dominating struggles with sin as a worship disorder opens the door to the incredibly good news of the gospel. The redemptive solution to the counselee's disoriented worship is God's redeeming grace; it recaptures and transforms them at the core of who they are (Eph. 2:8–9; Titus 2:11–12). Communicate to the counselee that there is a God who intervenes. He comes in grace and loves His children when they are still sinners and committed to rebellion (John 3:16; Rom. 5:8). Christ comes to rescue and bring comfort amid suffering, even when it is self-inflicted. He comes to live, suffer, die, be raised, ascend, and send his Spirit (Matt. 11:28–30; 2 Cor. 1:3–4). He presently intercedes and has promised to return and completely conform His people into His image (Phil. 1:6; Heb 7:25).

Show the counselee that because of Christ, they can be free from the guilt, folly, power, and presence of sin forever. Second Corinthians 5:17 promises that "*if anyone is in Christ, he is a new creation. The old has passed away; behold, the new has come.*" Romans 6:4 explains that "*we were buried therefore with him by baptism into death, in order that, just as Christ was raised from the dead by the glory of the Father, we too might walk in newness of life.*"

To help counselees embrace this transformation, counselors can ask, "What's one lie you believe about substances, like 'they're my only escape,' that you could replace with a truth from God's Word today? What Scripture might help you do that?" These questions invite them to shed falsehoods and cling to promises like Matthew 11:28, practically applying grace to their struggle. Similarly, asking, "What would it mean for you to see yourself as a new creation in Christ (2 Cor. 5:17), even with your struggles? How could that hope change your daily fight against addiction?" roots their identity in Christ's victory, stirring hope that reshapes their battle. Through such questions, the gospel becomes a living power to reorient their worship.

Progressive Sanctification

These changes are only possible when the person is willing to yield to Christ (Rom. 12:1). As they grow in wisdom and knowledge of the Word by the power of the Holy Spirit, God will change them within and enable them to become free from the yearnings of the soul that drive addiction (Col. 1:9–10). In the process of progressive sanctification, the counselee will battle against the fleshly desires that tempt them to return to the slavery of addiction (Gal. 5:16–17). Because the aftereffects of catastrophic suffering are so emotional, the counselee will have to work diligently at recognizing and overcoming the powerful desires of the flesh that they have tried to avoid through substance abuse (1 Pet. 5:8–9). They will have to practice putting off their old self, being renewed in their mind, and putting on the new self, which God creates to be like Christ in holiness (Eph. 4:22–24).

As we have seen, the Bible offers profound wisdom and practical guidance for addressing problems related to catastrophic suffering. Counselors can guide counselees toward practical steps and community strength to support this journey. For instance, asking, "When you feel tempted to use again, who in your church community could you reach out to for support? How can they help you honor God in that moment?" highlights the vital role of others in bearing burdens (Gal. 6:2), turning isolation into shared perseverance. Likewise, encouraging small, actionable faith with, "What is one small step you could take this week to turn away from substances and toward God instead, like praying a Psalm or reading a verse when the urge hits?" equips them to put off sin and put on righteousness in tangible ways. In the final chapter, we will reflect on the church's role in supporting those who endure such trials and the importance of community in the healing process. We can help individuals find hope and redemption in Christ by fostering a culture of care and compassion.

Consider and Apply

1. Discuss with the counselee how understanding addiction as a heart issue and a form of idolatry changes their perspective on substance abuse. Reflect on Luke 6:43–45 and discuss how addressing the root issues in the heart can lead to true and lasting change.
2. In what ways can being part of a supportive Christian community help the counselee in their journey towards recovery? Consider Proverbs 27:17 and Hebrews 10:24–25 and discuss how positive role modeling and accountability can aid them in their healing process from trauma and the substance abuse they fled to for refuge.
3. Discuss with the counselee how recognizing God's redeeming grace and His love for them, even while they persist in unrepentant sin, impacts their approach to overcoming addiction. Reflect on Ephesians 2:8–9 and Romans 5:8 and discuss how embracing God's grace can transform their life.
4. Work with the counselee to help them understand what steps they can take to actively participate in the process of progressive sanctification, putting off the old self and being renewed in their mind. Reflect on Ephesians 4:22–24 and Galatians 5:16–17 and discuss practical ways to battle against the desires of the flesh and grow in holiness. Help them create a concrete plan for change.

CHAPTER 13

Forgiveness and Repentance

Having examined how catastrophic suffering leads to struggles such as substance abuse, addiction, shame, anger, grief, loss, and fractured relationships, this chapter now focuses on forgiveness and repentance—central themes that are crucial for healing from catastrophic suffering. We will explore the biblical mandate for forgiveness, common misunderstandings about it, and the role of repentance in the process. By understanding and embracing these principles, sufferers can find freedom and restoration in their relationship with God and others.

Introducing Forgiveness to the Sufferer

As biblical counseling progresses and the person grows in their faith and sanctification, the issue of forgiveness must be addressed. Forgiveness is very often a point of contention in the biblical counseling process, as the counselee who has endured abuse, suffering, and all manner of affliction comes face to face with what God requires. Be assured that the counselee will have many questions about forgiveness and what it means for their future. How might past topics like guilt or addiction in a counselee's story shape their resistance to forgiveness, and how can you prepare to address this?

Counselors must be prepared to answer complex questions, such as why they must forgive the person or people who hurt them and, in some cases, destroyed significant parts or years of their lives. Before addressing a counselee's forgiveness, counselors should examine themselves: Have I forgiven as I've been forgiven (Col. 3:13)? This self-examination ensures their counsel flows from a heart aligned with God's grace. Forgiveness must be approached with humility, steeped in prayer and Scripture (James 1:5), recognizing their own forgiven debts (Col. 3:13). Expect resistance from the counselee; often, suffering hardens hearts, but trust the Spirit to soften them (Ezek. 36:26).

The Divine Mandate for Forgiveness

Forgiveness is a divine mandate rooted in Christ's redemptive work on the cross (Rom. 5:8). It reflects the character of God, who is merciful and full of grace, which He lavishes on His people (Ps. 103:10). Mercy is when a guilty person does not receive what they deserve. Every sinner forgiven by God has received His mercy (Ps. 103:10; Titus 3:5). Grace also reflects God's character (Ps. 145:8). Grace is unmerited favor, and every sinner receives God's grace when they are forgiven of their sin through their union with Christ. Grace is when a guilty person receives what they do not deserve (Rom 3:23–24; Titus 2:11). Forgiveness is not merely a duty but a sanctifying act, aligning the counselee's heart with God's as they grow in grace (2 Pet. 3:18). Remembering the great debts of which the counselee has been forgiven and understanding their own need for grace and mercy should be the catalyst for their willingness to forgive those who sinned against them (Eph. 4:32).

Forgiveness as a Command and a Choice

Anyone who has ever been victimized, including survivors of crime, accidents, childhood abuse, any unjust imprisonment, or survivors of warfare, must decide whether they will forgive those who harmed them or not. There is no middle ground in forgiveness: the counselee will choose to obey and forgive the people or person(s) who hurt them, or they will decide to withhold it.

Those victimized must realize that forgiving their oppressor is crucial to their healing. This sounds absurd to some suffering counselees, who may be angry at the suggestion that they forgive someone who has hurt them so badly. Consider taking the counselee through the parable of the unforgiving servant (Matt. 18:23–34) because this parable is rich with teaching on forgiveness.

In the parable, the king (who represents God) wishes to settle accounts, and the man in question (who represents everyone, including the counselee) owes an enormous sum of money—a sum so large there is no way he could have paid it back. Ensure the counselee understands that "talent" is a word of weight, not worth. The sheer number of talents makes this a staggering sum of money, and it is evident that it is impossible for the man to repay the debt (this represents their debt to God). The king could seek justice by commanding the man and his family to be sold into debtors' bondage so that some repayment could be paid, even though it would be only a very small drop in a very large bucket. The servant begs for mercy and promises to repay what he certainly knows he cannot. The king overlooks the obvious lie, is moved with compassion, cancels the entire debt, and releases the man from any punishment whatsoever (representing how God wholly and freely forgives the counselee of their sin debt). The forgiven slave went on his way and found someone who owed him a mere pittance compared to what he was forgiven. The debtor pleaded for mercy, but despite all the grace he had been given, he would not relent and had his fellow slave tossed in jail. When his fellow slaves saw what had happened, they were very angry and told the king everything. The king was furious because he forgave an enormous debt. At the very least, he thought the servant should have been willing to forgive his fellow debtor what was a pittance of debt because he had been forgiven such an enormous one. The king revokes the forgiveness and hands the servant over to be punished.

Encourage the counselee to see themselves as the servant who has been forgiven a debt they could never pay. To make this vivid, the counselor might contrast the counselee's unpayable sin debt, perhaps millions in modern terms, with the smaller offenses against them. You can suggest they journal their reflections on God's mercy versus their grudges. As difficult as it may be, even those who have endured immense pain and suffering at the hands of others are expected by God to forgive those who hurt them. They are to forgive as they have been forgiven.

Forgiveness is also a choice in which the counselee decides to transfer the responsibility for recompense and vengeance for sin committed against them to God and to let go of the desire for revenge (Rom. 12:19). This may be the most challenging aspect of forgiveness for a person who has been maliciously harmed.

An afflicted person struggling with forgiveness can be confident that those who harm others will not escape the consequences of their actions regardless of what happens in this life. One day, God will avenge all wrongs (Rom. 12:17–21). Forgiveness frees a suffering person from harboring anger and bitterness in their hearts toward their oppressor. It enables them to increase their trust in God, grow in love for others, and define their lives by God's love and mercy rather than by the abuse they suffered.[193]

Common Misunderstandings About Forgiveness

The counselee may be deeply disturbed by God's requirement to forgive because they do not understand what the Bible says about forgiveness. For example, it is common to think that forgiveness means someone must forget what happened to them. Some wonder if forgiveness implies that what was done to them was okay.

In some cases, they may still be suffering from the results of the abusive treatment. It is crucial that you make it clear that forgiveness does not mean excusing the evil committed against the counselee. Forgiveness does not mean what happened to them was acceptable or can be excused. Stress that God does not minimize the sin committed against a victim. Abuse of all kinds provokes God's wrath. It is not a tiny, unimportant thing to God; as has already been demonstrated above, God takes harm inflicted on His image bearers seriously. Forgiveness does not mean the counselee will forget what happened to them, nor should they avoid having those who victimized them punished by law. It is not vengeance to use the governing system God set in place to hold people accountable according to the law (Rom. 13) and put them in prison where they cannot harm others. A great evil has been committed, and in many cases, it is unlikely that those complicit in inflicting suffering would ever ask for forgiveness. While reconciliation is not always possible or recommended, pursuing forgiveness in their heart before God is possible. Forgiveness releases the heart before God, while reconciliation requires mutual repentance and safety, two distinct steps often conflated in suffering's aftermath. Beware of rushing forgiveness, minimizing the counselee's pain, or pushing reconciliation where it's unsafe; such missteps can deepen wounds rather than heal them.

The Process of Forgiveness

Overcoming every aspect of the effects of calamitous suffering in this book requires the counselee to immerse themselves in Scripture. Only in Scripture will they find the wisdom, insight, and understanding they need to work through their suffering and affliction (Ps. 1:2–3; 2 Tim. 3:16–17; James 1:5). They will also need an abundance of discernment (Prov. 2:3–5). Scripture provides the only unshakable and unchangeable foundation for the counselee to rebuild their life (Isa. 40:8).

The Scriptures offer the counselee the strength and guidance that will enable them to navigate the complex and often conflicting feelings and emotions they will process on their healing journey (Phil. 4:13). Praying the Scriptures brings the counselee hope and comfort, fostering peace to the turbulent soul. If they are unsure how to pray, suggest they focus on praying the Psalms back to God. They will quickly discover that many Psalms of lament provide a fairly consistent pattern that begins with the psalmist calling or crying out to God in their distress (Ps. 3:1–3; 63:1). They then present their complaint to God. These are typically raw and painful expressions of their suffering, pain, and confusion at their circumstances and, often, at the silence from God (Ps. 13:1; 22:1). The language of lamenting will likely encourage and surprise the afflicted counselee who may not understand God *wants* His children to come to Him in this way. The lamentation then moves to an expression of trust in God despite His silence and details his goodness, kindness, faithfulness, and other attributes that contrast their current problems. This affirms their faith that God has always been faithful to His people (Ps. 13:5; 22:4–5). The psalmist then asks the Lord for help, intervention, or deliverance in their specific situation. The tone of the request frequently reveals an urgency about their plight (Ps. 22:19–20; 69:1–3; 143:7–9). Often, the lament will conclude on a hopeful note, expressing confidence that God will respond or act. The psalmist speaks out in faith and promises to worship God with thanksgiving regardless of the outcome of his situation (Ps. 13:6; 22:22; 30:11–12).

Forgiveness may not be settled in one session, depending on how the person was harmed, the duration of their suffering, and the grievous nature of the sins committed against them. Sue Nicewander explains in her book, *Treasure in the Ashes,*

> Contrary to common belief, [sic] forgiveness must be renewed, perhaps many times. Each time an offense comes to mind… We have an occasion to renew that promise just as Jesus does every time we offend him (1 John 1:9–2:2). But that doesn't mean we didn't really forgive the first time. Think of forgiveness as a series of promise renewals.[194] One former trafficking victim said, "Forgiveness can sometimes be a process that needs repetition often. I have spent days and weeks choosing to re-forgive the horrific abuse I endured."[195]

Encourage the afflicted person to admit they are struggling with forgiveness. Scriptures such as Psalm 139:1–4 and Hebrews 4:15–16 reveal that God is already aware of their internal conflicts and is there to provide comfort and direction and help them in their time of need. Walking the counselee through passages such as 1 Peter 5:6–11 and Philippians 4:4–9 explicitly emphasizes how this is a spiritual battle and that God is present to take on all their pain, anger, anxieties, and other burdens. Focus on teaching the counselee to resist the urge to cling to anger and bitterness and instead fix their eyes on what God has done and is doing in their situation. The thought journal may again prove helpful here, as well as a supportive church community. Encourage counselors to connect the counselee with a trusted church member for prayer or accountability, easing the burden of forgiveness (Gal. 6:2).

The counselor can structure this process in three phases: (1) Acknowledge the wound and its pain (Ps. 51:3); (2) Release vengeance to God through prayer (Rom. 12:19); (3) Renew the heart with Scripture's truth (Eph. 4:31–32).

Forgiveness will be a journey of many small steps. It will not happen overnight. Remind the counselee that forgiveness is ultimately for the glory of God and the benefit of the afflicted. It releases them from the bitterness and emotional bondage they are holding on to and is a critical step in their ability to heal and move forward with life. Counselors can present this journey as a reflection of sanctification, where each step of forgiveness mirrors the transformative process of putting off bitterness, renewing the mind with Scripture, and putting on Christlikeness (Eph. 4:22–24). By framing it this way, you will help the counselee see God's redemptive hand at work, turning even their struggle to forgive into a path toward holiness.

Sally: A Case Study in Catastrophic Suffering- Forgiveness

Sally sat in the Mission's counseling room, her hands trembling as they clutched a tattered Bible, the weight of this session pressing down like a stone. At 23, sober but bearing trafficking's scars, Sally's anger burned fiercely: toward Billy, her brother, who at 9 raped her in their clubhouse, later prostituting her to friends and forcing an abortion at 13 with a knife to her throat. She raged against her circumstances—parents blind to her torment, a church chanting love while she bled in silence, a world that ensnared her in sex work after she fled at 15. The abortion haunted her, a child's life stolen by Billy's threats. Her anger raged at God, whose silence in the woods and that clinic car ride echoed in her screams of "Where were You?" Abigail, her biblical counselor, saw guilt gnawing at Sally, her silence, rebellion, and running away, but she knew self-forgiveness was not the answer. Sally's soul needed God's mercy (Rom. 8:1), not self-release, and Abigail gently turned her toward forgiveness, the lynchpin of her healing, a process that would stretch over weeks, even months.

Sally's rage flared at the thought—forgiving Billy, the men who paid him, and God who stood by. Abigail pressed forward, her presence steady across countless tear-soaked sessions. Forgiveness wasn't excusing evil; it was freedom, a command rooted in Christ's forgiveness of Sally's own sins (Eph. 4:32). Her lies, rebellion, and flight had been wiped clean at the cross (Col. 2:13–14). She was called to forgive as she had been forgiven, not because they deserved it, but because Christ forgave her. It wasn't trusting either; Billy's unchanged ways demanded no such risk. Tears streaked Sally's face as she wrestled, her chest heaving with bitter sobs over months of meetings. The idea churned in her gut like surrender, like Billy "gets away with it all," his smirking face in the clubhouse, the knife's cold edge, years of profit from her pain, all unpunished. Her hands gripped the Bible's edges, knuckles white, as if she could squeeze out justice herself. Abigail knelt beside her, unwavering, and reframed the lie: forgiveness didn't erase Billy's debt to God (Rom. 12:19), only her burden to carry it. Sally's breath hitched, her tears pooling on the table, as Abigail placed Psalm 13 in her hands, guiding her to lament, "How long, O Lord?" (v. 1), and pour out the hurt, letting bitterness seep away over weeks of halting prayers. With Romans 8:28, Abigail slowly renewed Sally's mind, weaving Billy's evil into God's sovereign good, a promise he wouldn't escape justice. When urged to pray for Billy out of obedience (Matt. 5:44), Sally recoiled, then relented. After months, she whispered, "Lord, judge him," a Christlike step rooted in Christ's mercy towards her.

Forgiving God gnawed at Sally deepest, her fists pounding the table one gray afternoon, accusing Him of failing her. Abigail paused, then gently corrected her over weeks: "Forgiving God" implied He'd sinned, but God, perfect and holy, cannot sin (Hab. 1:13; 1 John 1:5). Abigail knew Sally's anger at Him stemmed from a heart wrestling with His ways, not His wrongs (Isa. 55:8–9). Sally's brow furrowed, her sobs softening as Abigail traced God's sinless love through Scripture, renewing her trust in His goodness despite the silence she'd felt. Painstaking and slow, this shift marked the hardest hurdle victims like Sally face. When urged to pray for Billy, Sally's halting words grew steadier, her heart unshackling over time.

As she pondered facing Billy, dread shadowed Sally's eyes, but Abigail clarified that forgiveness wasn't reconciliation. Sally could release him to God's justice without meeting him; reconciliation required repentance, absent in his unrepentant state. Some relationships, like with Billy, couldn't and should not resume. His crimes, rape, trafficking, and his refusal to admit them, proved it. Abigail pointed to God's authorities (Rom. 13:1–4) for accountability, a protective step beyond vengeance, and Sally mulled it over, a daunting path forming. Then her thoughts turned to her parents, shame choking her for lies and rebellion. Abigail revisited Ephesians 4:32—forgiveness as she'd received it might bridge to them, though their shock at Billy's sins loomed. Sally pictured their frail faces as forgiveness, forged over months, began to free her.

The Role of Repentance in Forgiveness

Repentance and Sanctification

Repentance is a crucial aspect of the Christian faith, deeply rooted in the process of sanctification and heart transformation. True repentance goes beyond mere external expressions of remorse and involves a profound change in the counselee's thoughts, beliefs, and desires. For the wounded, repentance often unlocks forgiveness—turning from bitterness enables releasing others, a dual sanctification that counselors must nurture together. The Holy Spirit initiates this change, and it is characterized by a genuine sorrow for sin that leads to salvation, as opposed to worldly sorrow, which results in death (2 Cor. 7:10). For those who have been harmed by others, understanding and embracing this concept is essential, as it helps them to address their own heart issues and bring God glory by how they live (Rom. 2:4).

Ongoing Process of Repentance

Repentance is not a one-time event but an ongoing process that reflects a believer's commitment to forsake sin and pursue righteousness. This process involves continuously examining the heart, recognizing areas of sin, and seeking God's help to change (Phil. 2:12–13). As previously stated, those who have endured extreme suffering may struggle with feelings of anger, bitterness, and self-pity, in addition to numerous other sinful fruits, which can hinder their spiritual growth. By acknowledging these sinful attitudes and repenting, they can experience healing and freedom from the bondage of their past (Ps. 139:23–24).

Accepting Consequences and Making Restitution

Repentance requires a willingness on the counselee's part to accept the consequences of their own actions and to make restitution where possible, which is especially important for a person who suffered tragedy and hurt others due to their pain. Genuine repentance involves taking responsibility for one's behavior, seeking forgiveness from those wronged, and making amends when possible (Ps. 51:10; Eph. 4:22–24). This process can potentially restore relationships (when appropriate) but also demonstrates the transformative power of God's grace in the believer's life.

Developing a God-Centered Perspective

A key aspect of repentance is the development of a God-centered perspective, where the counselee's primary concern is the honor and glory of God (1 Cor. 10:31). For those who have experienced devastating suffering, this means shifting their focus from their woundedness to God's redemptive work in their lives (Rom. 8:28–29). By cultivating a heart that seeks to please God above all else, they can overcome the negative emotions and destructive behaviors resulting from their affliction. This transformation is evidenced by a growing desire to obey God's Word and reflect His character in their daily lives (John 14:15; Col. 3:23–24).

Humility and Dependence on God

Finally, repentance is marked by a deep sense of humility and dependence on God. Sufferers must recognize that actual change is only possible through the power of the Holy Spirit and the application of biblical principles (Gal. 5:16). This involves a daily commitment to deny oneself, take up the cross, and follow Christ (Luke 9:23). As they submit to God's authority and allow Him to work in their hearts, they will experience the ongoing renewal and sanctification that leads to spiritual maturity and wholeness.

As we have seen, forgiveness and repentance are transformative processes that bring healing and reconciliation. The next chapter will reflect on the church's role in supporting those who have endured catastrophic suffering. We can help individuals find hope and redemption in Christ by fostering a culture of care and compassion.

Consider and Apply

1. What steps can the counselee take to cultivate a heart that seeks to please God above all else? How can this transformation help them overcome negative emotions and destructive behaviors?
2. What specific barriers or challenges does your counselee face in forgiving those who have hurt them? How do these obstacles impact their emotional and spiritual well-being?
3. How can you help the counselee apply the biblical principles of forgiveness discussed in this chapter to their own life? Work with the counselee to identify practical steps they can take to begin or continue the process of forgiving those who have wronged them.
4. How does the concept of true repentance, as described in this chapter, differ from mere expressions of remorse? Reflect on the importance of a profound change in thoughts, beliefs, and desires initiated by the Holy Spirit.
5. How willing is the counselee to accept the consequences of their actions? How will you help the counselee realize the significance of taking responsibility for their behavior and seeking forgiveness from those they have wronged?
6. Make a plan for how you will help the counselee shift their focus from their own woundedness to God's redemptive work in their life.

CHAPTER 14

The Role of the Church

The local church is where biblical counseling and support for all the issues discussed in this book should occur. The church plays a vital role in healing those who have experienced catastrophic suffering. This chapter will explore the importance of community, spiritual disciplines, and practical support in fostering a culture of care. By embracing its calling to love and support one another, the church can create a safe and nurturing environment for those who have experienced deep suffering.

The Church as a Healing Community

Someone who has experienced harm, loss, and suffering will benefit significantly by belonging to a body of believers and participating in the local church, even if they do not know how to relate to "normal" people, awkwardly interact with people, or have difficulties in social situations. In the community of believers, the survivor will hear and learn God's truth, be encouraged, pray for others, worship God, discover their spiritual gifts, and learn how to minister to others.

Freedom Through the Gospel

In Luke 4:18, Jesus announced He came to free the captives. The counselees who have lived bound to their past need freedom but do not know how to find it, so they turn to secular means and methodologies. The church serves as the primary space where suffering people can find liberation from the guilt, shame, and bondage of their past. This freedom is not only part of the gospel but also applies to everyday life. As the body of Christ, under His headship (Eph. 1:22–23), the church is empowered by the Spirit (1 Cor. 12:12–13) to equip the broken for holiness, something no secular system can replicate. The church represents God on earth and is specifically charged with loving God and loving our neighbors.

The Power of God's Word in Restoration

In the church, the person whose life has been shattered by tragedy, suffering, and devastation will study, memorize, and learn the Word of God, essential for developing and maintaining spiritual growth and change. Psalm 19 is a hymn of praise to God in which the psalmist declares, "The law of the Lord is perfect, restoring the soul" (7a). Robert Somerville explains, "Our souls need restoring, and the word of God is able to do just that. The word restores our broken souls by building our faith in God."[196] The church unveils God's immutable goodness (Mal. 3:6; James 1:17), correcting the sufferer's impulse to judge Him by their pain, and leads them to rest in His unchanging love through preaching and song.

Spiritual Disciplines for the Afflicted

In the church, the afflicted person will learn the spiritual disciplines, including prayer, which is talking to God about thoughts, feelings, needs, heartaches, and joys. Prayer is an essential component in the life of every Christian, demonstrating humility and dependence on God. Many people struggle with knowing how to pray, and the counselee whose life is colored by confusion and despair may not know where to begin. The counselor can suggest that they start with short prayer times and talk to God about what is on their heart. They can begin by praying something short like Psalm 117 and build up to longer prayer times, eventually adding prayers for their families, friends, church, and themselves. The goal is to make prayer a normal part of every day. Counselors can pair the counselee with a mature believer for one-on-one prayer, modeling discipleship (James 5:16). For those paralyzed by social fear, begin with low-risk tasks, such as sitting near the back during worship, and build to small group participation as trust grows.

Discipleship: The Heart of Biblical Counseling

The church is the place for discipleship. Jim Berg says discipleship is a "… relationship between two believers with a very specific spiritual goal in mind. Discipleship is helping another believer make biblical change toward Christlikeness – helping others in the sanctification process."[197] Biblical counseling is discipleship. It is a targeted form of discipleship in which one person comes alongside another in a relationship intended to provide an opportunity for exhorting one another to become more Christ-like. Each counselee will have their own goals in this process, but the biblical counselor's goal is to help them with the sanctification process of growth and change. It is in this context that the person who has experienced catastrophic and life-altering suffering will find help and healing for the emotional and spiritual problems they experience as a result of their ordeal.

Discipleship for the abused might target fear of man (Prov. 29:25), guiding them to fear God alone through Scripture memory (e.g., Isa. 41:10). When abusers lurk within, the church enacts discipline (Matt. 18:15–17), confronting sin, pursuing repentance, or removing the unrepentant, offering survivors a shield and a voice. The counselor's goal is not just comfort, but a counselee equipped to comfort others (2 Cor. 1:3–7). In the process of biblical change, the counselee can become godly and useful to Christ, no matter their past.

The Church as God's Hands and Feet

Within the community of believers, those struggling with hopelessness and shattered lives will begin to find victory over their past and hope for the future. Through corporate lament (Psalm 44), the church turns survivors' cries into worship, teaching them to trust God's justice (Deut. 32:4) over their felt abandonment. Some blame God, as if He sinned, but the church teaches His perfection (1 John 1:5), guiding survivors to lament (Psalm 13:1) and trust His sinless ways (Isa. 55:8–9) through collective worship and truth. Robert Somerville explains how necessary the body of Christ is in the life of anyone who is suffering, especially one who is suffering from feelings of depression, something commonly experienced by those who have been abused and harmed by others. He says,

> There is hope because you are part of the Body of Christ – the church. You don't have to endure this alone. The church has many important roles: to practice Christ-centered worship, to train Christians to do the work of the ministry, to reach out with the good news about Jesus Christ to the community and to the world, and to minister to one another through love. God shows up in our lives through the body of Christ when fellow believers go into action and help us in our suffering. They are His hands and feet. They help us bear our burdens.[198]

When churches falter by missing the cries of the afflicted, they fall short of their calling. Yet, even then, God redeems through a faithful remnant (Rom. 11:5), offering a community where truth restores (Psalm 19:7) and love binds up wounds (Gal. 6:2). The local church is where the disheartened person receives comfort from their pastor and friends. They hear good counsel, are consoled, and nourish their faith. The church also upholds justice, confronting sin (Matt. 18:15–17) and supporting survivors in reporting to authorities (Rom. 13:1–4), reflecting God's heart for the oppressed (Psalm 82:3–4). The church walks with survivors to God-ordained authorities, providing counsel, prayer, and presence as they seek justice, embodying Psalm 82's call to defend the weak.

Overcoming Relational Challenges in the Church

A person who has been betrayed and mistreated may find it challenging to attend church. For those seeking refuge from harm, the online church provides a sense of safety through screens, acting as a lifeline until they feel courageous enough to join in person and fully embrace the church community. The counselor can bridge the gap by inviting them to watch with a trusted friend and then ease them into the fold with care (Heb. 10:24–25).

Depending on what devastation or suffering the person has experienced, church attendance may be viewed as risky. Those who have been crushed in spirit often find relationships more challenging than anticipated. For example, they may fear relationships because they don't trust anyone. Because relationships have historically only brought pain, they might push away potential friends because they do not want to be hurt. Their longing for love and acceptance can become confused and distorted, and the strong and sometimes negative emotions make relating to anyone feel daunting. They may be highly manipulative, testing others to see if they "really" care, or hypersensitive, overly dependent, or hyper-controlling in their relationships because that is how they habitually function. Fear of rejection tempts them to do whatever it takes to avoid rejection, leading to fear of man behaviors. When they begin to take risks and join in church activities or small groups, they may frequently find themselves in conflict with others. Sue Nicewander says, "A history of disapproval, harsh treatment, and feelings of emptiness can distort our view of God's beautiful purpose for relationships, causing confusion and deep anguish."[199] A sufferer might cringe at a kind word, expecting betrayal, or lash out to test loyalty. Over time, as the church models Christ's steadfast love (John 13:34–35), their clenched fists soften, learning that relationships can reflect God's beauty, not just their past pain. Despite the difficulties of relationships, the struggling person must hear that, despite how they feel, this does not mean they are a failure.

None of these opportunities for growth and change can be corrected or conquered apart from ongoing discipleship relationships in the local church. In the context of gospel-centered relationships, the counselee will learn to address these heart issues and learn how to have God-honoring friendships and relationships with others. They will know that friendships do not have to be filled with uncertainty and fear but can be beautiful and healthy. Eventually, the overcomer can begin to mentor others who have experienced catastrophic suffering. This is 2 Corinthians 1:3–7 in action.

Sally: A Case Study in Catastrophic Suffering: Resolution

Sally entered the church trembling each week, her past casting a long shadow. Her childhood church had echoed with love while she suffered, its elders oblivious to her cries. Now, in a new congregation, she found refuge. Pastor James preached about God's perfection (1 John 1:5), helping her redirect her anger at His perceived silence. She learned to lament rather than accuse (Psalm 13:1). A deacon shared Isaiah 41:10, addressing her fear of man (Proverbs 29:25), while sisters prayed with her, their hands steadying hers.

When Sally revealed her brother Billy's crimes from years past, the church didn't flinch. A small group, including Pastor James and Abigail, walked with Sally as she contemplated reporting Billy's crimes to the police. They provided counsel and prayer and were a constant presence, encouraging Sally to seek justice. Once Sally made the decision to go forward, the elders contacted the church he still attended, the one from their childhood, and encouraged them to confront him (Matt. 18:15–17). Billy denied the accusations and made malicious comments about Sally, painting her as an unstable woman who was a deeply troubled child. He urged them not to listen to her accusations. Billy lived states away, untouchable by the hands of Sally's elders, but Sally pressed forward; her resolve steeled. A gray-haired, gentle deacon drove her to the police station (Rom. 13:1–4), his quiet prayers filling the car as she went in and filed the initial report. Throughout the months that the trial dragged on, the church walked with her, comforting, consoling, and supporting her through the grueling testimony that forced her to relive every horrific detail. Abigail and Pastor James were at her side for court dates, embodying Psalm 82's justice, and were steadfast anchors through the legal storm.

Over the months, Sally began to slowly trust and open up to those in the church who supported her through the legal ordeal. She flourished under the love she was shown, and her hesitant prayers grew bold. During one biblical counseling meeting with Abigail, Sally told her that she thought God had allowed her trials so she could help others. Shortly thereafter, she began mentoring a teen, a new arrival at the Mission house, living out 2 Corinthians 1:3–7. Sally continued to be discipled by Abigail, and their time together decreased until she no longer needed intensive biblical counseling.

As this chapter has explored, the church is crucial in supporting those who have experienced catastrophic suffering. By embracing our calling to love and support one another, we can create a safe and nurturing environment for those in need. In the concluding chapter, we will summarize the key points discussed throughout this book and offer final reflections on the hope and redemption found in Christ.

Consider and Apply

1. Have the counselee write out the areas of their life where they feel bound or captive. How can you guide them to experience the freedom Jesus proclaimed, both spiritually and practically? What specific biblical truths and promises can you share to help them find liberation from guilt, shame, and past bondage?
2. Consider your counselee's current prayer habits. How can you encourage them to start with short, simple prayers and gradually build up to longer, more intentional prayer times? What resources, such as prayer journals or Scripture-based prayer prompts, can you provide to help them deepen their communication with God?
3. Learn the specific challenges your counselee faces in building relationships within the church. How can you support them in overcoming these barriers and encourage them to engage in church activities and small groups? What practical steps can you take to help them build healthy, God-honoring relationships and find a supportive community?
4. Think about how your counselee's healing journey can be a source of comfort and encouragement to others as described in 2 Corinthians 1:3–7. How can you help them see the value of their experiences and the comfort they have received from God? What steps can you guide them through to become effective mentors, offering emotional support, spiritual guidance, and practical help to those who are going through similar struggles?

CHAPTER 15

A Call to Biblical Sufficiency in Counseling Trauma

From the outset of this book, I have voiced concern for the current state of care for those who have endured catastrophic suffering. I am deeply troubled by the medicalization of suffering and the integration of secular psychological theories into biblical counseling, approaches that minimize the power and supremacy of God's Word. This book was written to confront these issues head-on, calling us back to the sufficiency of Scripture as we minister to those who have faced horrors most of us cannot fathom. We live in an era where "trauma" is a buzzword, and more people than ever seek help for their pain. Yet, as we conclude, I pray that you—counselors and counselees alike—see the limitations of worldly wisdom and embrace the unmatched hope of a purely biblical approach. The gospel is the ultimate source of healing and redemption, addressing the root of human suffering—sin—and offering a profound transformation through Christ's redemptive work that surpasses mere coping mechanisms or psychological interventions.

The Crisis of Modern Approaches to Suffering

Throughout this book, we've examined the secular view of catastrophic suffering, often labeled as post-traumatic stress disorder (PTSD) or complex post-traumatic stress disorder (C-PTSD). The Diagnostic and Statistical Manual of Mental Disorders (DSM), a socially constructed document based on consensus rather than scientific discovery, drives this medicalization. It categorizes human suffering into disorders requiring medical intervention, reflecting prevailing social, cultural, and political climates rather than eternal truth. This narrow lens overlooks the broader spiritual and moral implications of suffering, reducing profound experiences to clinical diagnoses and pathologizing normal responses to a fallen world.

Secular methodologies, relying heavily on psychological and physiological explanations, focus on symptom relief through medication and therapy. By doing so, they fail to address the spiritual dimensions of suffering, the need for spiritual healing, and the gospel's transformative power, which can lead individuals to identify primarily through their diagnoses, such as "PTSD sufferer" or "C-PTSD victim," overshadowing their God-given identity as image-bearers with inherent worth and purpose in Christ. While these approaches may offer temporary relief, they fall short of providing lasting healing, leaving unresolved pain and brokenness without addressing the spiritual roots. Even more concerning is the rise of "trauma-informed" practices and "clinically-informed biblical counseling," which blend these flawed secular ideas with Scripture. Such integration breeds confusion, undermines trust in God's Word, and fails to deliver the whole hope of the gospel. I encourage biblical counselors to critically evaluate these methodologies and their underlying assumptions, comparing them with biblical principles to discern whether they align with or contradict Scripture. Remain steadfast in your commitment to biblical sufficiency, even when faced with the allure of secular approaches.

A Biblical Understanding of Trauma

In contrast, this book defines trauma biblically—not as a disorder, but as suffering, distress of the soul, and affliction inherent to life in a broken world. Scripture reveals God's redemptive plan for humanity, emphasizing that catastrophic suffering and trials are part of living in a fallen world but can be redeemed through Christ (Rom. 8:28–29). Our calling as biblical counselors is to help those who have experienced or witnessed something horrible, violent, shocking, or painful, addressing both the spiritual and emotional dimensions of their suffering. This holistic approach considers the whole person—body, mind, and spirit (1 Thess. 5:23)—and focuses on the heart, where thoughts, beliefs, and desires reside. True healing comes from addressing the heart and its transformation through the power of the Holy Spirit (Ezek. 36:26), not just modifying behavior.

The Bible provides a comprehensive framework for understanding and ministering to catastrophic suffering (2 Tim. 3:16–17). It calls for the renewal of the mind, encouraging individuals to align their thoughts with God's truth (Rom. 12:2), which leads to lasting change and healing. Through these pages, I have presented a model of care that redefines trauma from a biblical perspective, emphasizing a new identity in Christ—where individuals are new creations, redeemed and loved by God (2 Cor. 5:17). Scripture is sufficient for all aspects of life, including the emotional and psychological struggles tied to catastrophic suffering, offering wisdom, guidance, and hope that surpasses the limitations of secular approaches. Biblical counselors recognize that this is a calling from God. He has entrusted you with the privilege and responsibility of walking alongside those who are suffering, offering hope, and pointing them to Christ.

Living Out Biblical Sufficiency

This call to biblical sufficiency begins with you, dear counselor. Regularly pray for wisdom and discernment in your counseling ministry, asking God to guide you in applying His Word to the lives of those you counsel. Rely on the Holy Spirit to work through you, trusting He will provide the words, insights, and compassion needed to minister effectively. Reflect on your own experiences of suffering and apply the truths of Scripture to your life, for the healing power of the gospel must also transform your heart and mind as you minister to others. Approach each counselee with empathy and understanding—listen to their stories and show genuine compassion for their pain. Be a consistent and reliable presence in their lives, offering practical support and connecting them with resources in the church community to assist them as needed.

Extend your ministry beyond individual sessions. Whether you are a pastor, biblical counselor, or lay leader, be intentional about integrating these principles into your church. Let it be known in your community that your church isn't a place that *has* a biblical counseling ministry—it *is* a biblical counseling ministry—a place of refuge where the gospel is given, the broken are welcomed, and lives are changed. The church community plays a vital role in the healing process for those who have endured catastrophic suffering and loss by offering support, encouragement, and accountability. Believers are called to bear one another's burdens (Gal. 6:2), providing practical help like meals, chores, or a listening ear to show Christ's love in tangible ways. Encourage your counselees to engage with their church community, helping them build relationships with other believers who can offer additional support. Develop discipleship programs to provide ongoing care and train leaders and members through workshops and mentorship to multiply this ministry. Regularly pray for the individuals you counsel, asking God to work in their hearts, bring healing, and draw them closer to Himself. My prayer is that your church becomes a beacon of hope, fully equipped to care for those who have endured catastrophic suffering.

The Hope of Christ in Every Trial

As we close, let us fix our eyes on the profound hope and redemption found in Christ. Jesus, who bore the ultimate suffering on the cross, understands our pain and offers restoration. In Him, no suffering is wasted; every trial serves His glory and our good (Rom. 8:28). Our hardships refine our faith, draw us nearer to Him, and equip us to comfort others (2 Cor. 1:3–4). Through His death and resurrection, He has conquered sin and death, turning our wounds into testimonies of His grace. The gospel brings hope to the hopeless, assuring sufferers that their pain is not in vain and that God has a purpose for what they have endured—a hope rooted not in temporary relief but in the eternal promise of restoration and renewal in Christ (Jer. 29:11).

Offer words of hope and encouragement to those you counsel: In Christ, you are a new creation; the old has passed away, and the new has come (2 Cor. 5:17). Your past experiences do not define you; your identity is found in Christ. You are deeply loved and chosen by God, adopted as His beloved child (Eph. 1:4–5). Through Christ's sacrifice, you are redeemed and forgiven (Col. 1:13–14). It is for freedom that Christ has set you free; your past does not hold you captive (Gal. 5:1). God heals the brokenhearted and binds up their wounds (Ps. 147:3), working to restore you. Healing is a journey—be patient with yourself, trusting that God is with you every step of the way, producing hope through perseverance (Rom. 5:3–4). Keep your eyes fixed on Jesus, the author and perfecter of your faith (Heb. 12:2), your ultimate source of hope and healing. Encourage them this way, urging them to continue seeking God, trusting His promises, and participating in the church community while growing in their faith through prayer, Bible study, and worship.

Final Charge

Stand firmly and immovably on the sufficiency of Scripture. While secular methods may provide temporary relief, true healing flows from a relationship with Christ and the unchanging truth of His Word. The DSM and similar tools may label and categorize, but they cannot touch the soul as Scripture does. Keep your focus on helping counselees experience heart transformation through the gospel, not just modifying behavior. As biblical counselors, you participate in God's redemptive work, an eternal impact that brings lasting peace and transformation. Reject the confusion of integration, rely solely on the Bible, and trust the Holy Spirit to bring transformation. By remaining steadfast in biblical sufficiency and embracing the privilege and responsibility of this calling, you can offer genuine hope and guidance. Always point counselees to the hope found in the gospel—God's love, grace, and redemption through Jesus Christ. May your life, ministry, and church reflect Christ's love and power, pointing the hurting to the One who makes all things new.

A Prayer for the Journey Ahead

I leave you with this prayer. Heavenly Father, we thank You for the wisdom and guidance found in Your Word. We pray that those who have endured unimaginable suffering may find hope and healing in Christ. Equip us as biblical counselors to be vessels of Your grace, offering help, hope, and support to those in need. Grant us wisdom and discernment as we apply Your Word, and may we rely on the Holy Spirit to work through us with compassion and insight. Use us to bring Your light to a hurting world, participating in Your redemptive plan. May our lives and ministries reflect Your love and power, pointing all to the hope of the gospel. In Jesus' name, we pray. Amen

APPENDIX A

Understanding the Medical Frameworks of Trauma—An Optional Deep Dive

This appendix provides an in-depth examination of secular trauma models for those interested in their technical details. These frameworks, focused on brain and body, may contrast with Scripture's heart-centered view, but understanding them equips the biblical counselor to engage secular ideas critically.

Brain Imaging and Trauma Research

While brain imaging seeks to see trauma's effects, polyvagal theory shows how the nervous system, including the brain and autonomic responses, grounds suffering in physiology, not the soul.

Diagnosing Trauma Through Brain Imaging

Types of brain imaging include magnetic resonance imaging (MRI), which enables doctors to examine changes in the volume and structure of various brain areas. Functional MRI (fMRI) is a scan that measures and maps brain activity, including blood flow in various brain areas.

Magnetoencephalography (MEG) is a rapid, sensitive, and accurate method for measuring electrical activity in the brain.[200,201] Positron emission tomography (PET),[202,203] electroencephalography (EEG),[204,205] and functional near-infrared spectroscopy (fNIRS) [206,207] are all used to capture structural and functional images[xxvi] of the brain to differentiate normal or abnormal brain structure and functioning. The brain imaging maps made from the scans are valuable in assessing the damage from stroke, epilepsy, traumatic brain injury (TBI), or Alzheimer's disease, and the progression of tumor growth or diseases of the brain.[208] These imaging techniques are also used in hopes of revealing the physical effects of trauma and PTSD on the brain.

There is substantial evidence that fMRI is a favored brain scan among trauma researchers, particularly for studying PTSD, childhood trauma, and mild TBI, due to its high spatial resolution, non-invasiveness, and ability to map functional changes in neural circuits (e.g., amygdala-prefrontal dysregulation).[209,210,211,212,213] "fMRI is a complex process that involves biophysics, neuroanatomy, neurophysiology, and statistics (experimental design, statistical modeling, and data analysis)."[214] Scientists are under tremendous pressure to produce results from these scans because they are costly and time-intensive. Therefore, some trauma researchers are quick to

---

[xxvi] Functional changes in neuroimaging scans refer to alterations in brain activity, connectivity, metabolism, or hemodynamic responses that reflect dynamic neural processes, distinguishing normal from abnormal brain functioning. MEG and EEG capture changes in electrical/magnetic activity (e.g., neural oscillations, event-related potentials), PET measures metabolic and neurochemical shifts (e.g., glucose uptake), fNIRS tracks cortical hemodynamic changes (e.g., blood oxygenation), and CT, primarily structural, assesses functional changes indirectly via perfusion (e.g., cerebral blood flow). These changes highlight physiological dysfunction in conditions like epilepsy, traumatic brain injury, or psychiatric disorders, providing insights into brain function beyond structural abnormalities.

Soroosh Afyouni, Stephen M. Smith, and Thomas E. Nichols, "Exploring the Frontiers of Neuroimaging: A Review of Recent Advances in Understanding Brain Functioning and Disorders," Brain Sciences 13, no. 4 (2023): 587, https://doi.org/10.3390/brainsci13040587.

Taha N. Alotaiby, Fatmah A. Alsubaie, Zainab A. Aljumaiah, Abdulmajeed A. Alrubian, and Saleh A. Alshebeili, "Electroencephalography Signal Processing: A Comprehensive Review and Analysis of Methods and Techniques," Sensors 23, no. 14 (2023): 6434, https://doi.org/10.3390/s23146434.

Lars Farde, "Imaging the Living Human Brain: Magnetic Resonance Imaging and Positron Emission Tomography," Proceedings of the National Academy of Sciences 94, no. 7 (1997): 2787–2788, https://doi.org/10.1073/pnas.94.7.2787.

Ki-Sueng Hong, Muhammad Jawad Khan, and Noman Naseer, "Functional Near-Infrared Spectroscopy and Its Clinical Application in the Field of Neuroscience: Advances and Future Directions," Frontiers in Neuroscience 14 (2020): 724, https://doi.org/10.3389/fnins.2020.00724.

Jian Zhang, Gianna Raffa, Zhimin Liang, Gabriel Garcia, Ali A. Asadi-Pooya, and Xiaohua Hu, "Magnetoencephalography in the Detection and Characterization of Brain Abnormalities Associated with Traumatic Brain Injury: A Comprehensive Review," Diagnostics 11, no. 9 (2021): 1628, https://doi.org/10.3390/diagnostics11091628

tout the images of the PTSD or trauma-affected brain compared to a normal brain. Some say there is abundant evidence for changes in the structure and function of different areas of the brain involved in fear response and anxiety.[215]

Others are more skeptical, citing sample sizes that are too small to capture reproducible brain–behavioral phenotype associations, low replicability of results, the introduction of bias into the research by clinicians, the inclusion of cross-sectional studies, and difficulties with data interpretation. Additionally, the scans generate massive amounts of data that can only be understood by custom computer programs. However, flaws in the program's software have produced images that suggest differences in brain activity where none exist. [216,217,218,219] There is even one well-known study in which the researchers did an fMRI scan on a dead Atlantic Salmon, and it lit up "as if it were somehow still dreaming of a spawning run." [220,221] The fMRI scan produced false-positive brain activity due to improper statistical thresholds, illustrating challenges in neuroimaging reliability.

A critical review of the research reveals that just because various "experts" proclaim their theories as fact does not make them factual. For example, McNally claims that while MRI studies show that "the stress aspect of PTSD is consistent with hippocampal atrophy, other facts strongly argue against this interpretation."[222] Researchers Quosh and Gergen state that there are problems with identifying the psychobiologic mechanisms of PTSD. They say,

> Even if most patients with a PTSD diagnosis shared a distinctive pattern of cortical functioning, there would be no grounds for concluding that PTSD has a neural basis. The diagnostic category is a cultural construction, and the very same "symptoms" could be constructed in numerous other ways. We might view the same population as "striving to cope," "highly alert," "multiply concerned," "intensively hopeful," or "ontologically insecure," or even "spiritually in need."[223]

Dr. Eaton Fores states,

> If the argument is: mental state *x* can be shown to have a physiological substrate, therefore it is pathological, the response is obvious. *All* mental states, without exception, have neurochemical substrates. This proves exactly nothing. No doubt there are neurochemical differences between conservatives and liberals, too. Who, however, is to decide which state is pathological?[224]

While brain imaging seeks to visualize trauma's impact, polyvagal theory explains how the brain and nervous system react, both rooting suffering in physiology rather than the soul, a premise Scripture reorients toward the heart's spiritual needs.

Linking the Brain to The Polyvagal Theory: Nervous System Basics

To help us understand the polyvagal theory and evaluate its implications for trauma, we must take a brief detour into territory that is likely unfamiliar to many of us: neurology and biopsychiatry. While I am not an expert in either field and don't pretend to be, my research has yielded a rich harvest of information critical to understanding PVT.

We must explore the biological framework it relies on, mainly how the body and brain interact in response to stress and fear. At the heart of PVT is the idea that the nervous system, specifically the vagus nerve and its connections to the brain, plays a key role in how humans respond to trauma, whether through fight, flight, freeze, or social engagement. This brings us to the central nervous system (CNS), which is foundational to understanding these processes. The central nervous system (CNS), comprising the brain and spinal cord, is an extensively studied bodily system, but we still don't know why some brains react differently to stress and trauma. Despite all the advances in modern medicine, researchers have noted that we know more about the universe than we do about the human brain. However, we must take a deeper look at the brain to help us understand the foundations of trauma-informed care and its rationale.

Simply stated, the brain is a complex organ that serves as the body's central processing and control center. It receives, sends, and combines chemical and electronic signals from the entire body and coordinates the whole body's movements, functions, and activities.[225,226,227] The brain is comprised of several key regions. The cerebrum, which is the largest part, is divided into two hemispheres. Covering the cerebrum is the cerebral cortex, the outermost layer responsible for higher cognitive functions, including reasoning, memory, language, and emotional regulation. The cortex has four lobes: the frontal lobe, key for planning and managing emotions, like controlling impulses; the parietal lobe, which handles sensory information like touch; the temporal lobe, important for memory and processing emotions; and the occipital lobe, for visual processing. Other brain areas, like the amygdala deep in the temporal lobe, also play a major role in emotions, such as reacting to fear.[228,229,230,231]

Deep within the temporal lobe, we find the amygdala. The amygdala is a pair of almond-shaped collections of nuclei located one in each brain hemisphere. They are considered part of the limbic system, which describes a group of brain structures surrounding the brain stem. The amygdala plays an essential role in processing emotions. While it was initially thought of as the "threat detector" and the initiator of the body's "fight-or-flight" response, its total functions are not fully understood.[232]

For our purposes, some researchers theorize that when a person has PTSD and perceives a threat at hand, the amygdala automatically becomes hyperactive or is "hijacked" and overrules the frontal lobe's logical thought processes, leading to irrational responses often out of proportion to an actual threat. Such statements imply causal mechanisms that have not yet been empirically tested.

Some people who have experienced complex trauma are said to be stuck in a loop of "amygdala hijacking," leading to ongoing reactivity, hypervigilance, impulsiveness, and unsettled feelings.[233,234] According to Scheeringa, this is nonsensical. He says, "To claim that a brain center, such as the amygdala, can be rewired by one life experience, or even dozens of experiences of psychological stress, is to discuss the hard structure of the brain at a comic book level of simplicity."[235] Additionally, the claim is that *only* the portion of the brain that controls emotional functions is hijacked, which is also false. There are numerous redundancies built into our brain centers that provide multiple pathways for communication. Finally, Scheeringa points out that this theory is more ideological than scientific. He asks, "If the amygdala gets rewired, why doesn't the cerebellum get rewired, and you forget how to walk? Your perception of danger is altered but not your perception of balance? Why doesn't trauma affect the areas that control your ability to read and speak?"[236] After analyzing the studies related to this claim, he concludes that trauma does not rewire the amygdala.

The hippocampus is also located in the temporal lobe and is part of the limbic system. It is your brain's memory center, much like a hard drive. It helps us make sense of events as we process memories and is believed to play a role in our ability to overcome fear responses. Trauma researchers theorize that in a person diagnosed with PTSD, the traumatic memories are not correctly "written" to the hippocampus; therefore, the trauma survivor can't always remember details, and there are often gaps in the timeline of traumatic events. Conversely, the person may be able to recall very vivid memories of what happened to them.[237,238,239]

Another area of the brain we need to examine is the medulla oblongata, also known as the medulla. The medulla is the lowest part of the brainstem where your brain connects to the spinal cord. Within the medulla is the nucleus ambiguus, a large group of neurons that mainly control swallowing and speech. Important to PVT, the nucleus ambiguus plays a role in parasympathetic cardiac inhibition through the 10th cranial nerve, which we will examine in greater detail shortly.[240] The neurons comprising the nucleus ambiguus are also proposed by Porges to control what he calls the social engagement system, which includes facial expressions, speech, and listening and is one of the risk responses in the PVT.[241]

The spinal cord carries nerve signals throughout the body that report essential information about sensations such as pain and hunger to the brain. It also carries signals to your body parts that control movement, reflexes, and involuntary functions, such as breathing and organ function. Thirty-one spinal nerves enter the cord where the spinal cord and brain meet at the brainstem.[242] In addition, twelve paired cranial nerves emerge from the brainstem at the base of the skull. These nerves are considered part of the peripheral nervous system (PNS), the second major division of the CNS. These nerves run throughout the body and carry messages to and from the brain and spinal cord.[243,244]

The 10th cranial nerve is commonly referred to as the vagus nerve. The vagus nerve, meaning "wandering" in Latin, is very long, resembling a thick cable or cord housing with thousands of fibers. It originates in the brain stem and ends in the colon. It is the body's main parasympathetic nerve, and an estimated three-quarters of all parasympathetic nerve fibers come from the 10th cranial nerve. Its fibers are organized into two bundles running down the neck's right and left sides.[245,246] An oversimplified explanation for how it functions is that some fibers send sensory information from the brain to the body via the peripheral nervous system, and other fibers send information from the body's organs to the brain by that same method.

The peripheral nervous system comprises two main subdivisions: the somatic nervous system (SNS) is associated with voluntary movements, such as turning the page of a book, and the autonomic nervous system (ANS) controls involuntary processes outside of conscious control, including digestion, breathing, and heartbeat. Additionally, the ANS regulates homeostasis, which maintains equilibrium within the body's systems.

The traditional view of the ANS is that it is divided into two parts. One is the sympathetic nervous system (SNS), named by the Second-Century Roman physician Galen. He taught that "the body has animal spirits that would be distributed in the body by tubes (peripheral nerves) that would enable concerted, coordinated (i.e., sympathetic) functioning of body organs."[247,248] van der Kolk notes that Galen observed that this system functioned with emotions (*sym pathos)*.[249] The nerves of the SNS are myelinated for fast transmission of data. Myelination is a lipid sheath that wraps around nerves to protect and speed up the transmission of signals.

The SNS is the "gas pedal." It prepares the body for quick reactions to stressful or scary events by triggering the pituitary and adrenal glands to excrete catecholamines, which include adrenaline, noradrenaline, and cortisol, which increases heart rate, respiration, and blood pressure.[250] We understand this as the "fight-or-flight" response.[251,252]

The other side of the ANS is the parasympathetic nervous system (PNS). The PNS is the "brake." It is responsible for slowing down the heart rate and respiration and calms the body by releasing the acetylcholine hormone, which slows the heart rate after a threat has passed.[253] This system, known as the "rest and digest" system, regulates body functions when we are calm and at rest.[254] The PNS nerves are *unmyelinated* and transmit signals more slowly than the myelinated nerves. To be clear, these are oversimplified descriptions that don't take into account the full range of activities undertaken by these two systems of the body. Still, they will suffice to help us understand PVT.

Core Components of the Polyvagal Theory: The Vagus Nerve and Behavioral Responses

Porges says belief in only the sympathetic and parasympathetic systems is "a very naive and simplistic model." He adds a third system, which he calls "the social engagement system."[255] PVT links the evolution of the mammalian autonomic nervous system, specifically the vagus nerve, to emotional regulation, social behavior, and fear responses. He wants us to think of them as neural circuits that respond to stress and trauma, follow an evolutionary hierarchy, and are triggered in order when a person is presented with a potential threat. [256,257]

The polyvagal theory, while an evolutionary framework, presents a rather grim view of human behavior by attributing it mainly to the autonomic nervous system's responses. Instead of highlighting the mind's role, it focuses heavily on the body's mechanisms, suggesting that physiological states drive our actions more than conscious thought. This bio-physiological perspective might seem to reduce the complexity of human behavior to mere bodily reactions, overshadowing the influence of the mind and psychological factors. According to van der Kolk, "The Polyvagal Theory provided us with a more sophisticated understanding of the biology of safety and danger."[258] According to PVT, a neural process operates below our level of awareness and continually scans our environment for safety cues and potential dangers. Porges says this differs from perception and coined the term *neuroception* to describe the process.[259,260] He says, "Neuroception happens before perception.

Neuroception is automatic and happens prior to any conscious awareness."[261] He also states, "Neuroception – our nervous system's risk evaluation – is functionally unpredictable (and it happens without our awareness). We don't know how our nervous system will respond."[262] Either the parasympathetic or sympathetic system will be triggered based on the signals the dorsal vagus nerve receives, indicating whether the individual is safe or in danger. While Porges has given it a new name, what he calls neuroception appears to be what others refer to as "threat detection." The concept of threat detection is not new, but it has been well-researched.[263,264]

Porges divides the vagus nerve and its evolutionary development into two distinct branches, the "dorsal vagus complex" of the parasympathetic system and the "ventral vagus complex." These are terms unique to Porges. The "ventral vagal complex" are myelinated nerves originating in the brain's nucleus ambiguus.[265] The ventral vagal complex regulates bodily functions above the diaphragm, including the heart, lungs, and facial muscles.[xxvii] Porges considers the ventral vagus system the "smart vagus" and the origin of what he calls "the social engagement system." Theoretically, this system can activate and calm the nervous system in milliseconds to adjust quickly to a situation based on neuroception. He claims the ventral vagal complex is unique to mammals and is our most recent evolutionary addition.[266] However, other evolutionary biologists disagree and have found these neurons in various non-mammalian species, most notably various fish and reptiles.[267]

The dorsal vagal complex is said to regulate organs below the diaphragm, including the stomach, kidneys, liver, pancreas, and gallbladder.[268,269,270] PVT views this branch as the "vegetative vagus." It is rooted in the ancient reptilian system that controls what we call "rest and digest" and triggers the defensive systems of immobilization ("freeze") and shutdown.[271] He says the key to PVT is understanding the importance of the social engagement system, which is supposedly mediated by the myelinated, above-the-diaphragm branch of the ventral vagus complex's vagus nerve. PVT theoretically explains how what is happening in the body (the physiological state) influences behavior and emotional states, thus, a person's ability to interact with others.

Other key components of PVT are said to be Heart Rate Variability (HRV) and Respiratory Sinus Arrhythmia (RSA). RSA refers to the natural variation in your heart rate that occurs during a breathing cycle. When you inhale, your

---

[xxvii] Porges links cardiac functioning to PVT, specifically linking respiratory sinus arrhythmia (RSA) and trauma response. I refer you to the work of Dr. Paul Grossman in which he explains why specifically Premises One and Two of PVT are false. https://www.researchgate.net/post/After-20-years-of-polyvagal-hypotheses-is-there-any-direct-evidence-for-the-first-3-premises-that-form-the-foundation-of-the-polyvagal-conjectures.

heart rate increases; when you exhale, it decreases, reflecting the parasympathetic nervous system's influence on the heart via the vagus nerve. RSA is often used to indicate parasympathetic nervous system activity and is considered a marker of the body's ability to adapt to stress. Heart Rate Variability (HRV) is the variation in time between heartbeats, which the autonomic nervous system regulates. Having a high HRV is generally considered to indicate a balance between the sympathetic and parasympathetic branches of the autonomic nervous system. HRV and RSA are considered signs of resilience, meaning the person can more quickly adapt to changes and recover from stressors. A resilient person is considered better able to manage their emotions, even in the face of significant stress.

While Porges's theory is currently the basis for understanding trauma and its effects on human physiology, PVT is not universally accepted. There are several problems with Porges's claims besides what I have already cited. First, while he describes the social engagement system, he never clearly defines it. Secondly, no scientific evidence exists to support the notion that the ventral vagus is crucial for "social engagement."[272] While the nerves above the diaphragm are involved in vocalizing, breathing, and swallowing, there is no evidence that they contribute to social interaction. Thirdly, these processes are far too complex to be handled by a few neurons in the nucleus ambiguus, as Porges claims they are. Fourthly, there is no supporting scientific evidence for PVT that other evolutionary biologists and neuroscientists have not debunked. One critic stated, "PVT does not fulfill the most basic scientific requirements (clarity, testable claims, empirical evidence, due credit to others' contributions), ignores or dismisses contrary evidence."[273] Finally, Dr. Paul Grossman, a cardiovascular autonomic psychophysiologist, has studied and repeatedly refuted Porges's Polyvagal Theory over the past 35 years. It is not my intent to be an apologist for Grossman or the numerous other evolutionary scientists and biologists who have studied all the aspects of PVT and consider it "lacking evidence," "fallacious," and Porges himself as "the purveyor of false information." Still, it is notable that those within his own camp do not endorse his theory.

Evidence-Based Treatments in Trauma-Informed Care

While imaging and PVT explore trauma's causes, these treatments apply those ideas, aiming to heal through secular methods, yet all share a focus on the body and mind over the soul. Under the TIC model, the treatment of specific mental health symptoms and syndromes strongly recommends what are called "evidence-based treatment options," which are therapeutic and sometimes pharmacological approaches." The therapy is typically based on one or more theories of psychological treatment, the most prominent being behavioral, cognitive, and psychodynamic.

The evidence-based treatment options are focused on aspects of post-traumatic stress disorder (PTSD) as part of a trauma-informed care approach. Researchers Ghafoori and Taylor found that although many treatments for traumatic stress and PTSD have been developed, "...no trauma-focused evidence-based therapy has been investigated in a sample of individuals who have experienced sex trafficking."[xxviii]

Cognitive-behavioral therapy (CBT) is based on "the cognitive model of emotional response"[274] and is utilized for people with PTSD. CBT "focuses on the relationship among thoughts, feelings, and behaviors; targets current problems and symptoms; and focuses on changing patterns of behaviors, thoughts, and feelings that lead to difficulties in functioning."[275] CBT "...combines cognitive therapy with behavioral interventions such as exposure therapy, thought stopping, or breathing techniques."[276] CBT helps people reduce the emotional impact of trauma by addressing the connections they form between safe reminders of their trauma and intense fear responses. It also assists individuals in reshaping negative beliefs about themselves and others and their sense of control that frequently develops as they attempt to make sense of their traumatic experiences. By focusing on these areas, CBT decreases avoidance behaviors and alleviates the emotional distress triggered by trauma-related cues. [277]

Cognitive processing therapy (CPT) is a type of cognitive-behavioral therapy found to be effective in treating post-traumatic stress disorder (PTSD).[278] This treatment "focuses initially on the question of why the trauma occurred and then the effects of the trauma on the clients' beliefs about themselves, others, and the world through the use of progressive worksheets." This therapeutic approach is often used with rape victims.[279]

Researchers Salami, Gordon, Coverdale, et al. state:

> Cognitive restructuring techniques are used to change maladaptive, hopeless thoughts regarding the self, the world, and the future. Available evidence favors CPT for victims of human trafficking. Cognitive therapies may be more effective in addressing the strong

---

[xxviii] Clawson, Salomon, & Grace, "Treating the Hidden Wounds," In, *Evidence-Based Mental Health Treatment for Victims of Human Trafficking,* 4. Due to the relatively new development of anti-human trafficking activities and initiatives and the recent recognition of the phenomenon of human trafficking in the field of mental health, there is little evidence-based research on the treatment of victims of human trafficking; yet experts in the field of human trafficking advocate for treatment approaches that embrace a trauma-informed-care model.

> feelings of guilt and shame experienced by survivors. The CPT approach proceeds more slowly and with less exposure to traumatic reminders, which may help keep survivors in therapy.[280]

Prolonged exposure therapy (PET) is a form of cognitive-behavioral therapy. It is a trauma-focused approach that was first developed for use with combat military veterans who had experienced extreme trauma on the battlefield.[281]

PET "...aims to reduce anxiety and fear through the confrontation of thoughts or actual situations related to the trauma the victim has experienced" to help the client fully process their traumatic experiences.[282] To the best of their knowledge, the client constructs a personal narrative of the event(s). They will reportedly experience uncomfortable feelings and emotions in PET; therefore, this therapy is not appropriate if the client is suicidal or homicidal.[283] To assist the client in coping with their emotional response to therapy, they will learn distraction methods, relaxation techniques, tactical breathing, and other complementary treatment processes.[284] The client is to recall and verbalize the trauma. The therapist asks them to repeat and clarify the story. As they do, the therapist asks them to focus on sights, sounds, smells, tastes, and tactile sensations associated with the trauma. For many victims, this is the first time the traumatic events have been discussed in detail. The therapist has them repeat the story until they are sure they are not omitting anything. As part of the therapy, the client is instructed to record their story and listen to it for 90 minutes daily, without distractions, until the next session. This process is repeated weekly until the client can verbalize the trauma without experiencing the emotions attached to the event(s).[285]

Stress inoculation therapy (SIT) is another form of CBT that combines psycho-education with anxiety management techniques such as relaxation training, breathing retraining, and thought-stopping, which are all treatments currently in use with sex trafficking victims.[286]

Narrative exposure therapy (NET) is effective in diverse populations that have experienced chronic and complex traumas.[287] In NET, an individual is taken through their entire autobiography via a timeline of events. The therapist guides the client through the trauma in a directive manner and helps them explore the traumatic events they experienced in detail and chronologically. Proponents of NET are careful to explain that exposure to traumatic events is different from reliving them, as they would in CBT and other therapeutic approaches for treating PTSD. The therapist provides the client with a transcribed, detailed account of their autobiography at the end of therapy to bear witness to the client's story and help them to speak in detail about the traumatic events in their life.[288]

Eye Movement Desensitization and Reprocessing (EMDR) "…combines general clinical practice with brief imaginal exposure and cognitive restructuring (rapid eye movement is induced during the imaginal exposure and cognitive restructuring phases)."[289] During an EMDR session, the client recalls a traumatic memory or thought and is asked to hold on to it while following the therapist's hand with their eyes as it moves back and forth over the client's field of vision (bilateral stimulation) or while listening to alternating sounds or tapping on the shoulders, knees, or hands, on alternate sides of the body. The client is also instructed to be aware of their physical responses to the memory. During bilateral stimulation, the therapist helps the client replace negative beliefs associated with trauma with positive ones and guides the client in noting any residual tension or discomfort that may arise during the process. EMDR is theorized to help the brain reprocess traumatic memories, thereby reducing their emotional impact. Because it is not clear how EMDR works, it is somewhat controversial in the therapeutic community.[290]

These various forms of therapy are currently used to help victims of sex trafficking, and yet other trauma experts claim it is not beneficial for a victim to have to relive their story to process it. The goal is for the victim to learn how to live in the present moment, regulate their brain processes away from hyperarousal and dissociation caused by fear, and teach them to live in the moment.[291] Trauma expert Vickie Peterson says:

> It is possible (and likely) that someone suffering from the effects of complex trauma is feeling anxious and depressed, in addition to other emotions, but there is a difference to the root cause. Many effective strategies that treat anxiety and depression don't work for trauma survivors. Meditation and mindfulness techniques that make one more aware of their environment sometimes can produce an opposite effect on a trauma survivor. Trauma survivors often don't need more awareness. They need to feel safe and secure in spite of what their awareness is telling them.[292]

Other recommended evidence-based secular treatments for trauma include functional family therapy (FFT), in which the therapist works to create a solid therapeutic alliance with the family. The therapist provides psychoeducation about trauma and introduces skills to interrupt negative family patterns and promote positive interactions. These skills are tailored to the family's unique needs and may include communication techniques, parenting skills, affect regulation, and conflict management. The therapist assists the family members in the healing process as well as understanding behaviors resulting from the effects of trauma.[293]

Assertive community treatment (ACT) involves a team of professionals, including psychiatrists, social workers, nurses, and substance use specialists, who work together to provide highly personalized, holistic care in the community and often in the client's home. ACT integrates various services, with plans tailored to each client's specific needs and goals, including mental health treatment, substance use treatment, housing support, and vocational assistance.[294]

Dialectical behavior therapy (DBT), developed initially to treat individuals who were highly suicidal, combines individual therapy, group skills training, and phone coaching to ensure comprehensive support for applying DBT skills in daily life.[295] There are four skills modules: mindfulness, distress tolerance, emotion regulation, and interpersonal effectiveness. DBT teaches mindfulness skills to help individuals stay present and grounded, which can reduce the impact of trauma-related triggers and help individuals manage distressing thoughts and emotions. Distress tolerance shows clients how not to make things worse in distress by using self-soothing and distraction to cope with challenging moments. Emotion regulation digs into understanding how emotions work, which helps clients improve their emotional well-being and navigate life's challenges more effectively. Interpersonal effectiveness gives tools to handle relationships, letting clients deal with trauma's fallout by managing interactions and setting limits.[296]

TIC also recognizes the use of pharmacological interventions (psychoactive medications) when they support recovery. The use of psychotropic medications such as sertraline, paroxetine, fluoxetine, and venlafaxine has received conditional recommendations for adults as a viable treatment option for PTSD according to the 2017 APA guidelines. Their conditional status implies they're considered when trauma-focused therapy alone falls short or when severe symptoms like anxiety, depression, or sleep issues significantly impair daily life. They may also be offered if a patient prefers pharmacological aid alongside or instead of therapy.[297] In practice, these meds serve as a supplementary tool, addressing specific symptoms to bolster overall recovery within a trauma-informed approach.

Recently, unconventional treatments, such as LSD, psilocybin, and MDMA (Ecstasy), are being researched and implemented with various therapies targeting PTSD via research studies.[298,299,300]All of these drugs are Schedule I psychedelics, meaning they are considered highly dangerous drugs with a high potential for abuse and no accepted medical benefit. All three have shown some positive results in research studies.[301] However, there are numerous concerns about the validity of the data from the studies, such as the design of the trials and the integrity of the data, which is in question due to the inadvertent unblinding of subjects. In the case of MDMA, the FDA has concerns about alleged ethical misconduct by the drug's sponsor, Lykos Therapeutics.[302] The FDA has also raised concerns about the potential abuse of these drugs, all of which are highly addictive. [303] Additionally, there are questions regarding the potential underreporting of adverse events involving the drugs, such as psychosis, anxiety, paranoia, depression, and cognitive impairment. There are also significant concerns about the impact of the drugs on the subject's health on a short-term basis and over the long term, as there is insufficient data regarding how they will affect the subject.

Ketamine infusions are also in the research phase for those labeled with PTSD. Ketamine is correctly used as an anesthetic for various medical procedures. It is a Schedule III drug, along with other drugs like Buprenorphine for the treatment of opioid addiction, Tylenol with Codeine, and anabolic steroids. It is considered to have a low risk of physical dependence leading to withdrawal; however, users can develop a craving for the euphoria it provides, contributing to tolerance and the need for increasing doses to achieve the same effects. It induces hallucinogenic effects, a trance-like state, sedation, amnesia, and pain relief. Research studies reveal that when used as a treatment for PTSD and C-PTSD, ketamine, delivered via IV infusion, causes rapid onset of effects and reduces symptoms within hours. Initial research shows that combined with CBT, ketamine infusion leads to more significant and sustained improvements in sufferers of PTSD. However, more research is needed to understand the risks, benefits, and complications fully.

Several limitations and challenges regarding the research must be considered, including relatively small sample sizes of 5 to 235 participants, which are susceptible to outliers and will not provide reliable data. Such small sample sizes can yield false negatives or false positives, and findings that may only apply to the studied group and not to a larger population.[304]

Other alternative therapies, such as trauma-sensitive yoga and acupuncture to reduce feelings of stress and anxiety, are being incorporated along with virtual reality exposure therapy (VRET). Some who consider themselves "progressive biblical counselors" also advocate and integrate TIC methodologies and DSM constructs into their counseling ministries. Others offer services such as micro-current neurofeedback therapy, cupping therapy, and emotional freedom therapy under the guise of "holistic biblical counseling."

Can a biblical counselor support and endorse these treatments for the distress of the soul? While TIC methodologies may not be harmful, are they beneficial? Sufferers who undergo psychological treatment are inundated with the secular view of man. None of these interventions properly diagnose the human condition, and all fail to view the problem or the counselee from a biblical perspective. The focus is on symptom relief, modifying behavior, and providing coping skills to manage stress and anxiety resulting from the extreme suffering, tragedy, or devastating events the person has endured.

What secular integrated therapies miss is that these are spiritual issues that require biblical solutions. Supporting or endorsing these treatments suggests that Scripture is insufficient for counseling and that secular methods are necessary for helping wounded people. Secular counseling, such as clinically-informed counseling (CIC), is based on theories and therapies that assume behaviors and emotions can be understood and treated through psychological methods without reference to God, sin, or the spiritual condition of the sufferer's soul. While some treatment methods embrace "spirituality," their goal is more to have the essence of morality without Deity. As such, there is no application of the Bible's solution to the problems, no direction toward spiritual renewal by the power of the Holy Spirit, and no focus on the Scriptural teaching for responding to the distress of the soul that follows catastrophic suffering.

Those who embrace integrated methodologies, such as those used in so-called clinically-informed biblical counseling (CIBC), attempt to blend humanistic theories with biblical truth. Endorsing these treatments would compromise the purity of biblical counseling by integrating incompatible worldviews. Dressing up or reframing secular techniques like mindfulness, EMDR, and various cognitive therapies with Scripture does not fundamentally alter the foundation of these therapies, which are psychological in nature. The reliance on secular psychological theories and evidence-based treatments suggests that human wisdom and clinical methods can effectively address the needs of the soul. It presents them as a necessary augmentation to the ministry of the Holy Spirit.

In contrast, biblical counseling offers a complete framework for understanding and addressing affliction, suffering, and God's redemptive purposes through the Word of God. Distress of the soul is fundamentally a spiritual issue that requires biblical solutions.

Brain imaging, polyvagal theory, and TIC treatments reveal a secular quest to map, explain, and mend trauma through the body and mind. However, as this appendix shows, their foundations— scientism and a materialist worldview—fall short of the soul's cry for redemption. For sufferers like Sally, these offer symptom relief but not eternal hope. Biblical counseling, rooted in Scripture's sufficiency (2 Tim. 3:16–17), views suffering as a whole-person experience—encompassing both body and soul—and offers Christ's transformative peace (John 16:33). Understanding these frameworks sharpens our witness, pointing the broken not to scans or therapies, but to the Savior who heals.

Endnotes

Introduction

1 David A. C. Powlison, "Crucial Issues in Contemporary Biblical Counseling," ed. Jay E. Adams, The Journal of Pastoral Practice 9, no. 3 (1988): 54.

2 Michael Scheeringa, The Trouble with Trauma: The Search to Discover How Beliefs Become Facts (Las Vegas: Central Recovery Press, 2021), 10.

Chapter One: The Fall of Mankind and the Roots of Suffering

3 John MacArthur, The MacArthur Bible Commentary (Nashville, TN: Thomas Nelson, 2005), 17.

4 Zondervan, The Zondervan NIV Bible Commentary: Volume 1: Old Testament, ed. F.F. Bruce (Grand Rapids: Zondervan Publishing House, 1994), 10-11; Barnes, Calvin, Clarke, et.al. "The Ultimate Commentary in Genesis," Chapter 3.

5 MacArthur, The MacArthur Bible Commentary, 17.

6 Timothy Juhnke, "Doctrines of Grace: Irresistible Grace," MP3 sermon, Faith Community Church, April 7, 2019, https://www.sermonaudio.com/sermoninfo.asp?SID=481920433192, accessed April 10, 2019.

7 MacArthur, The MacArthur Bible Commentary, 16.

8 Victor P. Hamilton, The Book of Genesis: Chapters 1–17, New International Commentary on the Old Testament (Grand Rapids: Wm. B. Eerdmans Publishing Co., 1990), 91.

9 Jan Grimell, "Contemporary Insights from Biblical Combat Veterans through the Lenses of Moral Injury and Post-Traumatic Stress Disorder,"

Journal of Pastoral Care & Counseling; JPCC 72, no. 4 (2018): 241–250, https://doi.org/10.1177/1542305018790218.

Chapter Two: Trauma and the Medicalization of Suffering

10 Laura K. Jones and Judith L. Cureton, "Trauma Redefined in the DSM-5: Rationale and Implications for Counseling Practice," The Professional Counselor 4, no. 3 (2014):257–71

11 "Trauma," Merriam-Webster (2022), https://www.merriam-webster.com/dictionary/trauma.

12 Substance Abuse and Mental Health Services Administration, Practical Guide for Implementing a Trauma-Informed Approach, (Rockville, MD: National Mental Health and Substance Abuse Policy Laboratory, 2023, vii; Substance Abuse and Mental Health Services Administration SAMHSA's Concept of Trauma and Guidance for a Trauma-Informed Approach (Rockville, MD: Substance Abuse and Mental Health Services Administration, 2014), 7–9.

13 Susan P. Robbins, "From the Editor—The DSM-5 and Its Role in Social Work Assessment and Research," Journal of Social Work Education 50, no. 2 (2014): 201–205, https://doi.org/10.1080/10437797.2014.885363, accessed April 13, 2023.

14 Lisa Fritscher, "Advantages and Disadvantages of the Diagnostic Statistical Manual," Verywell Mind, updated January 17, 2023, https://www.verywellmind.com/dsm-friend-or-foe-2671930 , accessed October 31, 2024.

15 Council for Evidence-Based Psychiatry. "Diagnostic System Lacks Validity." CEP, March 15, 2014. http://cepuk.org/unrecognised-facts/diagnostic-system-lacks-validity/, quoted in Jenn Chen, Biblical Counseling and Mental Disorder Diagnosis (Wapwallopen, PA: Shepherd Press, 2024), 42–43.

16 American Psychiatric Association, "Post-Traumatic Stress Disorder," in Diagnostic and Statistical Manual of Mental Disorders, 5th ed. (Arlington, VA: American Psychiatric Association Publishing, 2013), 271–278, https://doi.org/10.1176/appi.books.9780890425596;

17 Jennifer Erin Beste, God and the Victim: Traumatic Intrusion on Grace and Freedom (New York: Oxford University Press, 2007), 5.

18 Paul B. Armstrong, "Phenomenology," in The Johns Hopkins Guide for Literary Theory and Criticism, 2nd ed. (Baltimore: John Hopkins

University Press, 2005), http://litguide.press.jhu.edu/ , accessed October 27, 2022.

19 Justin Holcomb and Lindsay Holcomb, Rid of My Disgrace: Hope and Healing for Victims of Sexual Assault (Wheaton, IL: Crossway, 2011), 40.

20 Jon G. Allen, Coping With Trauma: A Guide To Self-Understanding (Washington, DC: American Psychiatric Press, 1995), 14.

21 Lillian Wilde, "Trauma Across Cultures: Cultural Dimensions of the Phenomenology of Post-Traumatic Experiences." Phenomenology and Mind 18 (2020). Published online May 1, 2022. http://journals.openedition.org/phenomenology/1609, accessed October 27, 2022.

22 Jennifer Bisram, "Migrants in New York City Shelters Falling Victim to Human Trafficking." CBS New York, February 23, 2024, https://www.cbsnews.com/newyork/news/nyc-migrants-asylum-seekers-human-trafficking-sex-trafficking/. Accessed November 13, 2024.

23 Matthew Reher, "Biblical Counseling and Memory" (paper presented at the ACBC 2024 Colloquium Essays, Neuroscience, the Body, and Biblical Counseling, Midwestern Baptist Theological Seminary, Kansas City, MO. July 18–19, 2024).

24 Lara B. Gerassi and Andrea J. Nichols, Sex Trafficking and Commercial Sexual Exploitation: Prevention, Advocacy, and Trauma-Informed Practice (New York: Springer Publishing Company, 2018), 15.

25 R. Harrington, (The "Railway Spine" Diagnosis and Victorian Responses to PTSD," Journal of Psychosomatic Research 40, no.1 (1996): 11–14, https://doi.org/10.1016/0022-3999(95)00514-5

26 R.J. McNally, "Progress and Controversy in the Study of Post-Traumatic Stress Disorder," Annual Review of Psychology 54 (2003): 229–252, https://www.ncbi.nlm.nih.gov/pmc/articles/PMC3141586/, accessed October 21, 2022.

27 Ibid., 229–252

28 Lillian Wilde, "Trauma Across Cultures: Cultural Dimensions of the Phenomenology of Post-Traumatic Experiences." Phenomenology and Mind 18 (2020). Published online May 1, 2022. http://journals.openedition.org/phenomenology/1609, accessed December 22, 2024.

29 Herb Kutchins and Stuart A. Kirk, Making Us Crazy: DSM: The Psychiatric Bible and the Creation of Mental Disorders (New York: Free Press, 1997), 22–25.

30 Curtis Solomon, I Have PTSD: Reorienting after Trauma (Wheaton, IL: New Growth Press, 2023), 22.

31 Substance Abuse and Mental Health Services Administration. 2015. Quick Guide for Clinicians: Trauma-Informed Care in Behavioral Health Services. Washington, DC: Department of Health and Human Services. 59.

32 WebMD Editorial Contributors. "What Are Symptoms of PTSD?" Medically reviewed by Carol DerSarkissian, MD, November 10, 2021. https://www.webmd.com/mental-health/what-are-symptoms-ptsd, accessed October 20, 2022.

33 Frank W. Weathers et al., The PTSD Checklist for DSM-5 (PCL-5) (National Center for PTSD, 2013), www.ptsd.va.gov.

34 Los Angeles County Department of Mental Health. "Our Services." Accessed April 4, 2025. https://dmh.lacounty.gov/our-services/.

35 U.S. Department of Veterans Affairs. National Center for PTSD. "PTSD: National Center for PTSD - List of All Measures." VA.gov | Veterans Affairs, March 25, 2025. https://www.ptsd.va.gov/professional/assessment/list_measures.asp#list1.

36 Michelle J. Bovin et al., "Psychometric Properties of the PTSD Checklist for Diagnostic and Statistical Manual of Mental Disorders–Fifth Edition (PCL-5) in Veterans," Psychological Assessment 28, no. 11 (2016): 1379–91, https://doi.org/10.1037/pas0000254.

37 American Psychiatric Association. 2022. Diagnostic and Statistical Manual of Mental Disorders: DSM-5-TR. 5th ed., text rev. Washington, DC: American Psychiatric Association Publishing, 301–6.

38 American Psychiatric Association, DSM-5-TR, 302–4

39 American Psychiatric Association, DSM-5-TR, 301.

40 American Psychiatric Association, DSM-5-TR, 302.

41 Ibid.

42 American Psychiatric Association, DSM-5-TR, 303.

43 American Psychiatric Association, DSM-5-TR, 303-304.

44 American Psychiatric Association, DSM-5-TR, 309.

45 American Psychiatric Association, Diagnostic and Statistical Manual of Mental Disorders, 4th ed. (Washington, DC: American Psychiatric Association, 2004), 427–428.

46 American Psychiatric Association, Diagnostic and Statistical Manual of Mental Disorders, 5th ed. (Washington, DC: American Psychiatric Association, 2013).

47 McNally, Progress and Controversy in the Study of Post-Traumatic Stress Disorder, 231.

48 Alvarado Parkway Institute, Behavioral Health System. "Seven Signs You Have Mild PTSD Rather Than Anxiety." APIBHS (blog), September 7, 2018. https://apibhs.com/2018/09/07/seven-signs-you-have-mild-ptsd-rather-than-anxiety, accessed October 21, 2020.

49 Richard J. McNally, "Progress and Controversy in the Study of Posttraumatic Stress Disorder." PowerPoint Presentation, 2003. https://pdfs.semanticscholar.org/1db8/9cfe8a2d7fd42bb1a6b68664f47aec957a11.pdf, accessed October 21, 2022.

50 Nick Haslam, "The Problem with Describing Every Misfortune as 'Trauma'," Chicago Tribune, August 15, 2016, https://www.chicagotribune.com/opinion/ct-trauma-microaggressions-trigger-warnings-20160815-story.html, accessed December 4, 2020.

51 Judith L. Herman, "Complex PTSD: A Syndrome in Survivors of Prolonged and Repeated Trauma," Journal of Traumatic Stress 5, no. 3 (1992): 377–391.

52 Jayne Leonard, "Complex PTSD: Symptoms, Behaviors, and Recovery." Medical News Today, August 28, 2018, https://www.medicalnewstoday.com/articles/322886. accessed February 20, 2019.

53 Rachael Rosser, "15:14 Episode 31." interview by Curtis Solomon, Biblical Counseling Coalition podcast, October 28, 2017, https://www.biblicalcounselingcoalition.org/podcast/ , accessed May 14, 2019.

54 Bessel A. van der Kolk, "Developmental Trauma Disorder," Psychiatric Annals 35, no. 5 (May 2005): 401–408, https://haruv.org.il/wp-content/uploads/2019/10/Developmental-trauma-disorder-van-der-kolk-2005.pdf. Accessed October 19, 2022.

55 Michael S. Scheeringa, The Body Does Not Keep the Score: How Popular Beliefs About Trauma Are Wrong (Amazon, 2024), 120, Kindle.

56 Michael S. Scheeringa, The Body Does Not Keep the Score: How Popular Beliefs About Trauma Are Wrong (Amazon, 2024), 120, Kindle.

57 Ibid., 125.

58 Ibid., 125.

59 Christine Courtois, "Complex Trauma, Complex Reactions: Assessment and Treatment," In Evidence-Based Mental Health Treatment for Victims of Human Trafficking, ed. Erin Williamson, Nicole M. Dutch and Heather J. Clawson (Washington, DC: U.S. Department of Health and Human Services, Office of the Assistant Secretary for Planning and Evaluation, 2010), 3.

60 Dr. Frank Ocher, "Complex Post-traumatic Stress Disorder," Trauma Disassociation, February 20, 2019, http://traumadissociation.com/complexptsd. accessed February 20, 2019.

61 Rachael Rosser, "Counseling Complex Traumatic Relationships," Biblical Counseling Coalition, November 15, 2018. https://www.biblicalcounselingcoalition.org/2018/11/15/counseling-complex-traumatic-relationships/. accessed April 26, 2019.

62 Craig M. Bennet, Abigail A. Baird, Michael B. Miller, and George L. Wolford, "Neural Correlates of Interspecies Perspective Taking in The Post-Mortem Atlantic Salmon: An Argument for Multiple Comparisons Correction," (Poster presentation, Human Brain Mapping Conference, San Francisco, 2009).

63 Michael Scheeringa, Analysis of The Body Keeps the Score: The Science That Trauma Activists Don't Want You to Know (Monee, IL: Central Recovery Press, 2023), 8.

64 Daniel Berger II, Mental Illness Volume Three, The Reality of the Physical Nature, (Taylors, SC: Alethia International Publications, 2016), Kindle ed., loc. 1036.

65 Caroline Leaf, "How Are the Mind & the Brain Different? A Neuroscientist Explains," MBGHealth, March 8, 2021, https://www.mindbodygreen.com/articles/difference-between-mind-and-brain-neuroscientist, accessed November 8, 2022.

66 Greg Gifford, "Mind vs. Brain: Gaining Biblical Clarity on the Difference," The Biblical Counseling Coalition, April 1, 2022, www.biblicalcounselingcoalition.org/2022/04/01/mind-vs-brain-gaining-biblical-clarity-on-the-difference/, accessed November 11, 2024.

67 Craig Troxel, With All Your Heart: Orienting Your Mind, Desires, and Will Toward Christ, (Wheaton, IL: Crossway, 2020), 32.

68 Centers for Disease Control and Prevention, "Adverse Childhood Experiences," accessed October 22, 2022. https://www.cdc.gov/violenceprevention/aces/index.html#:~:text=Adverse%20childhood%20experiences%20(ACEs)%20can,understand%20ACEs%20and%20prevent%20them.

69 Minnesota Department of Health. "Definition: What Is the ACE?" Accessed February 6, 2019. https://www.health.state.mn.us/communities/ace/index.html.

70 Bessel Van der Kolk, The Body Keeps the Score: Brain, Mind, and Body in the Healing of Trauma (New York: Viking, 2014), 93.

71 Bruce D. Perry, "Childhood Experience and the Expression of Genetic Potential: What Childhood Neglect to Tells Us about Nature and Nurture," Brain and Mind 3 (2002): 79 – 100, reprinted in The White Umbrella: Walking with Survivors of Sex Trafficking, Kindle ed. (Chicago: Moody Publishers, Wellspring Living, 2012), chap. 5.

72 L. Bowley, "Her Battle," in The White Umbrella: Walking with Survivors of Sex Trafficking, ed. Mary Frances Bowley, Kindle ed. (Chicago: Moody Publishers, Wellspring Living, 2012), chap. 5.

73 Steffen, Patrick R., Dawson Hedges, and Rebekka Matheson. "The Brain Is Adaptive Not Triune: How the Brain Responds to Threat, Challenge, and Change." Frontiers in Psychiatry 13 (April 1, 2022):802606. https://doi.org/10.3389/fpsyt.2022.802606

74 Perry, Childhood Experience, chap. 5.

75 Bowley, Her Battle. 52

76 Ibid., 52.

77 Bruce D. Perry and Ronnie Pollard, "Homeostasis, Stress, Trauma, and Adaptation," in The White Umbrella: Walking with Survivors of Sex Trafficking, Kindle ed. (Chicago: Moody Publishers, Wellspring Living, 2012), chap 5.

78 "What is C-PTSD?" Beauty After Bruises, October 31, 2019, https://www.beautyafterbruises.org/what-is-cptsd, accessed November 8, 2022.

79 "Understanding Complex Post Traumatic Stress Disorder: Symptoms, Causes," Heal Her Heart, https://www.healherheart.org/blogs/resources/understanding-complex-post-traumatic-stress-disorder-symptoms-causes-and-treatment-options accessed November 8, 2022.

80 Michael Scheeringa, (@m_scheeringa), "one-hundred percent of the dozens of ACEs studies have been cross-sectional," X, February 13, 2025, 9:45 a.m., https://x.com/m_scheeringa/status/1890064357427482936

81 Michael Scheeringa, "ACEs Aware Advocacy Program Tries to Influence Youths with Celebrity Gamer," Trauma Dispatch, August 26, 2024, https://www.michaelscheeringa.com/trauma-dispatch/aces-aware-advocacy-program-tries-to-influence-youths-with-celebrity-gamer, accessed November 5, 2024

82 Michael D. De Bellis, Andrew S. Baum, Boris Birmaher, Matcheri S. Keshavan, Clayton H. Eccard, Amy M. Boring, Frank J. Jenkins, and Neal D. Ryan, "A.E. Bennett Research Award. Developmental Traumatology, Part I: Biological Stress Systems," Biological Psychiatry 45, no. 10 (1999): 1259–1270.

83 Ibid.

84 Michael D. Debellis, "Developmental Traumatology: Neurobiological Development in Maltreated Children With PTSD," Psychiatric Times 16, no. 9 (September 1, 1999), https://www.psychiatrictimes.com/view/developmental-traumatology-neurobiological-development-maltreated-children-ptsd, accessed November 9, 2022.

85 Martin H. Teicher, "Scars That Won't Heal: The Neurobiology of Child Abuse," Scientific American, March 1, 2002, https://www.scientificamerican.com/article/scars-that-wont-heal-the-neurobiology-of-child-abuse, accessed November 9, 2020.

86 Sheeringa, "The Trouble with Trauma," 64.

87 State of California Department of Health Care Services, "The science of ACEs and toxic stress: ACEs and toxic stress can affect health, but toxic stress is treatable," ACEs Aware, 2023, https://www.acesaware.org/ace-fundamentals/the-science-of-aces-toxic-stress/

88 Steve W. C. Chang, "The Science of Connection: What Does 'the Social Brain' Really Mean?", Psychology Today, March 16, 2020, https://www.psychologytoday.com/us/blog/the-science-connection/202003/what-does-the-social-brain-really-mean, accessed April 6, 2023.

89 Eamon McCrory. "The Guide to Childhood Trauma and the Brain," The Better Care Network, Anna Freud National Centre for Children and Families, September 2020. https://bettercarenetwork.org/library/particular-threats-to-childrens-care-and-protection/child-abuse-and-neglect/the-guidebook-to-childhood-trauma-and-the-brain, accessed April 6, 2023.

90 Centers for Disease Control and Prevention, "What is Epigenetics?," CDC, last reviewed August 15, 2022 https://www.cdc.gov/genomics/disease/epigenetics.htm, accessed April 6, 2023.

91 Lindsay Curtis, "How Adverse Childhood Experiences (ACEs) May Lead to Trauma and PTSD," PsychCentral, updated August 25, 2021, https://psychcentral.com/ptsd/adverse-childhood-experiences-post-traumatic-stress-disorder. Accessed April 5, 2023.

92 Scheeringa, "Analysis of The Body Keeps the Score," 64.

93 Ibid., 35.

94 Centers for Disease Control and Prevention, "What is Epigenetics?," accessed April 6, 2023.

95 Tobias B. Halene, Gregor Hasler, Amanda Mitchell, and Schahram Akbarian, Psychiatric Genetics: A Primer for Clinicians and Basic

Scientists, ed. Thomas G. Schulze and Francis J. McMahon (New York: Oxford University Press, 2018).

96 Michael Scheeringa, "The Body Does Not Keep the Score," (2024), P. 75-76.

97 Richard M. Cross, "Affect Regulation, Attachment, and the Developing Social Brain: Implications for Assessment and Treatment of Dissociative Disorders," in The Handbook of Complex Trauma and Dissociation in Children (Routledge, 2025).

98 Lockwood, Patricia L., Matthew A. J. Apps, and Steve W. C. Chang. "Is There a 'Social' Brain? Implementations and Algorithms." Tends in Cognitive Sciences 24, no. 10 (October 1, 2020): 802-13. https://doi.org/10.1016/j.tics.2020.06.011.

99 Michael Scheeringa, The Trouble with Trauma: The Search to Discover How Beliefs Become Facts, (Las Vegas: Central Recovery Press, 2021), 9,11.

100 Soares, S., Rocha, V., Kelly-Irving, M., Stringhini, S., & Fraga, S. (2020). Adverse Childhood Events and Health Biomarkers: A Systematic Review. Frontiers in Public Health, 9. https://doi.org/10.3389/fpubh.2021.649825, accessed 4/5/2023.

101 Michael Scheeringa, @m_scheeringa "If ACE theory is true, tell us, please, what's the biological mechanism of how ACEs cause a horde of physical and mental conditions? " X (formerly known as Twitter), 9:43AM, 02/13/25, https://x.com/m_scheeringa/status/1890064357427482936

102 Michael Scheeringa, Analysis of The Body Keeps the Score: The Science That Trauma Activists Don't Want You to Know (Monee, IL: Central Recovery Press, 2023), 8.

103 Liem and Neuhuber, "Critique of the Polyvagal Theory," accessed December 15, 2022.

104 Substance Abuse and Mental Health Services Administration. "Practical Guide for Implementing a Trauma-Informed Approach." Rockville, MD: National Mental Health and Substance Use Policy Laboratory, 2023. https://library.samhsa.gov/sites/default/files/pep23-06-05-005.pdf.

105 Ibid., 4., Williamson, Dutch, and Clawson, Evidence-Based Mental Health Treatment.

106 Lara B. Gerassi and Andrea J. Nichols, eds., Sex Trafficking and Commercial Sexual Exploitation: Prevention, Advocacy, and Trauma-Informed Practice (New York: Springer Publishing Company, 2018), 107,

citing Elliot et al. (2005), Hardy et al. (2013), and Heffernan and Blithe (2014).

107 Trauma Informed Care Project, "What Is Trauma Informed Care?," http://www.traumainformedcareproject.org/ , accessed February 18, 2019 verified February 2, 2025.

108 Bruce Roeder, "About Biblical Counseling," Reigning Grace Counseling Center Intake Paperwork, Reigning Grace Counseling Center, n.d., https://www.rgcconline.org

109 Daniel Berger III, Saving Abnormal: The Disorder of Psychiatric Genetics (Taylors, SC: Alethia International Publications, 2020), 241.

Chapter Three: Biblical Anthropology and Human Nature

110 Albert Barnes, John Calvin, Adam Clarke, et al., "The Ultimate Commentary on Genesis," chap. 3, in The Ultimate Commentary Collection (publication details unavailable).

111 Wayne Grudem, "Systematic Theology: An Introduction to Biblical Doctrine," (Grand Rapids: Zondervan, 1994), 442.

112 Donald Grey Barnhouse, Genesis: A Devotional Exposition, vol. 1 (Grand Rapids: Zondervan Publishing House, 1973), 12; R. C. Sproul, Everyone's a Theologian: An Introduction to Systematic Theology Sanford, FL: Reformation Trus Publishing, 2014), 103.

113 Stephen J. Brammer, Kenneth Gangel, Ed. Max Anders, Holman Old Testament Commentary: Genesis, (Nashville: Broadman & Holman Publishers, 2003), 27.

114 Wayne Grudem, Systematic Theology: An Introduction to Biblical Doctrine (Grand Rapids, MI: Zondervan, 1994), 446–448; 805–808).

115 Ibid., 446–448; 805–808

116 Jay E. Adams, A Theology of Christian Counseling (Grand Rapids: Zondervan, 1979), 112.

117 Ibid., (Grand Rapids: Zondervan, 1979), 110.

118 Winston Smith. "Dichotomy or Trichotomy? How the Doctrine of Man Shapes the Treatment of Depression." The Journal of Biblical Counseling 18, no. 3 (Spring 2000): 22.

119 Sean Perron, @seanperron, "there is nothing wrong with telling an anxious person who is worked up to take a breath," X post, February 18, 2025, 9:18 a.m., https://x.com/seanperron/status/1891869805570863347

120 Nate Brooks, "The Bible Keeps Record of Trauma. But Is It Trauma Informed?" Christianity Today, November 4, 2022, https://www.christianitytoday.com, accessed December 8, 2022.

121 Mark R. McMinn and Timothy R. Phillips, Care for the Soul: Exploring the Intersection of Psychology & Theology (Downers Grove, IL: InterVarsity Press, 2001), 25.

122 Millard J. Erickson, Christian Theology, 3rd ed. (Grand Rapids, MI: Baker Academic, 2013), 178.

123 Samuel Stephens, "Christian Counseling and General Revelation: The Misuse of a Biblical Doctrine," (presentation, ACBC Annual Conference – O Church Arise: Reclaiming a Culture of Care, October 2021), https://www.biblicalcounseling.com.

124 Heath Lambert, A Theology of Biblical Counseling: The Doctrinal Foundations of Counseling Ministry, (Grand Rapids, MI: Zondervan, 2016), 3.

125 Keith Mathison, "Interpreting General and Special Revelation," Ligonier Ministries, May 25, 2012, https://learn.ligonier.org/articles/interpreting-general-and-special-revelation-reformed-approach-science-and-scripture

126 Louis Berkhof, Systematic Theology (Grand Rapids: Wm. B. Eerdmans Publishing Co.,1953) 440-441.

127 Eric C. Martin, "Science and Ideology," Internet Encyclopedia of Philosophy, https://iep.utm.edu/sci-ideo/#H6, accessed 4/5-2023.

128 Sixbert Sangwa and Mutabazi Placide, "The Bible and Science: The Relationship between Science and Christianity," Studia Philosophica 9, no. 1 (2021): 7–29, https://www.researchgate.net/profile/Sixbert-Sangwa-2/publication/353522381_The_Bible_and_Science_The_Relationship_between_Science_and_Christianity, accessed August 4, 2024, doi:10.23756/sp.v9i1.596.

129 Nate Brooks, Tate Cockrell, Brad Hambrick, Kristin Kellen, and Sam Williams, "What Is Redemptive Counseling / Clinically Informed Biblical Counseling?" (paper, Southeastern Baptist Theological Seminary Biblical Counseling Department, July 8, 2024), www.sebts.edu/wp-content/uploads/2024/07/What-is-RCCIBC.pdf, accessed August 4, 2024.

Chapter Four: A Biblical Model of Care

130 ACBC Dale Johnson, "Who is Man?" (plenary address, Association of Certified Biblical Counselors Annual Conference, "In His Image:

Recovering Human Dignity," Fort Worth, TX, October 3, 2022), audio recording. Definition: Johnson critiques the integration of secular psychological theories into biblical counseling, emphasizing the sufficiency of Scripture for addressing human soul care.

131 Louis Berkhof, Systematic Theology (Grand Rapids: Wm. B. Eerdmans Publishing Co., 1996), Kindle edition, "The Principia of Dogmatics: The Seat of Religion—It Has Its Seat in the Heart."

132 Lori Stanley Roeleveld, "What Does the Bible Say about the Mind?" Christianity.com, March 7, 2022, https://www.christianity.com/wiki/bible/what-bible-say-about-mind.html. Accessed April 4, 2023.

133 "How Did the Fall Affect Humanity?," Got Questions (blog), accessed April 14, 2019, https://www.gotquestions.org/fall-affect-humanity.html.

134 John Bunyan, Grace Abounding to the Chief of Sinners, (1666; repr., London: The Religious Tract Society edition, 1905), 85, transcribed by David Price, Project Gutenberg, released February 19, 2013, https://www.gutenberg.org/files/654/654-h/654-h.htm

135 Paul David Tripp, Instruments in the Redeemer's Hands, (Phillipsburg, NJ: P&R Publishing, 2002), 10.

136 Ibid., 13.

137 Pam Gannon and Cheryl Moore, In the Aftermath: Past the pain of Childhood Sexual Abuse (Bemidji, MN: Focus Publishing, 2002), 40.

138 Wayne Gruden, Systematic Theology: An Introduction to Biblical Doctrine (Grand Rapids, MI: Zondervan, 1994), 449.

139 Ibid., 153.

140 David Powlison, Recovering from Child Abuse: Healing and Hope for Victims (Greensboro, NC: New Growth Press, 2008), 4.

141 Lou Priolo, Self-Image: How to Overcome Inferiority Judgments (Phillipsburg, NJ: P&R Publishing, 2007), 7.

142 Powlison, Recovering from Child Abuse, 5.

Chapter Five: Redefining Trauma-Related Terms

143 Microsoft Copilot, "Diagnoses, Symptoms, Behaviors, and Descriptions Chart" and "BPD and RAD Diagnoses Chart," Copilot, 2024, https://download.bpd-and-rad-diagnoses-chart.

144 Mark Shaw, "Conveying God's Love, Wisdom, and Power Through Biblical Language," in A Call to Clarity: Critical Issues in Contemporary

Biblical Counseling, ed. Heath Lambert, (Jacksonville, FL: First Baptist Church Jacksonville, 2024), 90.

Chapter Six: Foundational Counseling Principles

145 David Powlison, "I'll Never Get Over It- Help For the Aggrieved, Journal of Biblical Counseling, volume 28:1, (2014): 8-27

146 Daniel Berger, "Post-Traumatic Stress is not a Disorder," DrDanielBerger.com, February 23, 2018, https://www.drdanielberger.com/single-post/2018/02/23/Post-Traumatic-Stress-is-not-a-Disorder, accessed December 19, 2024.

147 Sue Nicewander and Maria Brookins, Treasure in the Ashes: Our Journey Home from the Ruins of Sexual Abuse (Wapwallopen, PA: Shepherd Press, 2018), 170.

148 "The Roman Scourge," Bible History, 2024, http://bible-history.com/past/flagrum, accessed 12-19-24.

Chapter Seven: Biblical Response to Post-Event Fear and Anxiety

149 The American Heritage Dictionary of the English Language, Fifth Edition copyright 2022 by HarperCollins Publishers. https://ahdictionary.com/word/search.html?q=disease

150 David Powlison, Sexual Assault: Healing Steps for Victims (Greensboro, NC: New Growth Press, 2010), 18–19

151 Timothy S. Lane, PTSD: Healing for a Heart Held Captive (Greensboro, NC: New Growth Press, n.d.), 11–13

152 Lane, PTSD, 11–13

153 Pam Gannon and Cheryl Moore, In the Aftermath: Past the Pain of Childhood Sexual Abuse (Bemidji, MN: Focus Publishing, 2002), 78.

154 Paige MacDonald, "The Same Kind of Human," chap. 26, In Mary Francis Bowley, The White Umbrella, Walking with Survivors of Sex Trafficking (Chicago: Moody Publishers, 2012), chap. 5.

155 Gannon and Moore, In the Aftermath, 78.

156 Lou Priolo, Self-Image: How to Overcome Inferiority Judgments (Phillipsburg, NJ: P&R Publishing, 2007), 13.

157 Daniel Berger, The Influence of Nurture: How Environment Shapes Behavior (n.p.: Alethia Books, 2018), 185.

158 Gannon and Moore, In the Aftermath, 84.

159 Priolo, Self-Image, 16–17; Pamela V. Hunt, "8 Biblical Steps to Recover from Post-Traumatic Stress Disorder," Christian Post, accessed June 3, 2019, https://www.christianpost.com/news/8-biblical-steps-to-recover-from-post-traumatic-stress-disorder.html.

Chapter Eight: Biblical Responses to Grief and Loss

160 Paul David Tripp, Grief: Finding Hope Again (Greensboro, NC: New Growth Press, 2004), 8.

Chapter Nine: Biblical Responses to Guilt and Shame

161 Ken Campbell, Those Ugly Emotions: How to Manage Your Emotions (Fearn, Ross-shire, Scotland: Christian Focus Publications, 1999), 65.

162 Robert Somerville, If I'm a Christian, Why Am I Depressed? Finding Meaning and Hope in Suffering (Maitland, FL: Xulon Press, 2014), 95.

163 Somerville, If I'm a Christian, 96.

164 Daniel Berger, The Influence of Nurture: How Environment Shapes Behavior (n.p.: Alethia Books, 2018), 210.

165 Ibid., 210.

166 Campbell, Those Ugly Emotions, 68.

167 Athena Moberg, Yes, You Can! Overcome No Matter Where You're From: Straight Talk & Strategies for Adult Survivors of Childhood Sexual Abuse (n.p.: Athena Moberg Speaking International, LLC, 2015), chap. Titled "Shame," Kindle.

168 Edward T. Welch, Shame Interrupted: How God Lifts the Pain of Worthlessness and Rejection (Greensboro, NC: New Growth Press, 2012), 239.

169 Rachel Rhoadarmer, Mend: Journey to Sexual Healing (North Charleston, SC: CreateSpace Independent Publishing Platform, 2017), 28.

Chapter Ten: Biblical Responses to Anger and Bitterness

170 David Powlison, Good and Angry, (Greensburo, NC: New Growth Press, 2016), 8

171 The BibleStudyTools Staff, "Bitterness in the Bible," Bible Study Tools, September 7, 2018, https://www.biblestudytools.com/topical-verses/bitterness-in-the-bible/ accessed February 12, 2025.

172 Wayne A. Mack, Anger and Stress Management God's Way (Phillipsburg, NJ: P&R Publishing, 2017), 12.

173 Julie Ganschow, "Overcoming Anger" Module 500, Lesson 5, Reigning Grace Counseling Center, Reigning Grace Institute's Fundamentals of Biblical Counseling Training Program, 2024.

174 Christine McDonald, The Same Kind of Human: Seeing the Marginalized and Exploited Through the Eyes of Grace (n.p.: Amazon Digital Services LLC, 2016), chap. 24, Kindle.

175 Edward T. Welch, Depression: Looking Up from the Stubborn Darkness (Greensboro, NC: New Growth Press, 2011), 139.

176 Mack, Anger & Stress Management God's Way, 54–58

Chapter Eleven: Biblical Responses to Self-Harm and Substance Abuse

177 Edward T. Welch, "Self-Injury," in A Biblical Counseling Resource

178 Ibid.

179 Ibid., 7.

Chapter Twelve: Biblical Responses to Substance Abuse and Addiction

180 National Institute on Drug Abuse, "Trauma and Stress," National Institute on Drug Abuse, February 6, 2024, https://nida.nih.gov/research-topics/trauma-and-stress accessed February 5, 2025.

181 Pastoral Care Inc., "Statistics on Addictions," 2025, https://www.pastoral-careinc.com/statistics/statistics-on-addictions/, accessed February 2, 2025.

182 Office to Monitor and Combat Trafficking in Persons, "About Us," U.S. Department of State, June 2020, https://www.state.gov/about-us-office-to-monitor-and-combat-trafficking-in-persons/ accessed February 7, 2025.

183 National Institute on Drug Abuse, "Sex Differences in Substance Use," National Institute on Drug Abuse, April 1, 2020, https://nida.nih.gov/publications/research-reports/substance-use-in-women/sex-differences-in-substance-use accessed January 30, 2025.

184 Raven Badger, "Addressing Women's Sexual Health Disparities in Substance Use Disorder Treatment," Advances in Addiction & Recovery, Winter 2016, www.naadac.org/assets/2416/

aa&r_winter2016_addressing_womens_sexual_health_disparities_in_substance_use_disorder_treatment.pdf

185 The Addiction Connection, "Residential Programs," https://www.theaddictionconnection.org/residential-programs/

186 Lara B. Gerassi, Andrea J. Nichols, Sex Trafficking and Commercial Sexual Exploitation: Prevention, Advocacy, and Trauma-Informed Practice, (New York: Springer Publishing Company, 2018), 40; Mark Shaw, The Heart of Addiction: A Biblical Perspective (Bemidji, MN: Focus Publishing, 2008), chap. 13, Kindle.

187 Gerassi and Nichols, Sex Trafficking and Commercial Sexual Exploitation, 107–115.

188 Shaw, The Heart of Addiction, chap. 19.

189 Ibid., chaps. 5, 12.

190 Timothy S. Lane, "Godly Intoxication," in Addictions: A Banquet in the Grave (Phillipsburg, NJ: P&R Publishing, 2001), 5.

191 Shaw, The Heart of Addiction, chap 1.

192 Edward T. Welch, "Addictions: New Ways of Seeing, New Ways of Walking Free," The Journal of Biblical Counseling 19, no. 3, (Spring 2001): 19–30, published by The Christian Counseling and Educational Foundation, Glenside, PA.

Chapter Thirteen: Forgiveness and Repentance

193 David Powlison, Recovering from Child Abuse: Healing and Hope for Victims (Greensboro, NC: New Growth Press, 2008), 17.

194 Sue Nicewander and Maria Brookins, Treasure in the Ashes: Our Journey Home from the Ruins of Sexual Abuse (Wapwallopen, PA: Shepherd Press, 2018), 221.

195 Athena Moberg, "Unforgiveness," in Straight Talk & Strategies for Adult Survivors of Childhood Sexual Abuse, (n.p.: Independently published, n.d.).

Chapter Fourteen: The Role of the Church in Healing

196 Robert Somerville, If I'm a Christian, Why Am I Depressed? (n.p.: Xulon Press, 2014), 37–38

197 Jim Berg, Changed Into His Image: God's Plan for Tranforming Your Being (Greenville, SC: BJU Press, 2018), 10.

198 Somerville, If I'm a Christian, Why Am I Depressed?, 40.

199 Nicewander and Moore, Treasure in the Ashes, 189.

Appendix

200 Zhang, J., et al. "Magnetoencephalography in the Detection and Characterization of Brain Abnormalities Associated with Traumatic Brain Injury: A Comprehensive Review." *Diagnostics* 11, no. 9 (2021): 1628. https://doi.org/10.3390/diagnostics11091628.

201 Gross, J. "Magnetoencephalography in Cognitive Neuroscience: A Primer." *Neuron* 104, no. 2 (2019): 189–204. https://doi.org/10.1016/j.neuron.2019.07.001.

202 Farde, L. "Imaging the Living Human Brain: Magnetic Resonance Imaging and Positron Emission Tomography." *Proceedings of the National Academy of Sciences* 94, no. 7 (1997): 2787–2788. https://doi.org/10.1073/pnas.94.7.2787.

203 Mele, G., et al. "Simultaneous Electroencephalography-Functional Magnetic Resonance Imaging for Assessment of Human Brain Function." *Frontiers in Neurology* 13 (2022): 934265. https://doi.org/10.3389/fneur.2022.934265

204 Alotaiby, T. N., et al. "Electroencephalography Signal Processing: A Comprehensive Review and Analysis of Methods and Techniques." *Sensors* 23, no. 14 (2023): 6434. https://doi.org/10.3390/s23146434.

205 Chowdhury, S., et al. "Electroencephalography (EEG) Physiological Indices Reflecting Human Physical Performance: A Systematic Review Using Updated PRISMA." *Journal of Integrative Neuroscience* 22, no. 3 (2023): 76. https://doi.org/10.31083/j.jin2203076.

206 Hong, K. S., et al. "Functional Near-Infrared Spectroscopy and Its Clinical Application in the Field of Neuroscience: Advances and Future Directions." *Frontiers in Neuroscience* 14 (2020): 724. https://doi.org/10.3389/fnins.2020.00724.

207 Zhang, Y., et al. "Impact of Repetitive Transcranial Magnetic Stimulation on Cortical Activity: A Systematic Review and Meta-Analysis Utilizing Functional Near-Infrared Spectroscopy." *Journal of NeuroEngineering and Rehabilitation* 21, no. 1 (2024): 103. https://doi.org/10.1186/s12984-024-01392-7.

208 Sally Satel and Scott Lilienfield, Brainwashed: The Seductive Appeal of Mindless Neuroscience (New York: Basic Books, 2013), 11.

209 "A Functional Magnetic Resonance Imaging Meta-Analysis of Childhood Trauma." ScienceDirect. Accessed April 18, 2025. https://www.sciencedirect.com/science/article/abs/pii/S0149763423004496.

210 "Scientist Uses Brain Scans to Search for Ways to Ease the Effects of Trauma." University of Wisconsin-Milwaukee, August 12, 2023. https://uwm.edu/news/scientist-uses-brain-scans-to-search-for-ways-to-ease-the-effects-of-trauma/.

211 Logothetis, Nikos K. "What We Can Do and What We Cannot Do with fMRI." Nature 453, no. 7197 (2008): 869–878. https://doi.org/10.1038/nature06976.

212 Meda, Shashwath A., Vince D. Calhoun, and Michael C. Stevens. "Functional Magnetic Resonance Imaging: An Invaluable Tool in Translational Neuroscience." NCBI Bookshelf. Accessed April 18, 2025. https://www.ncbi.nlm.nih.gov/books/NBK533144/.

213 Bandettini, Peter A. "Overview of Functional Magnetic Resonance Imaging." PMC, April 1, 2017. https://pmc.ncbi.nlm.nih.gov/articles/PMC5573747/.

214 Emery N. Brown and Marlene Behrmann, "Controversy in Statistical Analysis of Functional Magnetic Resonance Imaging Data," Proceedings of the National Academy of Sciences of the United States of America 114, no. 17 (2017): E3368–E3369, https://doi.org/10.1073/pnas.1705513114.

215 Emily R. Duval, Arash Javanbakht, and Israel Liberzon, "Neural circuits in anxiety and stress disorders: a focused review," Therapeutics and Clinical Risk Management 11 (2015): 115–126,

216 S. Marek, B. Tervo-Clemmens, F.J. Calabro, et al., "Reproducible Brain-Wide Association Studies Require Thousands of Individuals," Nature 603, (2022): 654–660, https://doi.org/10.1038/s41586-022-04492-9, accessed October 27, 2022.

217 Anders Eklund, Thomas E. Nichols, and Hans Knutsson, "Cluster failure: Why fMRI inferences for spatial extent have inflated false-positive rates," Proceedings of the National Academy of Sciences 113, no. 28 (2016): 7900–7905, https://doi.org/10.1073/pnas.1602413113.

218 Michael R. Egnor, "Why A 'Budding' Neuroscientist Is Skeptical of Brain Scans." Mind Matters News, April 5, 2021. Accessed October 27, 2022. https://mindmatters.ai/2021/04/no-fmri-brain-scans-are-not-reading-our-minds/

219 Benjamin O. Turner, Erick J. Paul, Michael B. Miller, and Aron K. Barbey, "Small Sample Sizes Reduce the Replicability of Task-Based fMRI Studies," Communications Biology 1, no. 62 (December 2018):

1–10, https://pubmed.ncbi.nlm.nih.gov/30271944/, accessed October 26, 2022.

220 Bennett, Craig M., Abigail A. Baird, Michael B. Miller, and George L. Wolford. "Neural Correlates of Interspecies Perspective Taking in the Post-Mortem Atlantic Salmon: An Argument for Multiple Comparisons Correction." Journal of Serendipitous and Unexpected Results 1, no. 1 (2009): 1–5. https://www.jsur.org/v1n1p1.pdf.

221 Eklund, Anders, Thomas E. Nichols, and Hans Knutsson. "Cluster Failure: Why fMRI Inferences for Spatial Extent Have Inflated False-Positive Rates." Proceedings of the National Academy of Sciences 113, no. 28 (2016): 7900–7905. https://doi.org/10.1073/pnas.1602413113.

222 McNally, Progress and Controversy in the Study of Post-Traumatic Stress Disorder, 240.

223 Constanze Quosh and Kenneth Gergen. "Constructing Trauma and Its Treatment: Knowledge, Power and Resistance." In Meaning in Action, edited by Toshio Sugiman, Kenneth J. Gergen, Wolfgang Wagner, and Yoko Yamada, 103–104. Tokyo: Springer, 2008. https://doi.org/10.1007/978-4-431-74680-5_6.

224 Eaton T. Fores, "There Are No 'Chemical Imbalances.'" Academy for the Study of the Psychoanalytic Arts, The Eaton T. Fores Research Center, 2003. Accessed October 26, 2022. https://psychrights.org/research/digest/TheBrain/NoChemicalImbalances.htm.

225 Tim Newman, "All About the Central Nervous System," Medically reviewed by Seunggu Han, M.D. Medical News Today, Updated on November 29, 2023. https://www.medicalnewstoday.com/articles/307076, accessed 11/14/2024

226 Toshniwal Paharia, Pooja Toshniwal Paharia. "What is the Nervous System?" News-Medical. https://www.news-medical.net/health/What-is-the-Nervous-System.aspx (accessed November 14, 2024).

227 Marc Dingman, Ph.D. "2-Minute Neuroscience: Divisions of The Nervous System," Neuroscientifically Challenged, 2002, https://neuroscientificallychallenged.com/posts/2-minute-neuroscience-divisions-of-the-nervous-system, accessed November 11, 2024.

228 "A Functional Magnetic Resonance Imaging Meta-Analysis of Childhood Trauma." ScienceDirect. Accessed April 18, 2025. https://www.sciencedirect.com/science/article/abs/pii/S0149763423004496.

229 "Post-Traumatic Stress Disorder: The Neurobiological Impact of Psychological Trauma." Taylor & Francis Online, April 1, 2022. https://www.tandfonline.com/doi/full/10.31887/DCNS.2011.13.3/msteenkamp.
230 "Scientist Uses Brain Scans to Search for Ways to Ease the Effects of Trauma." University of Wisconsin-Milwaukee, August 12, 2023. https://uwm.edu/news/scientist-uses-brain-scans-to-search-for-ways-to-ease-the-effects-of-trauma/.
231 Huang, Z. Josh, and Hongkui Zeng. "It Takes the World to Understand the Brain." Science 350, no. 6256 (2015): 42–44. https://pmc.ncbi.nlm.nih.gov/articles/PMC4664961/.
232 Jacek Dębiec, and Joseph LeDoux, "The Amygdala and the Neural Pathways of Fear," in Post-traumatic Stress Disorder: Basic Science and Clinical Practice, ed. P. J. Shiromani, T.M. Keane, and J.E. LeDoux (Humana Press/Springer Nature, 2009), 23–38. https://doi.org/10.1007/978-1-60327-329-9_2. https://psycnet.apa.org/record/2009-04091-002, accessed December 15, 2022.
233 "A Functional Magnetic Resonance Imaging Meta-Analysis of Childhood Trauma." ScienceDirect. Accessed April 18, 2025. https://www.sciencedirect.com/science/article/abs/pii/S0149763423004496.
234 "Post-Traumatic Stress Disorder: The Neurobiological Impact of Psychological Trauma." Taylor & Francis Online, April 1, 2022. https://www.tandfonline.com/doi/full/10.31887/DCNS.2011.13.3/msteenkamp.
235 Michael Scheeringa, Analysis of The Body Keeps the Score, 12.
236 Ibid., 12.
237 Bremner, J. Douglas. "Traumatic Stress: Effects on the Brain." Dialogues in Clinical Neuroscience 8, no. 4 (2006): 445–461. https://pmc.ncbi.nlm.nih.gov/articles/PMC3181836/.
238 Liberzon, Israel, and Chandra Sekhar Sripada. "The Functional Neuroanatomy of PTSD: A Critical Review." Progress in Brain Research 167 (2008): 151–169. https://doi.org/10.1016/S0079-6123(07)67011-3.
239 Shin, Lisa M., Scott L. Rauch, and Roger K. Pitman. "Amygdala, Medial Prefrontal Cortex, and Hippocampal Function in PTSD." Annals of the New York Academy of Sciences 1071, no. 1 (2006): 67–79. https://doi.org/10.1196/annals.1364.007.
240 Bogdana Petko, Prasanna Tadi, "Neuroanatomy, Nucleus Ambiguus." [Updated July 25, 2022]. In: StatPearls [Internet]. Treasure Island (FL): StatPearls Publishing; 2022 Jan-Available from: https://www.ncbi.nlm.nih.gov/books/NBK547744/, accessed December 15, 2020.

241 Liem and Neuhuber, "Critique of the Polyvagal Theory," accessed December 15, 2022.

242 American Association of Neurological Surgeons, "Anatomy of the Spine and Peripheral Nervous System," 2022. Located at https://www.aans.org/en/Patients/Neurosurgical-Conditions-and-Treatments/Anatomy-of-the-Spine-and-Peripheral-Nervous-System, accessed November 11, 2022.

243 "Cranial Nerves," Cleveland Clinic, February 22, 2022, https://my.clevelandclinic.org/health/body/21998-cranial-nerves, accessed November 10, 2022.

244 Dingman, Ph.D., "2-Minute Neuroscience: Divisions of The Nervous System," Neuroscientifically Challenged, 2002. https://neuroscientificallychallenged.com/posts/2-minute-neuroscience-divisions-of-the-nervous-system, accessed November 11, 2022.

245 N. Hammer, J. Glatzner, C. Feja, C. Kuhne, J. Meixensberger, U. Planitzer, S. Schiefenbaum, B.N.Tillmann, D. Winkler, "Human Vagus Nerve Branching in the Cervical Region." PLoS One 10, no. 2 (2015): e0118006, https://www.ncbi.nlm.hih.gov/books/NBK537171, accessed November 13, 2022.

246 Christina Caron, "This Nerve Influences Nearly Every Internal Organ. Can It Improve Our Mental State too?" The New York Times, June 2, 2022. https://www.nytimes.com/2022/06/02/well/mind/vagus-nerve-mental-health.html, accessed November 17, 2022.

247 D.S. Goldstein, "Sympathetic Nervous System," in Encyclopedia of Stress, 2nd ed., ed. George Fink (Academic Press, 2007), 697–703, https://doi.org/10.1016/B978-012373947-6.00370-6.), accessed November 15, 2022.

248 David S. Goldstein, "The Autonomic Nervous System Has Parts," YouTube video 8:53, from Introduction to Autonomic Medicine Course (video 3 of 24), posted by The American Autonomic Society, November 14, 2016, https://www.youtube.com/watch?v=8mEBFEffectM, accessed November 14, 2022.

249 Van der Kolk, The Body Keeps the Score, 125.

250 Kendra Cherry, "What Is the Fight-or-Flight Response? Experiencing Physical Symptoms in Response to Stress," updated November 07, 2022, Medically reviewed by Steven Gans, MD. VeryWell Mind. https://www.verywellmind.com/what-is-the-fight-or-flight-response-2795194, accessed November 16, 2022.

251 Marc Dingman, Ph.D. "2-Minute Neuroscience: The Sympathetic Nervous System" YouTube video, Neuroscientifically Challenged.

https://neuroscientificallychallenged.com/posts/2-minute-neuroscience-sympathetic-nervous-system, accessed November 16, 2022.

252 Nicoletta Lanese and Scott Dutfield, "Fight or Flight: The Sympathetic Nervous System," Live Science, February 9, 2022, https://www.livescience.com/65446-sympathetic-nervous-system.html, accessed November 11, 2022.

253 "Difference Between Sympathetic And Parasympathetic," Byju's, 2022, https://byjus.com/biology/difference-between-sympathetic-and-parasympathetic/, accessed November 16, 2022.

254 Marc Dingman, Ph.D., "2-Minute Neuroscience: The Parasympathetic Nervous System," YouTube video, Neuroscientifically Challenged. https://neuroscientificallychallenged.com/posts/2-minute-neuroscience-parasympathetic-nervous-system, accessed November 16, 2022.

255 Stephen Porges and Gunther Schmidt, "Polyvagal Theory: How Your Body Makes the Decision," YouTube video, 1:30:09, posted by Trauma Research UK, May 28, 2016, https://www.youtube.com/watch?v=ivLeal-hBHPM&t=8s, accessed February 2, 2020.

256 Ibid.

257 Stephen W. Porges and Deb Dana, eds., Clinical Applications of the Polyvagal Theory: The Emergence of Polyvagal-Informed Therapies (New York: W. W. Norton & Company, 2018).58

258 van der Kolk, The Body Keeps the Score, 126.

259 Stephen W. Porges, "Social Engagement and Attachment," Annals of the New York Academy of Sciences, 1008, no. 1 (2003): 31–47.

260 Stephen W. Porges, "Neuroception: A Subconscious System for Detecting Threats and Safety," Zero to Three 24, no. 5 (2004): 19–24.

261 Stephen W. Porges and Deb Dana, eds., Clinical Applications of the Polyvagal Theory: The Emergence of Polyvagal-Informed Therapies (New York: W. W. Norton & Company, 2018).58

262 Stephen Porges and Ruth Buczynski, "Polyvagal Theory and Trauma," National Institute for the Clinical Application of Behavioral Medicine, https://www.nicabm.com/topic/polyvagal-theory-explained/ , accessed November 23, 2022.

263 Lilianne R. Mujica-Parodi, Jiook Cha, and Jonathan Gao, "From Anxious to Reckless: A Control Systems Approach Unifies Prefrontal-Limbic Regulation Across the Spectrum of Threat Detection," Frontiers in Systems Neuroscience 11, art. 18 (2017). https://www.frontiersin.org/articles/10.3389/fnsys.2017.00018/full, accessed December 14, 2022.

264 D. Caroline Blanchard, Guy Griebel, Roger Pobbe, and Robert J. Blanchard, "Risk Assessment as an Evolved Threat Detection and Analysis Process," Neuroscience & Biobehavioral Reviews 35, no. 4 (March 2011): 991–998, https://pubmed.ncbi.nlm.nih.gov/21056591/, accessed December 14, 2022.

265 Stephen Porges, "Polyvagal Theory: A Biobehavioral Journey to Sociality," Comprehensive Psychoneuroendocrinology 7 (August 2021): 100069, https://www.sciencedirect.com/science/article/pii/S2666497621000436, accessed December 14, 2022.

266 Porges and Buczynski, "Polyvagal Theory and Trauma."

267 Edwin Taylor, Cleo A. C. Leite, Marina Satori, Tobias Wang, Augusto S. Abe, and Dane A. Crossley II, "The Phylogeny and Ontogeny of Autonomic Control of the Heart and Cardiorespiratory Interactions in Vertebrates," Journal of Experimental Biology 217, no. 5 (March 2014): 690–703,

268 National Institute for the Clinical Application of Behavioral Medicine, with Stephen W. Porges and Ruth Buczynski, "Polyvagal Theory and Trauma," NICABM, 2022, https://www.nicabm.com/topic/polyvagal-theory-explained/, accessed November 23, 2022.

269 Davide Casiraghi, "The Polyvagal Theory for Dummies," Movement Meets Life, October 13, 2013, https://www.movementmeetslife.com/en/posts/polyvagal-theory-for-dummies, accessed November 23, 2022.

270 Stephen W. Porges, "The polyvagal perspective," Biological Psychology 74, no. 2 (2007): 116–143

271 Theodore P. Beauchaine, Lisa Gatzke-Kopp, and Hilary K. Mead, "Polyvagal Theory and Developmental Psychopathology: Emotion and Dysregulation and Conduct Problems from Preschool to Adolescence," Biological Psychology 74, no. 2 (February 2007): 174–184, https://doi.org/10.1016/j.biopsycho.2005.08.008, accessed November 29, 2022.

272 Scheeringa, Analysis of The Body Keeps the Score, 59.

273 Olea Sylvestris, "'Polyvagal Theory' is Pseudoscience. Here's why. The Deeper You Dig, the Worse It Gets," Medium, November 3, 2022, https://medium.com/@clymene/polyvagal-theory-is-pseudoscience-heres-why-139d8b41608d, accessed December 14, 2022.

274 Gerassi and Nichols, Sex Trafficking, 110.

275 American Psychological Association, "Cognitive Behavioral Therapy (CBT) for Treatment of PTSD," Clinical Practice Guidelines for the

Treatment of Posttraumatic Stress Disorder, accessed April 8, 2025, https://www.apa.org/ptsd-guideline/treatments/cognitive-behavioral-therapy.

276 Ibid., 5.

277 American Psychological Association, "Cognitive Behavioral Therapy (CBT) for Treatment of PTSD," Clinical Practice Guidelines for the Treatment of Posttraumatic Stress Disorder, accessed April 8, 2025, https://www.apa.org/ptsd-guideline/treatments/cognitive-behavioral-therapy

278 Psychology Today, "Cognitive Processing Therapy," https://www.psychologytoday.com/us/therapy-types/cognitive-processing-therapy. Accessed February 18, 2019.

279 George F. Rhoades, Jr., "Understanding and Treatment of Sexual Trauma and Trafficking," American Psychological Association Division 56 (Trauma Psychology), n.d., https://www.apatraumadivision.org/images/kcfinder/files/rhoades_slides.pdf, accessed March 9, 2019; EMDR Institute, "What Is EMDR Therapy? Frequently Asked Questions," https://www.emdr.com/frequent-questions/, accessed June 12, 2019.

280 Walters Kluwer Health, "Mental Health Treatment for Victims of Human Trafficking," Medical Xpress, March 7, 2018, https://medicalxpress.com/news/2018-03-mental-health-treatment-victims-human.html, accessed March 9, 2019.

281 Marla Friedman, "Facing the Horrors Inside: Introduction to Prolonged Exposure Therapy for PTSI," In Public Safety, February 2018, https://inpublicsafety.com/2018/02/facing-the-horrors-inside-introduction-to-prolonged-exposure-therapy-for-ptsi/, accessed March 9, 2019.

282 Office of Mental Health and Addiction Services, "Trauma,"5.

283 Friedman, "Facing the Horrors Inside," https://inpublicsafety.com/2018/02/facing-the-horrors-inside-introduction-to-prolonged-exposure-therapy-for-ptsi/, accessed March 9, 2019.

284 Ibid.

285 Ibid.

286 Edna B. Foa, Seth J. Gillihan, & Richard A. Bryant, "Challenges and Successes in Dissemination of Evidence-Based Treatments for Posttraumatic Stress: Lessons Learned from Prolonged Exposure Therapy for PTSD," In Mental Health Services for Individuals Who Have Experienced Sex Trafficking, by Bita Ghafoori, (conference paper, November 2017), 5.

287 American Psychological Association, "Psychology Matters: Glossary," in Williamson, Dutch, and Clawson, Evidence-Based Mental Health Treatment, 5.

288 Katy Robjant, Jackie Roberts, and Cornelius Katona, "Treating Posttraumatic Stress Disorder in Female Victims of Trafficking Using Narrative Exposure Therapy: A Retrospective Audit," Frontiers in Psychiatry 8, art. 63, (June 1, 2017), https://doi.org/10.3389/fpsyt.2017.00063, accessed March 9, 2019.

289 American Psychological Association, "Psychology Matters: Glossary," in Williamson, Dutch, and Clawson, Evidence-Based Mental Health Treatment, 5.

290 Rhoades, "Understanding and Treatment," accessed June 12, 2019,

291 Ed Stetzer, "Healing Victims of Human Trafficking," Christianity Today, March 2017, https://www.christianitytoday.com/edstetzer/2017/march/healing-victims-of-human-trafficking-long-slow-road-to-tran.html. Accessed February 11, 2018.

292 Vicki Peterson, "We Can't Keep Treating Anxiety from Complex Trauma the Same Way We Treat Generalized Anxiety," The Mighty, June 30, 2018, https://themighty.com/2018/06/anxiety-from-complex-trauma/, accessed January 13, 2019.

293 Connecticut Department of Children and Families, "Functional Family Therapy (FFT): A Trauma-Informed Treatment," https://portal.ct.gov/-/media/dcf/trauma-informed_care/pdf/fftphasesandtrauma1pager2pdf.pdf, accessed November 20, 2024.

294 Missouri Department of Mental Health, "Assertive Community Treatment," https://dmh.mo.gov/behavioral-health/treatment-services/specialized-programs/assertive-community-treatment, accessed November 20, 2024.

295 Erica Laub, "DBT For PTSD: How It Works, Examples, & Effectiveness," Choosing Therapy, April 19, 2022. https://www.choosingtherapy.com/dbt-for-ptsd/, accessed November 20, 2024.

296 Behavioral Tech Institute, "Dialectical Behavior Therapy - Training & Education," October 26, 2023, https://behavioraltech.org/.)

297 American Psychological Association, Clinical Practice Guideline for the Treatment of Posttraumatic Stress Disorder (PTSD) in Adults (Washington, DC: American Psychological Association, 2017), 2, https://www.apa.org/ptsd-guideline/treatments/recommendations-summary-table.pdf.

298 Jennifer M. Mitchell et al., "MDMA-Assisted Therapy for Severe PTSD: A Randomized, Double-Blind, Placebo-Controlled Phase 3 Study," Nature Medicine 27 (2021): 1025–1033, https://doi.org/10.1038/s41591-021-01336-3.

299 Erwin Krediet et al., "Reviewing the Potential of Psychedelics for the Treatment of PTSD," International Journal of Neuropsychopharmacology 23, no. 6 (2020): 385–400, https://doi.org/10.1093/ijnp/pyaa018.

300 National Center for PTSD, "Psychedelic-Assisted Therapy for PTSD," U.S. Department of Veterans Affairs, August 26, 2024, https://www.ptsd.va.gov/professional/treat/txessentials/psychedelic_assisted_therapy.asp.

301 Shakila Meshkat, Richard J. Zeifman, Kathleen Stewart, Reinhard Janssen-Aguilar, Wendy Lou, Rakesh Jetly, Candice M. Monson, Venkat Bhat, "Psilocybin-Assisted Massed Cognitive Processing Therapy for Chronic Posttraumatic Stress Disorder: Protocol for an Open-Label Pilot Feasibility Trial," PLOS ONE, (January 17, 2025), https://doi.org/10.1371/journal.pone.031374, accessed February 18, 2025; Samoon Ahmad, "New Study Finds MDMA Effective in Treatment of PTSD: How Empathogens Work for Patients with Post-Traumatic Stress," Psychology Today, November 10, 2023, https://www.psychologytoday.com/us/blog/post-traumatic-stress-disorder/202311/new-study-finds-mdma-effecting-in-treatnent-of-ptsd, accessed February 17, 2025; NeuroLaunch Editorial Team, "LSD Trauma Therapy: Exploring Psychedelic-Assisted Treatment for PTSD," NeuroLaunch, October 1, 2024, https://neurolaunch.com/lsd-trauma-therapy/ , accessed February 28, 2025.

302 Claire Bugos, "FDA Advisors Shot Down MDMA as Treatment for PTSD. What Went Wrong?," Verywell Health, updated June 10, 2024, https://www.verywellhealth.com/fda-panel-rejects-mdma-therapy-for-ptsd-8659953, accessed February 18, 2025; C. Lemarchand, R. Chopin, M. Paul, A. Braillon, L. Cosgrove, I. Cristea, et al., "Fragile Promise of Psychedelics in Psychiatry," BMJ 387 (2024): e080391, https://doi.org/10.1136/bmj-2024-080391, accessed February 18, 2025; Leslie Morland and Joshua Woolley, "Psychedelic-Assisted Therapy for PTSD," PTSD: National Center for PTSD, U.S. Department of Veterans Affairs, January 15, 2025, https://www.ptsd.va.gov/professional/treat/txessentials/psychedelics_assisted_therapy.asp#four, accessed February 18, 2025; Collin M. Price, Walter Dunn, and Steve Marder, "Understanding the Challenges of Masking in Psychedelic Clinical Trials: A Comprehensive Review," 20th Annual Scientific Meeting Posters, Semel Institute for Neuroscience & Human Behavior at UCLA, 2024, https://isctm.org/public_access/20th_Annual/Poster/Price_Poster_NI.pdf, accessed February 28, 2025.

303 Ahmad, "New Study Finds MDMA Effective," accessed February 17, 2025.

304 Ralf-Dieter Hilgers, FranzKönig, Geert Molenberghs, and Stephen Senn, "Design and Analysis of Clinical Trials for Small Rare Disease Populations," Journal of Rare Diseases Research & Treatment, November 23, 2016, https://www.rarediseasesjournal.com/articles/design-and-analysis-of-clinical-trials-for-small-rare-disease-populations.html, accessed February 18, 2025; Institute of Medicine (US) Committee on Strategies for Small-Number-Participant Clinical Research Trials, Small Clinical Trials: Issues and Challenges, ed. Charles H. Evans Jr. and Suzanne T. Ildstad (Washington, DC: National Academies Press, 2001), https://pubmed.ncbi.nlm.nih.gov/25057552/, accessed February 18, 2025; J. Raymond, T. E. Darsaut, J. Eneling, et al., "The Small Trial Problem," Trials 24, art. 426 (June 22, 2023), https://doi.org/10.1186/s13063-023-07348-3, accessed February 18, 2025; Pär Kragsterman, "Clinical Trial Phases: Complete Guide to All 4 Stages," Collective Minds, February 11, 2025, https://about.cmrad.com/articles/clinical-trial-phases-complete-guide-to-all-4-stages, accessed February 18, 2025.

Bibliography

Adams, Jay E. A Theology of Christian Counseling. Grand Rapids, MI: Zondervan, 1979.

Alotaiby, Tarek N., Fahad A. Alkhamis, Sultan Alhusaini, Khalid J. Alghamdi, and Meshaal S. Alsallum. "Electroencephalography Signal Processing: A Comprehensive Review and Analysis of Methods and Techniques." Sensors 23, no. 14 (2023): 6434. https://doi.org/10.3390/s23146434.

Alvarado Parkway Institute, Behavioral Health System. "Seven Signs You Have Mild PTSD Rather Than Anxiety." APIBHS (blog), September 7, 2018. https://apibhs.com/2018/09/07/seven-signs-you-have-mild-ptsd-rather-than-anxiety.

American Association of Neurological Surgeons. "Anatomy of the Spine and Peripheral Nervous System." 2022. https://www.aans.org/en/Patients/Neurosurgical-Conditions-and-Treatments/Anatomy-of-the-Spine-and-Peripheral-Nervous-System.

American Heritage Dictionary of the English Language, The. 5th ed. Boston: HarperCollins Publishers, 2022. https://ahdictionary.com/word/search.html?q=disease.

American Psychiatric Association. Diagnostic and Statistical Manual of Mental Disorders. 4th ed. Washington, DC: American Psychiatric Association, 2004.

———. Diagnostic and Statistical Manual of Mental Disorders. 5th ed. Arlington, VA: American Psychiatric Association Publishing, 2013.

———. Diagnostic and Statistical Manual of Mental Disorders: DSM-5-TR. 5th ed., text rev. Washington, DC: American Psychiatric Association Publishing, 2022.

———. Clinical Practice Guideline for the Treatment of Posttraumatic Stress Disorder (PTSD) in Adults. Washington, DC: American Psychiatric Association, 2017. https://www.apa.org/ptsd-guideline/treatments/recommendations-summary-table.pdf.

American Psychological Association. "Cognitive Behavioral Therapy (CBT) for Treatment of PTSD." Clinical Practice Guidelines for the Treatment of Posttraumatic Stress Disorder. Accessed April 8, 2025. https://www.apa.org/ptsd-guideline/treatments/cognitive-behavioral-therapy.

Armstrong, Paul B. "Phenomenology." In The Johns Hopkins Guide for Literary Theory and Criticism, 2nd ed. Baltimore: Johns Hopkins University Press, 2005. http://litguide.press.jhu.edu/.

Badger, Raven. "Addressing Women's Sexual Health Disparities in Substance Use Disorder Treatment." Advances in Addiction & Recovery, Winter 2016. https://www.naadac.org/assets/2416/aa&r_winter2016_addressing_womens_sexual_health_disparities_in_substance_use_disorder_treatment.pdf.

Bandettini, Peter A. "Overview of Functional Magnetic Resonance Imaging." PMC, April 1, 2017. https://pmc.ncbi.nlm.nih.gov/articles/PMC5573747/.

Barnes, Albert, John Calvin, Adam Clarke, et al. "The Ultimate Commentary on Genesis." In The Ultimate Commentary Collection. N.p.: n.p., n.d.

Barnhouse, Donald Grey. Genesis: A Devotional Exposition. Vol. 1. Grand Rapids, MI: Zondervan Publishing House, 1973.

Beauchaine, Theodore P., Lisa Gatzke-Kopp, and Hilary K. Mead. "Polyvagal Theory and Developmental Psychopathology: Emotion Dysregulation and Conduct Problems from Preschool to Adolescence." Biological Psychology 74, no. 2 (February 2007): 174–184. https://doi.org/10.1016/j.biopsycho.2005.08.008.

Bennett, Craig M., Abigail A. Baird, Michael B. Miller, and George L. Wolford. "Neural Correlates of Interspecies Perspective Taking in the Post-Mortem

Atlantic Salmon: An Argument for Multiple Comparisons Correction." Journal of Serendipitous and Unexpected Results 1, no. 1 (2009): 1–5. https://www.jsur.org/v1n1p1.pdf.

Berger, Daniel, II. Mental Illness Volume Three: The Reality of the Physical Nature. Kindle ed. Taylors, SC: Alethia International Publications, 2016.

Berger, Daniel, III. Saving Abnormal: The Disorder of Psychiatric Genetics. Taylors, SC: Alethia International Publications, 2020.

Berger, Daniel. "Post-Traumatic Stress is not a Disorder." DrDanielBerger.com, February 23, 2018. https://www.drdanielberger.com/single-post/2018/02/23/Post-Traumatic-Stress-is-not-a-Disorder.

———. The Influence of Nurture: How Environment Shapes Behavior. N.p.: Alethia Books, 2018.

Berg, Jim. Changed Into His Image: God's Plan for Transforming Your Being. Greenville, SC: BJU Press, 2018.

Berkhof, Louis. Systematic Theology. Grand Rapids, MI: Wm. B. Eerdmans Publishing Co., 1953.

———. Systematic Theology. Kindle ed. Grand Rapids, MI: Wm. B. Eerdmans Publishing Co., 1996.

Beste, Jennifer Erin. God and the Victim: Traumatic Intrusion on Grace and Freedom. New York: Oxford University Press, 2007.

Bible History. "The Roman Scourge." 2024. http://bible-history.com/past/flagrum.

BibleStudyTools Staff, The. "Bitterness in the Bible." Bible Study Tools, September 7, 2018. https://www.biblestudytools.com/topical-verses/bitterness-in-the-bible/.

Bisram, Jennifer. "Migrants in New York City Shelters Falling Victim to Human Trafficking." CBS New York, February 23, 2024. https://www.cbsnews.com/newyork/news/nyc-migrants-asylum-seekers-human-trafficking-sex-trafficking/.

Blanchard, D. Caroline, Guy Griebel, Roger Pobbe, and Robert J. Blanchard. "Risk Assessment as an Evolved Threat Detection and Analysis Process." Neuroscience & Biobehavioral Reviews 35, no. 4 (March 2011): 991–998. https://pubmed.ncbi.nlm.nih.gov/21056591/.

Bovin, Michelle J., Stephanie Y. Wells, Ann M. Rasmusson, Terence M. Keane, and Brian P. Marx. "Psychometric Properties of the PTSD Checklist for Diagnostic and Statistical Manual of Mental Disorders–Fifth Edition (PCL-5) in Veterans." Psychological Assessment 28, no. 11 (2016): 1379–91. https://doi.org/10.1037/pas0000254.

Bowley, L. "Her Battle." In The White Umbrella: Walking with Survivors of Sex Trafficking, edited by Mary Frances Bowley, chap. 5. Kindle ed. Chicago: Moody Publishers, Wellspring Living, 2012.

Brammer, Stephen J., Kenneth Gangel, and Max Anders, eds. Holman Old Testament Commentary: Genesis. Nashville, TN: Broadman & Holman Publishers, 2003.

Bremner, J. Douglas. "Traumatic Stress: Effects on the Brain." Dialogues in Clinical Neuroscience 8, no. 4 (2006): 445–461. https://pmc.ncbi.nlm.nih.gov/articles/PMC3181836/.

Brooks, Nate. "The Bible Keeps Record of Trauma. But Is It Trauma Informed?" Christianity Today, November 4, 2022. https://www.christianitytoday.com.

Brooks, Nate, Tate Cockrell, Brad Hambrick, Kristin Kellen, and Sam Williams. "What Is Redemptive Counseling / Clinically Informed Biblical Counseling?" Paper, Southeastern Baptist Theological Seminary Biblical Counseling Department, July 8, 2024. https://www.sebts.edu/wp-content/uploads/2024/07/What-is-RCCIBC.pdf.

Brown, Emery N., and Marlene Behrmann. "Controversy in Statistical Analysis of Functional Magnetic Resonance Imaging Data." Proceedings of the National Academy of Sciences of the United States of America 114, no. 17 (2017): E3368–E3369. https://doi.org/10.1073/pnas.1705513114.

Bugos, Claire. "FDA Advisors Shot Down MDMA as Treatment for PTSD. What Went Wrong?" Verywell Health, updated June 10, 2024. https://www.verywellhealth.com/fda-panel-rejects-mdma-therapy-for-ptsd-8659953.

Bunyan, John. Grace Abounding to the Chief of Sinners. 1666. Reprint, London: The Religious Tract Society, 1905. Transcribed by David Price. Project Gutenberg, released February 19, 2013. https://www.gutenberg.org/files/654/654-h/654-h.htm.

Campbell, Ken. Those Ugly Emotions: How to Manage Your Emotions. Fearn, Ross-shire, Scotland: Christian Focus Publications, 1999.

Caron, Christina. "This Nerve Influences Nearly Every Internal Organ. Can It Improve Our Mental State too?" New York Times, June 2, 2022. https://www.nytimes.com/2022/06/02/well/mind/vagus-nerve-mental-health.html.

Casiraghi, Davide. "The Polyvagal Theory for Dummies." Movement Meets Life, October 13, 2013. https://www.movementmeetslife.com/en/posts/polyvagal-theory-for-dummies.

Centers for Disease Control and Prevention. "Adverse Childhood Experiences." Accessed October 22, 2022. https://www.cdc.gov/violenceprevention/aces/index.html.

———. "What is Epigenetics?" Last reviewed August 15, 2022. https://www.cdc.gov/genomics/disease/epigenetics.htm.

Chang, Steve W. C. "The Science of Connection: What Does 'the Social Brain' Really Mean?" Psychology Today, March 16, 2020. https://www.psychologytoday.com/us/blog/the-science-connection/202003/what-does-the-social-brain-really-mean.

Chen, Jenn. Biblical Counseling and Mental Disorder Diagnosis. Wapwallopen, PA: Shepherd Press, 2024.

Cherry, Kendra. "What Is the Fight-or-Flight Response? Experiencing Physical Symptoms in Response to Stress." Verywell Mind, updated November 7, 2022. https://www.verywellmind.com/what-is-the-fight-or-flight-response-2795194.

Chowdhury, S., R. Biswas, A. H. Mallick, and S. N. Hasan. "Electroencephalography (EEG) Physiological Indices Reflecting Human Physical Performance: A Systematic Review Using Updated PRISMA." Journal of Integrative Neuroscience 22, no. 3 (2023): 76. https://doi.org/10.31083/j.jin2203076.

Cleveland Clinic. "Cranial Nerves." February 22, 2022. https://my.clevelandclinic.org/health/body/21998-cranial-nerves.

Connecticut Department of Children and Families. "Functional Family Therapy (FFT): A Trauma-Informed Treatment." https://portal.ct.gov/-/media/dcf/trauma-informed_care/pdf/fftphasesandtrauma1pager2pdf.pdf.

Council for Evidence-Based Psychiatry. "Diagnostic System Lacks Validity." CEP, March 15, 2014. http://cepuk.org/unrecognised-facts/diagnostic-system-lacks-validity/.

Courtois, Christine. "Complex Trauma, Complex Reactions: Assessment and Treatment." In Evidence-Based Mental Health Treatment for Victims of Human Trafficking, edited by Erin Williamson, Nicole M. Dutch, and Heather J. Clawson, 3. Washington, DC: U.S. Department of Health and Human Services, Office of the Assistant Secretary for Planning and Evaluation, 2010.

Cross, Richard M. "Affect Regulation, Attachment, and the Developing Social Brain: Implications for Assessment and Treatment of Dissociative Disorders." In The Handbook of Complex Trauma and Dissociation in Children. Routledge, 2025.

Curtis, Lindsay. "How Adverse Childhood Experiences (ACEs) May Lead to Trauma and PTSD." PsychCentral, updated August 25, 2021. https://psychcentral.com/ptsd/adverse-childhood-experiences-post-traumatic-stress-disorder.

De Bellis, Michael D., Andrew S. Baum, Boris Birmaher, Matcheri S. Keshavan, Clayton H. Eccard, Amy M. Boring, Frank J. Jenkins, and Neal D. Ryan. "A.E. Bennett Research Award. Developmental Traumatology, Part I: Biological Stress Systems." Biological Psychiatry 45, no. 10 (1999): 1259–1270.

De Bellis, Michael D. "Developmental Traumatology: Neurobiological Development in Maltreated Children With PTSD." Psychiatric Times 16, no. 9

(September 1, 1999). https://www.psychiatrictimes.com/view/developmental-traumatology-neurobiological-development-maltreated-children-ptsd.

Dębiec, Jacek, and Joseph LeDoux. "The Amygdala and the Neural Pathways of Fear." In Post-traumatic Stress Disorder: Basic Science and Clinical Practice, edited by P. J. Shiromani, T. M. Keane, and J. E. LeDoux, 23–38. Humana Press/Springer Nature, 2009. https://doi.org/10.1007/978-1-60327-329-9_2.

Dingman, Marc, Ph.D. "2-Minute Neuroscience: Divisions of The Nervous System." Neuroscientifically Challenged, 2002. https://neuroscientificallychallenged.com/posts/2-minute-neuroscience-divisions-of-the-nervous-system.

———. "2-Minute Neuroscience: The Parasympathetic Nervous System." YouTube video. Neuroscientifically Challenged. https://neuroscientificallychallenged.com/posts/2-minute-neuroscience-parasympathetic-nervous-system.

———. "2-Minute Neuroscience: The Sympathetic Nervous System." YouTube video. Neuroscientifically Challenged. https://neuroscientificallychallenged.com/posts/2-minute-neuroscience-sympathetic-nervous-system.

Duval, Emily R., Arash Javanbakht, and Israel Liberzon. "Neural Circuits in Anxiety and Stress Disorders: A Focused Review." Therapeutics and Clinical Risk Management 11 (2015): 115–126.

Eklund, Anders, Thomas E. Nichols, and Hans Knutsson. "Cluster Failure: Why fMRI Inferences for Spatial Extent Have Inflated False-Positive Rates." Proceedings of the National Academy of Sciences 113, no. 28 (2016): 7900–7905. https://doi.org/10.1073/pnas.1602413113.

EMDR Institute. "What Is EMDR Therapy? Frequently Asked Questions." https://www.emdr.com/frequent-questions/.

Erickson, Millard J. Christian Theology. 3rd ed. Grand Rapids, MI: Baker Academic, 2013.

Farde, Lars. "Imaging the Living Human Brain: Magnetic Resonance Imaging and Positron Emission Tomography." Proceedings of the National Academy of Sciences 94, no. 7 (1997): 2787–2788. https://doi.org/10.1073/pnas.94.7.2787.

Foa, Edna B., Seth J. Gillihan, and Richard A. Bryant. "Challenges and Successes in Dissemination of Evidence-Based Treatments for Posttraumatic Stress: Lessons Learned from Prolonged Exposure Therapy for PTSD." In Mental Health Services for Individuals Who Have Experienced Sex Trafficking, by Bita Ghafoori, 5. Conference paper, November 2017.

Fores, Eaton T. "There Are No 'Chemical Imbalances.'" Academy for the Study of the Psychoanalytic Arts, The Eaton T. Fores Research Center, 2003. https://psychrights.org/research/digest/TheBrain/NoChemicalImbalances.htm.

Friedman, Marla. "Facing the Horrors Inside: Introduction to Prolonged Exposure Therapy for PTSI." In Public Safety, February 2018. https://inpublicsafety.com/2018/02/facing-the-horrors-inside-introduction-to-prolonged-exposure-therapy-for-ptsi/.

Fritscher, Lisa. "Advantages and Disadvantages of the Diagnostic Statistical Manual." Verywell Mind, updated January 17, 2023. https://www.verywellmind.com/dsm-friend-or-foe-2671930.

Gannon, Pam, and Cheryl Moore. In the Aftermath: Past the Pain of Childhood Sexual Abuse. Bemidji, MN: Focus Publishing, 2002.

Ganschow, Julie. "Overcoming Anger." Module 500, Lesson 5, Reigning Grace Counseling Center, Reigning Grace Institute's Fundamentals of Biblical Counseling Training Program, 2024.

Gerassi, Lara B., and Andrea J. Nichols. Sex Trafficking and Commercial Sexual Exploitation: Prevention, Advocacy, and Trauma-Informed Practice. New York: Springer Publishing Company, 2018.

Gifford, Greg. "Mind vs. Brain: Gaining Biblical Clarity on the Difference." The Biblical Counseling Coalition, April 1, 2022. https://www.biblicalcounselingcoalition.org/2022/04/01/mind-vs-brain-gaining-biblical-clarity-on-the-difference/.

Goldstein, David S. "The Autonomic Nervous System Has Parts." YouTube video, 8:53. From Introduction to Autonomic Medicine Course (video 3 of 24). Posted by The American Autonomic Society, November 14, 2016. https://www.youtube.com/watch?v=8mEBFEffectM.

———. "Sympathetic Nervous System." In Encyclopedia of Stress, 2nd ed., edited by George Fink, 697–703. Academic Press, 2007. https://doi.org/10.1016/B978-012373947-6.00370-6.

Got Questions. "How Did the Fall Affect Humanity?" Accessed April 14, 2019. https://www.gotquestions.org/fall-affect-humanity.html.

Grimell, Jan. "Contemporary Insights from Biblical Combat Veterans through the Lenses of Moral Injury and Post-Traumatic Stress Disorder." Journal of Pastoral Care & Counseling 72, no. 4 (2018): 241–250. https://doi.org/10.1177/1542305018790218.

Gross, Joachim. "Magnetoencephalography in Cognitive Neuroscience: A Primer." Neuron 104, no. 2 (2019): 189–204. https://doi.org/10.1016/j.neuron.2019.07.001.

Grudem, Wayne. Systematic Theology: An Introduction to Biblical Doctrine. Grand Rapids, MI: Zondervan, 1994.

Halene, Tobias B., Gregor Hasler, Amanda Mitchell, and Schahram Akbarian. Psychiatric Genetics: A Primer for Clinicians and Basic Scientists. Edited by Thomas G. Schulze and Francis J. McMahon. New York: Oxford University Press, 2018.

Hamilton, Victor P. The Book of Genesis: Chapters 1–17. New International Commentary on the Old Testament. Grand Rapids, MI: Wm. B. Eerdmans Publishing Co., 1990.

Hammer, N., J. Glatzner, C. Feja, C. Kuhne, J. Meixensberger, U. Planitzer, S. Schiefenheim, B. N. Tillmann, and D. Winkler. "Human Vagus Nerve Branching in the Cervical Region." PLoS One 10, no. 2 (2015): e0118006. https://www.ncbi.nlm.nih.gov/books/NBK537171.

Harrington, R. "The 'Railway Spine' Diagnosis and Victorian Responses to PTSD." Journal of Psychosomatic Research 40, no. 1 (1996): 11–14. https://doi.org/10.1016/0022-3999(95)00514-5.

Haslam, Nick. "The Problem with Describing Every Misfortune as 'Trauma.'" Chicago Tribune, August 15, 2016. https://www.chicagotribune.com/opinion/ct-trauma-microaggressions-trigger-warnings-20160815-story.html.

Heal Her Heart. "Understanding Complex Post Traumatic Stress Disorder: Symptoms, Causes." https://www.healherheart.org/blogs/resources/understanding-complex-post-traumatic-stress-disorder-symptoms-causes-and-treatment-options.

Herman, Judith L. "Complex PTSD: A Syndrome in Survivors of Prolonged and Repeated Trauma." Journal of Traumatic Stress 5, no. 3 (1992): 377–391.

Hilgers, Ralf-Dieter, Franz König, Geert Molenberghs, and Stephen Senn. "Design and Analysis of Clinical Trials for Small Rare Disease Populations." Journal of Rare Diseases Research & Treatment, November 23, 2016. https://www.rarediseasesjournal.com/articles/design-and-analysis-of-clinical-trials-for-small-rare-disease-populations.html.

Holcomb, Justin, and Lindsay Holcomb. Rid of My Disgrace: Hope and Healing for Victims of Sexual Assault. Wheaton, IL: Crossway, 2011.

Hong, Kyung S., Jae-Ho Choi, and Tong-Ho Kang. "Functional Near-Infrared Spectroscopy and Its Clinical Application in the Field of Neuroscience: Advances and Future Directions." Frontiers in Neuroscience 14 (2020): 724. https://doi.org/10.3389/fnins.2020.00724.

Huang, Z. Josh, and Hongkui Zeng. "It Takes the World to Understand the Brain." Science 350, no. 6256 (2015): 42–44. https://pmc.ncbi.nlm.nih.gov/articles/PMC4664961/.

Hunt, Pamela V. "8 Biblical Steps to Recover from Post-Traumatic Stress Disorder." Christian Post. Accessed June 3, 2019. https://www.christianpost.com/news/8-biblical-steps-to-recover-from-post-traumatic-stress-disorder.html.

Institute of Medicine (US) Committee on Strategies for Small-Number-Participant Clinical Research Trials. Small Clinical Trials: Issues and Challenges. Edited by Charles H. Evans Jr. and Suzanne T. Ildstad. Washington, DC: National Academies Press, 2001. https://pubmed.ncbi.nlm.nih.gov/25057552/.

Johnson, Dale. "Who is Man?" Plenary address at the Association of Certified Biblical Counselors Annual Conference, "In His Image: Recovering Human Dignity," Fort Worth, TX, October 3, 2022. Audio recording.

Jones, Laura K., and Judith L. Cureton. "Trauma Redefined in the DSM-5: Rationale and Implications for Counseling Practice." The Professional Counselor 4, no. 3 (2014): 257–271.

Juhnke, Timothy. "Doctrines of Grace: Irresistible Grace." MP3 sermon, Faith Community Church, April 7, 2019. https://www.sermonaudio.com/sermoninfo.asp?SID=481920433192.

Kragsterman, Pär. "Clinical Trial Phases: Complete Guide to All 4 Stages." Collective Minds, February 11, 2025. https://about.cmrad.com/articles/clinical-trial-phases-complete-guide-to-all-4-stages.

Krediet, Erwin, Eric Vermetten, and T. J. de Vries. "Reviewing the Potential of Psychedelics for the Treatment of PTSD." International Journal of Neuropsychopharmacology 23, no. 6 (2020): 385–400. https://doi.org/10.1093/ijnp/pyaa018.

Kutchins, Herb, and Stuart A. Kirk. Making Us Crazy: DSM: The Psychiatric Bible and the Creation of Mental Disorders. New York: Free Press, 1997.

Lambert, Heath. A Theology of Biblical Counseling: The Doctrinal Foundations of Counseling Ministry. Grand Rapids, MI: Zondervan, 2016.

Lane, Timothy S. PTSD: Healing for a Heart Held Captive. Greensboro, NC: New Growth Press, n.d.

———. "Godly Intoxication." In Addictions: A Banquet in the Grave, 5. Phillipsburg, NJ: P&R Publishing, 2001.

Lanese, Nicoletta, and Scott Dutfield. "Fight or Flight: The Sympathetic Nervous System." Live Science, February 9, 2022. https://www.livescience.com/65446-sympathetic-nervous-system.html.

Laub, Erica. "DBT For PTSD: How It Works, Examples, & Effectiveness." Choosing Therapy, April 19, 2022. https://www.choosingtherapy.com/dbt-for-ptsd/.

Leaf, Caroline. "How Are the Mind & the Brain Different? A Neuroscientist Explains." MBGHealth, March 8, 2021. https://www.mindbodygreen.com/articles/difference-between-mind-and-brain-neuroscientist.

Lemarchand, C., R. Chopin, M. Paul, A. Braillon, L. Cosgrove, I. Cristea, et al. "Fragile Promise of Psychedelics in Psychiatry." BMJ 387 (2024): e080391. https://doi.org/10.1136/bmj-2024-080391.

Leonard, Jayne. "Complex PTSD: Symptoms, Behaviors, and Recovery." Medical News Today, August 28, 2018. https://www.medicalnewstoday.com/articles/322886.

Liberzon, Israel, and Chandra Sekhar Sripada. "The Functional Neuroanatomy of PTSD: A Critical Review." Progress in Brain Research 167 (2008): 151–169. https://doi.org/10.1016/S0079-6123(07)67011-3.

Liem, Lucas, and Bernhard Neuhuber. "Critique of the Polyvagal Theory." Accessed December 15, 2022.

Logothetis, Nikos K. "What We Can Do and What We Cannot Do with fMRI." Nature 453, no. 7197 (2008): 869–878. https://doi.org/10.1038/nature06976.

Los Angeles County Department of Mental Health. "Our Services." Accessed April 4, 2025. https://dmh.lacounty.gov/our-services/.

MacArthur, John. The MacArthur Bible Commentary. Nashville, TN: Thomas Nelson, 2005.

Mack, Wayne A. Anger and Stress Management God's Way. Phillipsburg, NJ: P&R Publishing, 2017.

Marek, S., B. Tervo-Clemmens, F. J. Calabro, et al. "Reproducible Brain-Wide Association Studies Require Thousands of Individuals." Nature 603 (2022): 654–660. https://doi.org/10.1038/s41586-022-04492-9.

Martin, Eric C. "Science and Ideology." Internet Encyclopedia of Philosophy. https://iep.utm.edu/sci-ideo/#H6.

Mathison, Keith. "Interpreting General and Special Revelation." Ligonier Ministries, May 25, 2012. https://learn.ligonier.org/articles/interpreting-general-and-special-revelation-reformed-approach-science-and-scripture.

McCrory, Eamon. “The Guide to Childhood Trauma and the Brain.” The Better Care Network, Anna Freud National Centre for Children and Families, September 2020. https://bettercarenetwork.org/library/particular-threats-to-childrens-care-and-protection/child-abuse-and-neglect/the-guidebook-to-childhood-trauma-and-the-brain.

McDonald, Christine. The Same Kind of Human: Seeing the Marginalized and Exploited Through the Eyes of Grace. N.p.: Amazon Digital Services LLC, 2016. Kindle.

McMinn, Mark R., and Timothy R. Phillips. Care for the Soul: Exploring the Intersection of Psychology & Theology. Downers Grove, IL: InterVarsity Press, 2001.

McNally, Richard J. “Progress and Controversy in the Study of Post-Traumatic Stress Disorder.” Annual Review of Psychology 54 (2003): 229–252. https://www.ncbi.nlm.nih.gov/pmc/articles/PMC3141586/.

———. “Progress and Controversy in the Study of Posttraumatic Stress Disorder.” PowerPoint Presentation, 2003. https://pdfs.semanticscholar.org/1db8/9cfe8a2d7fd42bb1a6b68664f47aec957a11.pdf.

Meda, Shashwath A., Vince D. Calhoun, and Michael C. Stevens. “Functional Magnetic Resonance Imaging: An Invaluable Tool in Translational Neuroscience.” NCBI Bookshelf. Accessed April 18, 2025. https://www.ncbi.nlm.nih.gov/books/NBK533144/.

Mele, G., G. Cavaliere, M. Alfano, et al. “Simultaneous Electroencephalography-Functional Magnetic Resonance Imaging for Assessment of Human Brain Function.” Frontiers in Neurology 13 (2022): 934265. https://doi.org/10.3389/fneur.2022.934265.

Merriam-Webster. “Trauma.” 2022. https://www.merriam-webster.com/dictionary/trauma.

Meshkat, Shakila, Richard J. Zeifman, Kathleen Stewart, Reinhard Janssen-Aguilar, Wendy Lou, Rakesh Jetly, Candice M. Monson, and Venkat Bhat. “Psilocybin-Assisted Massed Cognitive Processing Therapy for Chronic Posttraumatic Stress

Disorder: Protocol for an Open-Label Pilot Feasibility Trial." PLOS ONE, January 17, 2025. https://doi.org/10.1371/journal.pone.031374.

Microsoft Copilot. "Diagnoses, Symptoms, Behaviors, and Descriptions Chart" and "BPD and RAD Diagnoses Chart." Copilot, 2024. https://download.bpd-and-rad-diagnoses-chart.

Minnesota Department of Health. "Definition: What Is the ACE?" Accessed February 6, 2019. https://www.health.state.mn.us/communities/ace/index.html.

Mitchell, Jennifer M., Michael Bogenschutz, Scott Aaronson, et al. "MDMA-Assisted Therapy for Severe PTSD: A Randomized, Double-Blind, Placebo-Controlled Phase 3 Study." Nature Medicine 27 (2021): 1025–1033. https://doi.org/10.1038/s41591-021-01336-3.

Moberg, Athena. Yes, You Can! Overcome No Matter Where You're From: Straight Talk & Strategies for Adult Survivors of Childhood Sexual Abuse. N.p.: Athena Moberg Speaking International, LLC, 2015. Kindle.

———. "Unforgiveness." In Straight Talk & Strategies for Adult Survivors of Childhood Sexual Abuse. N.p.: Independently published, n.d.

Mujica-Parodi, Lilianne R., Jiook Cha, and Jonathan Gao. "From Anxious to Reckless: A Control Systems Approach Unifies Prefrontal-Limbic Regulation Across the Spectrum of Threat Detection." Frontiers in Systems Neuroscience 11, art. 18 (2017). https://www.frontiersin.org/articles/10.3389/fnsys.2017.00018/full.

National Center for PTSD. "Psychedelic-Assisted Therapy for PTSD." U.S. Department of Veterans Affairs, August 26, 2024. https://www.ptsd.va.gov/professional/treat/txessentials/psychedelic_assisted_therapy.asp.

National Institute for the Clinical Application of Behavioral Medicine, with Stephen W. Porges and Ruth Buczynski. "Polyvagal Theory and Trauma." NICABM, 2022. https://www.nicabm.com/topic/polyvagal-theory-explained/.

National Institute on Drug Abuse. "Sex Differences in Substance Use." April 1, 2020. https://nida.nih.gov/publications/research-reports/substance-use-in-women/sex-differences-in-substance-use.

———. “Trauma and Stress.” February 6, 2024. https://nida.nih.gov/research-topics/trauma-and-stress.

Newman, Tim. “All About the Central Nervous System.” Medical News Today, updated November 29, 2023. https://www.medicalnewstoday.com/articles/307076.

Nicewander, Sue, and Maria Brookins. Treasure in the Ashes: Our Journey Home from the Ruins of Sexual Abuse. Wapwallopen, PA: Shepherd Press, 2018.

Office of Mental Health and Addiction Services. “Trauma.” [Details incomplete; assumed to be a report or webpage, cited as provided.]

Office to Monitor and Combat Trafficking in Persons. “About Us.” U.S. Department of State, June 2020. https://www.state.gov/about-us-office-to-monitor-and-combat-trafficking-in-persons/.

Ocher, Frank. “Complex Post-traumatic Stress Disorder.” Trauma Dissociation, February 20, 2019. http://traumadissociation.com/complexptsd.

Pastoral Care Inc. “Statistics on Addictions.” 2025. https://www.pastoralcareinc.com/statistics/statistics-on-addictions/.

Perron, Sean. (@seanperron). “There is nothing wrong with telling an anxious person who is worked up to take a breath.” X post, February 18, 2025, 9:18 a.m. https://x.com/seanperron/status/1891869805570863347.

Perry, Bruce D. “Childhood Experience and the Expression of Genetic Potential: What Childhood Neglect Tells Us about Nature and Nurture.” Brain and Mind 3 (2002): 79–100. Reprinted in The White Umbrella: Walking with Survivors of Sex Trafficking, chap. 5. Kindle ed. Chicago: Moody Publishers, Wellspring Living, 2012.

Perry, Bruce D., and Ronnie Pollard. “Homeostasis, Stress, Trauma, and Adaptation.” In The White Umbrella: Walking with Survivors of Sex Trafficking, chap. 5. Kindle ed. Chicago: Moody Publishers, Wellspring Living, 2012.

Peterson, Vicki. “We Can’t Keep Treating Anxiety from Complex Trauma the Same Way We Treat Generalized Anxiety.” The Mighty, June 30, 2018. https://themighty.com/2018/06/anxiety-from-complex-trauma/.

Petko, Bogdana, and Prasanna Tadi. "Neuroanatomy, Nucleus Ambiguus." In StatPearls. Treasure Island, FL: StatPearls Publishing, 2022. https://www.ncbi.nlm.nih.gov/books/NBK547744/.

Porges, Stephen W. "Neuroception: A Subconscious System for Detecting Threats and Safety." Zero to Three 24, no. 5 (2004): 19–24.

———. "The Polyvagal Perspective." Biological Psychology 74, no. 2 (2007): 116–143.

———. "Polyvagal Theory: A Biobehavioral Journey to Sociality." Comprehensive Psychoneuroendocrinology 7 (August 2021): 100069. https://www.sciencedirect.com/science/article/pii/S2666497621000436.

Porges, Stephen W., and Deb Dana, eds. Clinical Applications of the Polyvagal Theory: The Emergence of Polyvagal-Informed Therapies. New York: W. W. Norton & Company, 2018.

Porges, Stephen W., and Gunther Schmidt. "Polyvagal Theory: How Your Body Makes the Decision." YouTube video, 1:30:09. Posted by Trauma Research UK, May 28, 2016. https://www.youtube.com/watch?v=ivLealhBHPM&t=8s.

Powlison, David A. C. "Crucial Issues in Contemporary Biblical Counseling." Edited by Jay E. Adams. The Journal of Pastoral Practice 9, no. 3 (1988): 54.

Powlison, David. "Good and Angry*. Greensboro, NC: New Growth Press, 2016.

———. "I'll Never Get Over It—Help For the Aggrieved." Journal of Biblical Counseling 28, no. 1 (2014): 8–27.

———. Recovering from Child Abuse: Healing and Hope for Victims. Greensboro, NC: New Growth Press, 2008.

———. Sexual Assault: Healing Steps for Victims. Greensboro, NC: New Growth Press, 2010.

Price, Collin M., Walter Dunn, and Steve Marder. "Understanding the Challenges of Masking in Psychedelic Clinical Trials: A Comprehensive Review." 20th

Annual Scientific Meeting Posters, Semel Institute for Neuroscience & Human Behavior at UCLA, 2024. https://isctm.org/public_access/20th_Annual/Poster/Price_Poster_NI.pdf.

Priolo, Lou. Self-Image: How to Overcome Inferiority Judgments. Phillipsburg, NJ: P&R Publishing, 2007.

Psychology Today. "Cognitive Processing Therapy." https://www.psychologytoday.com/us/therapy-types/cognitive-processing-therapy.

Quosh, Constanze, and Kenneth Gergen. "Constructing Trauma and Its Treatment: Knowledge, Power and Resistance." In Meaning in Action, edited by Toshio Sugiman, Kenneth J. Gergen, Wolfgang Wagner, and Yoko Yamada, 103–104. Tokyo: Springer, 2008. https://doi.org/10.1007/978-4-431-74680-5_6.

Raymond, J., T. E. Darsaut, J. Eneling, et al. "The Small Trial Problem." Trials 24, art. 426 (June 22, 2023). https://doi.org/10.1186/s13063-023-07348-3.

Reher, Matthew. "Biblical Counseling and Memory." Paper presented at the ACBC 2024 Colloquium Essays, Neuroscience, the Body, and Biblical Counseling, Midwestern Baptist Theological Seminary, Kansas City, MO, July 18–19, 2024.

Rhoadarmer, Rachel. Mend: Journey to Sexual Healing. North Charleston, SC: CreateSpace Independent Publishing Platform, 2017.

Rhoades, George F., Jr. "Understanding and Treatment of Sexual Trauma and Trafficking." American Psychological Association Division 56 (Trauma Psychology), n.d. https://www.apatraumadivision.org/images/kcfinder/files/rhoades_slides.pdf.

Robbins, Susan P. "From the Editor—The DSM-5 and Its Role in Social Work Assessment and Research." Journal of Social Work Education 50, no. 2 (2014): 201–205. https://doi.org/10.1080/10437797.2014.885363.

Roeder, Bruce. "About Biblical Counseling." Reigning Grace Counseling Center Intake Paperwork. Reigning Grace Counseling Center, n.d. https://www.rgcconline.org.

Robjant, Katy, Jackie Roberts, and Cornelius Katona. "Treating Posttraumatic Stress Disorder in Female Victims of Trafficking Using Narrative Exposure Therapy: A

Retrospective Audit." Frontiers in Psychiatry 8, art. 63 (June 1, 2017). https://doi.org/10.3389/fpsyt.2017.00063.

Roeleveld, Lori Stanley. "What Does the Bible Say about the Mind?" Christianity.com, March 7, 2022. https://www.christianity.com/wiki/bible/what-bible-say-about-mind.html.

Rosser, Rachael. "15:14 Episode 31." Interview by Curtis Solomon. Biblical Counseling Coalition podcast, October 28, 2017. https://www.biblicalcounselingcoalition.org/podcast/.

———. "Counseling Complex Traumatic Relationships." Biblical Counseling Coalition, November 15, 2018. https://www.biblicalcounselingcoalition.org/2018/11/15/counseling-complex-traumatic-relationships/.

Sangwa, Sixbert, and Mutabazi Placide. "The Bible and Science: The Relationship between Science and Christianity." Studia Philosophica 9, no. 1 (2021): 7–29. https://www.researchgate.net/profile/Sixbert-Sangwa-2/publication/353522381_The_Bible_and_Science_The_Relationship_between_Science_and_Christianity.

Satel, Sally, and Scott Lilienfield. Brainwashed: The Seductive Appeal of Mindless Neuroscience. New York: Basic Books, 2013.

Scheeringa, Michael. Analysis of The Body Keeps the Score: The Science That Trauma Activists Don't Want You to Know. Monee, IL: Central Recovery Press, 2023.

———. The Body Does Not Keep the Score: How Popular Beliefs About Trauma Are Wrong. Amazon, 2024. Kindle.

———. "ACEs Aware Advocacy Program Tries to Influence Youths with Celebrity Gamer." Trauma Dispatch, August 26, 2024. https://www.michaelscheeringa.com/trauma-dispatch/aces-aware-advocacy-program-tries-to-influence-youths-with-celebrity-gamer.

———. (@m_scheeringa). "If ACE theory is true, tell us, please, what's the biological mechanism of how ACEs cause a horde of physical and mental conditions?" X, February 13, 2025, 9:43 a.m. https://x.com/m_scheeringa/status/1890064357427482936.

———. The Trouble with Trauma: The Search to Discover How Beliefs Become Facts. Las Vegas: Central Recovery Press, 2021.

Shaw, Mark. The Heart of Addiction: A Biblical Perspective. Bemidji, MN: Focus Publishing, 2008. Kindle.

———. "Conveying God's Love, Wisdom, and Power Through Biblical Language." In A Call to Clarity: Critical Issues in Contemporary Biblical Counseling, edited by Heath Lambert, 90. Jacksonville, FL: First Baptist Church Jacksonville, 2024.

Shin, Lisa M., Scott L. Rauch, and Roger K. Pitman. "Amygdala, Medial Prefrontal Cortex, and Hippocampal Function in PTSD." Annals of the New York Academy of Sciences 1071, no. 1 (2006): 67–79. https://doi.org/10.1196/annals.1364.007.

Soares, S., V. Rocha, M. Kelly-Irving, S. Stringhini, and S. Fraga. "Adverse Childhood Events and Health Biomarkers: A Systematic Review." Frontiers in Public Health 9 (2020): 649825. https://doi.org/10.3389/fpubh.2021.649825.

Solomon, Curtis. I Have PTSD: Reorienting after Trauma. Wheaton, IL: New Growth Press, 2023.

Somerville, Robert. If I'm a Christian, Why Am I Depressed? Finding Meaning and Hope in Suffering. Maitland, FL: Xulon Press, 2014.

Sproul, R. C. Everyone's a Theologian: An Introduction to Systematic Theology. Sanford, FL: Reformation Trust Publishing, 2014.

State of California Department of Health Care Services. "The Science of ACEs and Toxic Stress: ACEs and Toxic Stress Can Affect Health, but Toxic Stress Is Treatable." ACEs Aware, 2023. https://www.acesaware.org/ace-fundamentals/the-science-of-aces-toxic-stress/.

Steffen, Patrick R., Dawson Hedges, and Rebekka Matheson. "The Brain Is Adaptive Not Triune: How the Brain Responds to Threat, Challenge, and Change."

Frontiers in Psychiatry 13 (April 1, 2022): 802606. https://doi.org/10.3389/fpsyt.2022.802606.

Stephens, Samuel. "Christian Counseling and General Revelation: The Misuse of a Biblical Doctrine." Presentation at the ACBC Annual Conference – O Church Arise: Reclaiming a Culture of Care, October 2021. https://www.biblicalcounseling.com.

Stetzer, Ed. "Healing Victims of Human Trafficking." Christianity Today, March 2017. https://www.christianitytoday.com/edstetzer/2017/march/healing-victims-of-human-trafficking-long-slow-road-to-tran.html.

Substance Abuse and Mental Health Services Administration. Practical Guide for Implementing a Trauma-Informed Approach. Rockville, MD: National Mental Health and Substance Use Policy Laboratory, 2023. https://library.samhsa.gov/sites/default/files/pep23-06-05-005.pdf.

———. Quick Guide for Clinicians: Trauma-Informed Care in Behavioral Health Services. Washington, DC: Department of Health and Human Services, 2015.

———. SAMHSA's Concept of Trauma and Guidance for a Trauma-Informed Approach. Rockville, MD: Substance Abuse and Mental Health Services Administration, 2014.

Sylvestris, Olea. "'Polyvagal Theory' is Pseudoscience. Here's Why. The Deeper You Dig, the Worse It Gets." Medium, November 3, 2022. https://medium.com/@clymene/polyvagal-theory-is-pseudoscience-heres-why-139d8b41608d.

Taylor, Edwin, Cleo A. C. Leite, Marina Satori, Tobias Wang, Augusto S. Abe, and Dane A. Crossley II. "The Phylogeny and Ontogeny of Autonomic Control of the Heart and Cardiorespiratory Interactions in Vertebrates." Journal of Experimental Biology 217, no. 5 (March 2014): 690–703.

Teicher, Martin H. "Scars That Won't Heal: The Neurobiology of Child Abuse." Scientific American, March 1, 2002. https://www.scientificamerican.com/article/scars-that-wont-heal-the-neurobiology-of-child-abuse.

Toshniwal Paharia, Pooja. “What is the Nervous System?” News-Medical. https://www.news-medical.net/health/What-is-the-Nervous-System.aspx.

Trauma Informed Care Project. “What Is Trauma Informed Care?” http://www.traumainformedcareproject.org/.

Tripp, Paul David. Grief: Finding Hope Again. Greensboro, NC: New Growth Press, 2004.

———. Instruments in the Redeemer’s Hands. Phillipsburg, NJ: P&R Publishing, 2002.

Troxel, Craig. With All Your Heart: Orienting Your Mind, Desires, and Will Toward Christ. Wheaton, IL: Crossway, 2020.

Turner, Benjamin O., Erick J. Paul, Michael B. Miller, and Aron K. Barbey. “Small Sample Sizes Reduce the Replicability of Task-Based fMRI Studies.” Communications Biology 1, no. 62 (December 2018): 1–10. https://pubmed.ncbi.nlm.nih.gov/30271944/.

U.S. Department of Veterans Affairs. National Center for PTSD. “PTSD: National Center for PTSD - List of All Measures.” VA.gov | Veterans Affairs, March 25, 2025. https://www.ptsd.va.gov/professional/assessment/list_measures.asp#list1.

Van der Kolk, Bessel A. The Body Keeps the Score: Brain, Mind, and Body in the Healing of Trauma. New York: Viking, 2014.

———. “Developmental Trauma Disorder.” Psychiatric Annals 35, no. 5 (May 2005): 401–408. https://haruv.org.il/wp-content/uploads/2019/10/Developmental-trauma-disorder-van-der-kolk-2005.pdf.

Wallace, Jocelyn. Anxiety and Panic Attacks: Trusting God When You’re Afraid. Greensboro, NC: New Growth Press, 2013.

Walters Kluwer Health. “Mental Health Treatment for Victims of Human Trafficking.” Medical Xpress, March 7, 2018. https://medicalxpress.com/news/2018-03-mental-health-treatment-victims-human.html.

Weathers, Frank W., et al. The PTSD Checklist for DSM-5 (PCL-5). National Center for PTSD, 2013. www.ptsd.va.gov.

Welch, Edward T. "Addictions: New Ways of Seeing, New Ways of Walking Free." The Journal of Biblical Counseling 19, no. 3 (Spring 2001): 19–30.

———. Depression: Looking Up from the Stubborn Darkness. Greensboro, NC: New Growth Press, 2011.

———. "Self-Injury." In A Biblical Counseling Resource. [Details incomplete; assumed to be a published resource by Welch.]

———. Shame Interrupted: How God Lifts the Pain of Worthlessness and Rejection. Greensboro, NC: New Growth Press, 2012.

Wilde, Lillian. "Trauma Across Cultures: Cultural Dimensions of the Phenomenology of Post-Traumatic Experiences." Phenomenology and Mind 18 (2020): 1609. http://journals.openedition.org/phenomenology/1609.

Zhang, J., X. Liu, Z. Wang, et al. "Magnetoencephalography in the Detection and Characterization of Brain Abnormalities Associated with Traumatic Brain Injury: A Comprehensive Review." Diagnostics 11, no. 9 (2021): 1628. https://doi.org/10.3390/diagnostics11091628.

Zhang, Y., J. Liu, Y. Wang, et al. "Impact of Repetitive Transcranial Magnetic Stimulation on Cortical Activity: A Systematic Review and Meta-Analysis Utilizing Functional Near-Infrared Spectroscopy." Journal of NeuroEngineering and Rehabilitation 21, no. 1 (2024): 103. https://doi.org/10.1186/s12984-024-01392-7.

Zondervan. The Zondervan NIV Bible Commentary: Volume 1: Old Testament. Edited by F. F. Bruce. Grand Rapids, MI: Zondervan Publishing House, 1994

Afterword

Writing "Trauma Redeemed: A Biblical Response to Medicalized Suffering" has been a journey of deep introspection, prayer, and reliance on God's wisdom. My heart's desire is that this book serves as a beacon of hope and a source of practical guidance for biblical counselors who help counselees navigate the complex and often overwhelming experience of catastrophic suffering.

A Return to Biblical Sufficiency

I have sought to emphasize the sufficiency of Scripture in addressing catastrophic suffering. I am convinced that God's Word remains the ultimate source of truth and healing in a world that increasingly turns to secular methodologies and medicalized approaches. The Bible provides not only a comprehensive understanding of human nature and suffering but also offers the hope, healing, and redemption found in Christ.

Understanding Human Nature

Our exploration of biblical anthropology has been crucial in understanding the dual nature of humans as both material and immaterial beings. Recognizing that we are embodied souls created in God's image allows us to approach counseling with a holistic perspective, addressing both the physical and spiritual aspects of suffering. This understanding challenges the reductionist views of secular psychology and emphasizes the importance of heart transformation.

Practical Counseling Principles

I have endeavored to provide practical steps for counselors to navigate the complexities of fear, anxiety, grief, guilt, and shame. By grounding our approach in Scripture, we can offer genuine hope and help to those who have experienced deep, catastrophic suffering. The emphasis on renewing the mind, embracing one's identity in Christ, and the transformative power of forgiveness and repentance are central to the healing process.

A Call to the Church

The role of the church in healing has been emphasized as a vital component of the counseling process. The church is not only a place of worship but also a community of support, discipleship, and practical help. By fostering healthy relationships, providing spiritual disciplines, and offering practical assistance, the church can be a beacon of hope for those navigating the aftermath of catastrophic suffering.

Final Reflections

As we close this book, I am reminded that pain and suffering are not the final word. In Christ, there is hope, redemption, and transformation. The journey may be long and challenging, but with God's Word as our guide and His Spirit as our comforter, we can help our counselees find healing and restoration. My prayer is that this book inspires and equips biblical counselors to faithfully minister to the wounded, offering the hope and help that surpasses the limitations of secular approaches.

Thank you for joining me on this journey. May God bless you as you continue to seek His wisdom and grace in your counseling ministry.

In His Service,
Julie Ganschow

www.ingramcontent.com/pod-product-compliance
Lightning Source LLC
Chambersburg PA
CBHW072338090426
42741CB00012B/2839